Y0-EHY-216

Volume 19

Advances in
Librarianship

Volume 19

Advances in
Librarianship

Edited by

Irene Godden

The Libraries
Colorado State University
Fort Collins, Colorado

Academic Press

San Diego   New York   Boston   London   Sydney   Tokyo   Toronto

Copyright © 1995 by ACADEMIC PRESS, INC.

Academic Press, Inc.
A Division of Harcourt Brace & Company
525 B Street, Suite 1900, San Diego, California 92101-4495

United Kingdom Edition published by
Academic Press Limited
24-28 Oval Road, London NW1 7DX

International Standard Serial Number: 0065-2830

International Standard Book Number: 0-12-024619-8

PRINTED IN THE UNITED STATES OF AMERICA
95 96 97 98 99 00 BC 9 8 7 6 5 4 3 2 1

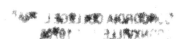

Contents

Quality Improvement in Libraries: Total Quality Management and Related Approaches
Joanne H. Boelke

A Changing Profession: Central Roles for Academic Librarians
Sheila D. Creth

Alternative Conceptualizations of the Information Economy
Sandra Braman

Systems, Quo Vadis?
An Examination of the History, Current Status, and Future Role of Regional Library Systems
Sarah Ann Long

The Future of Technical Services: An Administrative Perspective

Nancy H. Allen and James F. Williams II

Literary Text in an Electronic Age: Implications for Library Services

Marianne I. Gaunt

International Cooperation in Cataloging: Progress and Constraints
Jay H. Lambrecht

Contributors

Numbers in parentheses indicate the pages on which the authors' contributions begin.

Nancy H. Allen (159), University of Denver, Denver, Colorado 80208

Joanne H. Boelke (43), Library Services and Information Technology, Mankato State University, Mankato, Minnesota 56002

Julie J. Boucher (1), Library Research Service, Colorado State Library, Denver, Colorado 80203-1799

Sandra Braman (99), Institute of Communications Research, University of Illinois–Champaign/Urbana, Champaign, Illinois 61820

Sheila D. Creth (85), University of Iowa, Iowa City, Iowa 52242

Margo Crist (23), University of Michigan Library, Ann Arbor, Michigan 48109-1205

Marianne I. Gaunt (191), Rutgers University Libraries, Rutgers–The State University, New Brunswick, New Jersey 08903

William A. Gosling (23), University of Michigan Library, Ann Arbor, Michigan 48109-1205

Brenda Johnson (23), University of Michigan Library, Ann Arbor, Michigan 48109-1205

Jay H. Lambrecht (217), University Library, University of Illinois at Chicago, Chicago, Illinois 60680

Keith Curry Lance (1), Library Research Service, Colorado State Library, Denver, Colorado 80203-1799

Sarah Ann Long (117), North Suburban Library System, Wheeling, Illinois 60090

Wendy P. Lougee (23), University of Michigan Library, Ann Arbor, Michigan 48109-1205

Beth Forrest Warner (23), University of Michigan Library, Ann Arbor, Michigan 48109-1205

James F. Williams II (159), University of Colorado at Boulder, Boulder, Colorado 80309

Preface

Of the nine chapters in this nineteenth volume of *Advances in Librarianship*, six deal with emerging futures for the profession and its services and with the technology as well as the economics that is shaping those services. Two others discuss management issues, such as the availability of management statistics for academic libraries and the continued efforts to obtain quality improvements, while one provides an international perspective on cooperation in cataloging programs.

Lance and Boucher in "Decision-Making by the Numbers" identify major sources for general statistics, benchmarks, performance measures, and cost analysis results. Sources for data on specific topics, such as automated systems and networks, buildings, electronic access to information, fiscal trends, and salaries, are also given. Quality, timeliness, and utility of existing statistics are assessed, and the promise of emerging studies is critically reviewed. The expertise of the authors, who compile statistics on behalf of the Colorado Department of Education State Library and Adult Education Office, is reflected in the concise but thorough format, which should make this review a very useful tool for academic library managers as well as others involved in the assessment of outcomes and benchmark exercises.

Gosling et al. chronicle how the University of Michigan's library, in partnership with other campus information providers, is developing new methods of information delivery. The institutional environment and the information technology environment are described, as are specific projects.

Boelke in her review of "Quality Improvement in Libraries" covers the general characteristics of TQM and related approaches, lists background publications and bibliographies, and analyzes the applications of various elements of TQM as reported in the library literature. The relationship of TQM to current library organizational issues, and some of the pros and cons encountered in actual applications, are considered throughout, making this article extremely useful as a realistic and thorough introduction to the subject. A summary section on training opportunities, electronic resources for TQM discussion, activities in professional associations, and developments in selected countries outside the United States will also be helpful to those seeking ongoing sources for monitoring further developments.

Every present and future academic librarian and library administrator as well as library educators should read Creth's scenario for "A Changing Profession." As even a cursory review of the professional literature will reveal, academic organizational structures are changing and key traditional library services are being rethought in response to developments in technology, as well as increased pressures for reform of higher education and its components. Creth reviews why it is essential for library professionals to recognize the changes that will and must occur in their role and responsibilities, and makes clear that it is they who will need to redefine the requirements for academic librarianship and to lead in establishing new partnerships. Her article is particularly valuable in that it provides a checklist of new knowledge, skills, attitudes, and expectations needed to make the required changes to ensure a central role for academic librarians in creating and maintaining the information future.

Issues relating to the economics of information are critical to librarianship, as they affect our survival as institutions. Braman, in a fascinating article which should be a "must read" for everyone in the profession, defines the emerging broader field of "information economics," explains its terminology, and reviews major theories. It is recommended that librarians articulate an "enriched network economics perspective," if they are to be potential players in the emerging international information economy.

Public library systems, established in most if not all the states by the late 1960s, have made major progress in achieving one of their primary goals: extending access to library services. Their role in the 1990s is changing, and the changes range from a shift in emphasis of mission and work performed to questions of whether the role of systems can and should be absorbed by other entities. Long discusses the genesis of systems, past and present system configurations, external factors, and funding issues affecting library systems today, and suggests possible futures. Her extensive use of the interview method in addition to a literature review has resulted in the inclusion of a wide variety of viewpoints, which should make lively and provocative reading for those who wonder with the author about "Systems, Quo Vadis" in a time when one of the most successful structural models in the development of public libraries is changing.

The major operative change agents affecting the current operations and shaping the potential future of technical services in academic libraries are discussed by Allen and Williams, who provide an extensive review of the literature coupled with a thoughtful analysis. They conclude that while a new order for dissemination of information is certain, libraries in the transitional roles will continue to be central to the delivery of information, expanding and changing, but not obviating the need for the traditional technical services function of organization and integration.

As full text delivered over computing networks is becoming increasingly available, implications for collection development, bibliographic control, preservation, and direct user services, as well as copyright questions, are becoming more complex, and disciplinary differences are beginning to emerge. Gaunt specifically addresses electronic literary texts, a group for which the move from print to electronic form is much more than just a change in production and delivery systems, but rather a change that will alter the very definition of "text," de facto forcing a reconceptualization of the very field of literary study itself. The literature and major projects and implications are reviewed and new directions indicated.

In the international arena, Lambrecht discusses how far we have come in gaining international cooperation in cataloging, and how much more work it will take to attain the ideal of international cataloging based on universal standards. He reviews the standards designed to achieve international cooperation, discusses problems and conflicts, and concludes with specific proposals for improved cooperation in the future.

Decision-Making by the Numbers: Available Data for Academic Library Managers

Keith Curry Lance and Julie J. Boucher
Library Research Service
Colorado State Library
Denver, Colorado 80203-1799

Academic library managers require a variety of data to inform their decision-making. Such information ranges from general statistics, benchmarks, and performance measures to cost analysis results to data on a wide variety of specific topics, such as automated systems and networks, buildings, electronic access to information, fiscal trends, and salaries. This chapter identifies major sources of each type of data, assessing the quantity, quality, timeliness, and utility of existing sources and commenting on the promise of new and developing sources.

I. General Statistics

General statistics of academic libraries are compiled by a variety of organizations: professional associations, government agencies, and the private sector. Historically, data have been collected primarily on library staff, collections, and finances. But, in recent years, additional data on library services and the role of technology in libraries have been collected by many such organizations. The following descriptions of the major statistical sources for college and university libraries focus on what sets them apart from one another: their participants, history, frequency, content, and utility.

A. The Professional Associations: ARL, ACRL, AAHSLD, and AALL

Most of the nation's major college and university libraries rely on statistics compiled and reported by their two leading associations: the Association of Research Libraries (ARL) and the Association of College and Research Libraries (ACRL). Libraries that specialize in serving health science centers and law schools rely on annual data reports from the Association of Academic Health Sciences Library Directors (AAHSLD) and the American Association of Law Librarians (AALL), respectively.

1. ARL

From 1907–1908 through 1961–1962, data on the leading American university libraries were published as *The Gerould Statistics*, so named after their originator, James T. Gerould of the University of Minnesota.[1] From 1963–1964 through 1972–1973, they were published as *ARL Academic Library Statistics*.[2] Since 1973–1974, these data have appeared under the simple and straightforward title *ARL Statistics*, reflecting the association's membership beyond academic libraries.

In recent years, ARL has conducted two general statistical surveys. The first, maintaining a longstanding time series, collects basic data on staffing, holdings, expenditures, and interlibrary loans. The second, collecting "supplementary" statistics and administered with the first, provides additional data on services (e.g., circulation, in-house use, reference) and timely topics (e.g., library instruction, facilities and equipment, electronic access to information). (Note: ARL's salary survey will be addressed in a later section.)

For each data element, the ARL report provides summary statistics, and, for several critical items, respondents are ranked.

The strengths of the ARL statistics are the timeliness of the report, the availability of a time series in machine-readable form, and the oversight of the association's Committee on Statistics and Measurement.

Unlike academic library statistics reported by government agencies and other associations, ARL statistics are issued on a reliable, annual schedule.

The ARL time series, 1907–1908 to the present, is unparalleled among other sources of academic library data. This time series is made even more useful by its availability on diskette.

The ARL statistics project is overseen by the Committee on Statistics and Measurement, a body composed of some of the field's most insightful and experienced managers and data users.

The most notable weakness of the ARL statistics is their historical emphasis on measuring inputs or resources instead of outputs, services, or performance. But, in fairness, this criticism is no less applicable to other data collections on academic libraries.

---

[1] See R. Molyneux (1986). *The Gerould Statistics, 1907/08–1961/62.* Association of Research Libraries, Washington, DC.

[2] See K. Stubbs and D. Buxton (1981). *Cumulated ARL University Library Statistics 1962-63 through 1978-79.* Association of Research Libraries, Washington, DC.

2. ACRL

Since 1979, the ACRL, a division of the American Library Association, has collected statistics from 120 university libraries biennially. Libraries included are those at institutions in Carnegie Classifications Research I, Research II, Doctoral Granting I, and Doctoral Granting II that do not report to ARL. This survey gathers statistics on collections, interlibrary loan, personnel, expenditures, number of doctorates awarded, faculty, and enrollment. Percentages and ratios are calculated for various categories. Summary data include the high, mean, median, low, and total reported for each statistic as well as the number of libraries reporting. Additional tables report the rank order of responding libraries on 24 variables.

ACRL data are available on disk to purchasers of the printed report.[3] The strengths of the ACRL statistics are the availability of a time series (biennial from 1981–1982 to 1992–1993, at this writing) and the care and cooperation demonstrated by the principals who make the project possible: the staff of ACRL and the Library Research Center at the University of Illinois at Urbana-Champaign.

The major weakness of the ACRL statistics is a sin of omission. Like the Public Library Data Service of ACRL's sister ALA division, the Public Library Association, the ACRL statistics focus on the larger and richer organizational members of the division. There is no true counterpart to ARL or ACRL statistics for 4-year colleges and community colleges. The closest counterparts for selected liberal arts colleges are the annual data-sharing projects of the "Oberlin Group," Associated Colleges of the Midwest, and the Great Lakes Colleges Association.[4]

3. AAHSLD

Since 1978, the AAHSLD has published *Annual Statistics of Medical School Libraries in the United States and Canada*. The survey on which this report is based is administered to all libraries of medical schools that are "institutional" or "affiliate institutional" members of the Association of American Medical Colleges and to all osteopathic medical schools in the United States.

[3] Contact ACRL at 50 E. Huron St., Chicago, IL 60611, voice (800) 545–2433 × 2519.

[4] For information about the "Oberlin Group," contact Larry Frye, Lilly Library, Wabash College, 301 W. Wabash Ave., Crawfordsville, IN 47933, voice (317) 362–2242, fax (317) 362–7986, Internet Fryel@Wabash.edu. Although this ad hoc, relatively informal data sharing consortium does not publish a formal report, it does make its data file available on disk. Notably, too, since at least 1992, this survey has included several items relating to electronic access to information, such as number of machine-readable bibliographic records and expenditures on electronic materials, online searches, and automation. For information about similar projects sponsored by Associated Colleges of the Midwest and the Great Lakes Colleges Association, contact Sarah M. McGowan, Ripon College Library, 300 Seward St., Ripon, WI 54971-1499, voice (414) 748–8175, Internet MCGOWAVS@atsACAD.RIPON.EDU.

In addition to the types of data and rankings reported in the ARL and ACRL statistical reports, the AAHSLD report includes data on database access and sections on performance measures and salaries for selected positions. Like ARL and ACRL, AAHSLD makes its data available on disk to purchasers of their printed report.[5]

A key strength of the AAHSLD survey is its annual review process. A group meets annually to consider adding, changing, or eliminating items. While maintaining a time series of comparable core data is one of their major priorities, this group tries to be responsive to the changing data needs of health sciences libraries.

The most noticeable weakness of the AAHSLD report is its appearance. While attractively and solidly bound, the data tables themselves are not of high presentation quality.

4. AALL

Like medical school libraries, law school libraries have their own data collection, courtesy of the American Bar Association's Office of the Consultant on Legal Education and the American Association of Law Libraries. This survey is conducted annually by the ABA office, and the results are reported in the summer issue of the *Law Library Journal.*[6] It has several noteworthy strengths:

Topics on which data are collected are similar to those for other types of academic libraries: staffing, expenditures, holdings, and services. But, many specific data elements are cast differently; perhaps with more of an eye to the future than other such surveys. For example, major categories of expenditures include serials, databases, and "information resources," which include other formats—such as books.

While the groups for which summary statistics are reported are based on numbers of volumes held, volume equivalencies are employed in measuring nonprint materials added and held.

This survey also contains one of the first widely collected data elements measuring services made possible by electronic access to information: the number of hours of online computer-assisted legal research.

Another distinguishing characteristic of this survey is that this is the only one whose results appear as a regular part of a major professional journal, ensuring that these statistics are disseminated widely and are available to most interested parties without additional initiative or expense.

[5] Contact the Association of Academic Health Sciences Library Directors at 1133 M.D. Anderson Blvd., Houston, TX 77030, (713) 790–7060.

[6] See J. Hanrahan (1994).1992-93 Statistical Survey of ABA Law School Libraries and Librarians. *Law Library Journal* **83** (summer), 617–661. Contact the American Association of Law Libraries at 53 W. Jackson Blvd., Suite 940, Chicago, IL 60604, voice (312) 939–4764, fax (312) 431–1097.

This data source has only two noticeable weaknesses: While clearly readable, the data tables themselves are not of high presentation quality. And, unfortunately, this data set is not available on disk.

B. Federal and State Government: IPEDS, PALS, and Other State Reports

While professional associations provide for the data needs of their members, academic libraries that are not major players in those organizations must rely largely on data collected by government agencies. The federal government conducts a regular survey of academic libraries, and some state library and higher education agencies do the same.

1. Integrated Postsecondary Education Data System (IPEDS)

Libraries in all institutions of postsecondary education—everything from doctorate-granting universities to trade and technical schools—are surveyed by the National Center for Education Statistics through the IPEDS. This biennial survey gathers statistics on staffing, expenditures, collections, loan transactions, and other services. The results are published in an E.D. TABS report. There is usually a 2-year gap between the year for which data are collected and the year this report is issued. For instance, *Academic Libraries in the U.S., 1990* was published in 1992. But, because of problematic reporting on a couple of data elements, the 1992 data report will not be published until sometime in 1995.

The strengths of this survey are its comprehensiveness and *potential* for high data quality and the availability of such data in machine-readable form.

All postsecondary education institutions are surveyed, and NCES seeks to maintain strict quality control procedures.

This is the only collection of academic library statistics conducted electronically, using software which generates on-the-spot error and warning messages when statistically suspect figures are entered.

Likewise, the electronic data file resulting from this survey is very complete, indicating both unit and item nonresponse and when imputation has taken place. This file is available on diskette[7] and the E.D. TABS tables are available via the Office of Educational Research and Improvement's free electronic bulletin board system.[8]

[7] Contact Jeffrey Williams in the Library Statistics Unit, National Center for Education Statistics, U.S. Department of Education, 555 New Jersey Avenue, Washington, DC 20208, voice (202) 219–1362, fax (202) 219–1751, Internet jwilliam@inet.ed.gov.

[8] Communications software parameters for the OERI Electronic Bulletin Board System are speed 300/1200/2400 baud, 8 data bits, 1 stop bit, no parity, full duplex. Dial toll-free (800) 222–4922. For assistance with problems, call the system operator at (202) 219–1547.

Its weaknesses concern its timeliness, accessibility, and responsiveness to the changing data needs of academic library managers.

The data file is released so late that it is useful for little beyond historical research. There is always a trade-off between timeliness and data quality, but the delays of recent years have prevented academic library managers from making optimum use of these data without laying to rest concerns about data quality. Fortunately, solutions to this problem are being sought energetically and cooperatively by the Library Statistics Unit of the National Center for Education Statistics, the American Library Association's Office for Research and Statistics, and a committee including representatives of the Association of Research Libraries, the Association of College and Research Libraries, the Oberlin Group, and others representing segments of the academic library community for which there is no other data collection.

The printed report includes only summary data by the highest degree awarded by state and—as late as 1990—omits critical analytical variables, such as student enrollment, faculty size, and educational and general (E&G) expenditures. For library-by-library statistics, one must turn to the data file from which the E.D. TABS report is generated.

Data on two variables—gate count (i.e., library visits) and reference questions—are alarmingly poor. While all other data elements are collected for a year, these two are requested for a "typical week." An examination of 1992 data indicates that many respondents are giving annual rather than weekly figures for these two items. It is hoped that, by 1996, the software used to collect these data will have an error/warning message that will be triggered by such cases.

The survey's planning timeline is so long (2 years) that it has yet to even begin addressing the pressing need to measure electronic access to information provided via academic libraries.

2. Peer Academic Library Statistics (PALS) Project

One of the major uses of IPEDS data by academic libraries is peer comparisons. In Colorado, for example, each institution has a list of peers which is set periodically by that state commission on higher education. Since 1992, the Library Research Service, a unit of the Colorado State Library, has asked the over 300 nationwide peers of the state's academic libraries to submit copies of their completed IPEDS library survey forms and additional figures, such as FTE enrollment and E&G expenditures. The LRS enters these data into a spreadsheet, calculates per student figures and other ratios, and generates reports that are shared not only with Colorado institutions, but with their participating peers nationwide.[9]

The strengths of this project are its timeliness and utility.

Instead of waiting for up to 2 years for federal reports of library data, the LRS contacts PALS libraries directly when the IPEDS survey is being administered. This strategy enables the LRS to put PALS reports in the hands of academic library managers well before the federal report is issued.

PALS reports include presentation-quality tables of reported data and calculated per student and other ratios for 10–15 peer institutions nationwide. Most participants in the PALS project find these reports to be readily useful without additional packaging of the information.

The major weakness of this project is its reliance on voluntary reporting. Because participation in PALS is voluntary, some reports are more complete than others. For a variety of reasons, some libraries that participate in the IPEDS survey choose not to submit copies of the completed survey to the LRS. If the federal IPEDS data file was available on a timely basis, data on all libraries needed for PALS reports could be extracted from it.

3. Other State Reports

In many states, academic library statistics are published regularly. In at least seven states, the state library agency issues a single statistical report for all types of libraries. These publications include:

Directory of Michigan Library Statistics,
Statistics of Ohio Libraries,
Directory and Statistics of Oregon Libraries,
Pennsylvania Library Statistics,
Vermont Library Directory,
West Virginia Library Commission Statistical Report, and
Wisconsin Library Service Record.

Of these seven, the Michigan, Ohio, Oregon, and Wisconsin reports treat academic library statistics fairly comprehensively, whereas the Pennsylvania, Vermont, and West Virginia reports provide statistics on only a few critical data elements. Because the IPEDS library survey is only conducted in even-numbered years, states that report academic library statistics annually must

[9] Contact Keith Lance or Julie Boucher at the Library Research Service, Colorado State Library, 201 E. Colfax Avenue, Suite 309, Denver, CO 80203–1799, voice (303) 866–6737 or 866–6927, fax (303)866–6940, Internet <klance@cde.co.gov> or <jboucher@cde.co.gov>.

replicate the IPEDS survey for odd-numbered years. Many states which do this take advantage of the opportunity to ask additional questions.

In at least three states, academic library statistics are published separately. Two of these publications are:

Statistics and Input–Output Measures for Colorado Academic Libraries and *Directory of College and University Libraries in New York State.*

A similar publication of academic library statistics is done in California, but only for the California State University system.

All three of these reports are fairly comprehensive, including most, if not all, data elements in the IPEDS library survey. The Colorado report is issued for even-numbered years only, as it is based on IPEDS results.

C. The Private Sector: John Minter Associates

Since at least 1985, John Minter Associates, Inc. of Boulder, Colorado has been the major—if not only—private sector vendor of IPEDS library data.[10] This company offers several value-added products of great potential utility to academic library managers:

Academic Library Survey Response is a two-volume work—the first volume for public colleges and universities, and the second for private institutions. In addition to IPEDS library statistics, this work contains a variety of additional useful identifying data: enrollment (FTE and head count), campus environment (urban, suburban, or rural), location (six types from cities over 500,000 to rural communities under 2500), highest degree awarded, and Carnegie classification. To date, this is the only library-by-library tabulation of the complete national results from the IPEDS library survey.

ReadyStats is an online 24-hour file server via which subscribing academic libraries may obtain access to the latest NCES-released IPEDS library data and participate in a data exchange with peer subscribers. If subscribers send lists of peers when registering, Minter will solicit data from them.

The strengths of Minter's products and services are that they offer additional, valuable data (beyond that reported in the IPEDS library survey) as well as an immediate solution to the IPEDS timeliness problem.

The weaknesses of Minter's products and services are their low profile among academic library managers, the associated costs, and, as a result, current levels of participation. While *ReadyStats* fees are relatively modest (in 1993,

[10] Contact John Minter Associates at 2400 Central Ave, B-2, Boulder, CO 80301, voice (800) 444–8110, fax (800) 395–9476. Ask about current fees and services.

$295 for access to the latest NCES releases, $195 to exchange IPEDS data directly), many academic library managers resist paying anything "extra" for something they feel they should be getting for "free" from NCES. (Alas, these products and services are not available via NCES at this writing, and there is little reason to hope they will be anytime soon.) Others are simply unaware that this company or these value-added products exist.

II. Benchmarks and Performance Measures

In recent years, many academic library managers have found the usual peer comparisons of key statistics to be less valuable. In some cases, these managers have concluded—all too accurately—that the impact of such comparisons on higher education administrators is diminishing. One reason for this declining effectiveness is the mere familiarity of such arguments. Increasingly, however, there is another reason for such concern. As higher education dollars stagnate or even shrink—especially in the public sector—calls for accountability have increased. As a result, academic library managers and their colleagues campus wide feel pressed to demonstrate the performance of their operations, especially in relation to peer institutions.

The result has been several interesting attempts to create "benchmarks" and "performance measures" which make it easier to respond to calls for greater accountability. For academic libraries, there have been three noteworthy, but diverse, manifestations of this climate: a publication of "statistical norms" from the private sector, a "benchmarking" project led by campus accountants, and the development of "performance measures" by one of the major groups of academic libraries. The products of these efforts have been decidedly mixed.

A. Statistical Norms for College and University Libraries

Since 1988, John Minter Associates has published *Statistical Norms for College and University Libraries* on the same biennial basis as the IPEDS library survey from which it is derived. Although these "statistical norms" lack the sort of organizational endorsement that would gain them general recognition as benchmarks or performance measures, they can certainly be used as de facto ones by individual libraries. Three types of ratios are reported:

percent of a whole (e.g., collection expenditures as a percent of total operating expenditures),
percent change from year to year, and
per student ratios.

These ratios are presented for several classifications, including:

Carnegie classifications—for the nation as a whole, for the public and private
    sectors, and by regional association,
numbers of librarians and other professionals, and
the top 25 libraries in each Carnegie classification.

For each classification scheme, seven percentiles are reported (i.e., 10th, 15th,
25th, 50th, 75th, 85th, and 90th).

The strengths of *Statistical Norms* are its inclusiveness of all academic
libraries, its relative timeliness, and the comprehensiveness of its ratios and
classifications. Its weaknesses are the same low profile and cost associated
with other Minter products and its presentation quality. Like the AAHSLD
statistical report, it is attractively and solidly bound, but its tables are not of
presentation quality. (The font is quite small to accommodate more figures
per page.)

B. NACUBO Benchmarking Project

In the fall of 1991, the National Association of College and University Business Officers (NACUBO) began its Benchmarking Project. The project's
objective is to provide comparative data that encourages administrators to
examine critically costs and outputs in over 35 functional areas, one of which
is library services. By the project's 1993 cycle, one of every six ARL libraries
was participating, despite growing concerns in the library community about
the meaningfulness and utility of the data being collected.

Participating libraries questioned a number of NACUBO's so-called
"performance measures," such as "number of book and serial backfiles per
student and faculty FTE," "number of microform per student and faculty
FTE," and library "departmental cost per library holding." In an age that
values "just-in-time" access to information over "just-in-case" development
of large collections, how appropriate are such figures as "measures of service
quality?" Fortunately, the ARL Committee on Statistics and Measurement
stepped in to raise this question to NACUBO, and, in 1994, the committee
made advising the Benchmarking Project a major part of its agenda. The
committee is also exploring the possibility of ARL developing its own, more
appropriate benchmarks of library performance.

Reports issued by NACUBO provide two tables for each "performance
measure." The first table gives the maximum, minimum, median, and mean
values for the measure as well as the standard deviation and number of
reporting libraries. These statistics are reported for all responding institutions
in five institutional sectors: public research, private research, public comprehensive, private comprehensive, and liberal arts. The second table gives indi-

vidual institution results anonymously. Unfortunately, these results are not categorized by sector.

All academic libraries involved in the NACUBO Benchmarking Project are advised to cast a critical eye on the library "performance measures" and to keep abreast of ARL's involvement.[11]

C. AAHSLD Performance Measures

Perhaps the best examples of academic library performance measures are those developed by the Association of Academic Health Sciences Library Directors. AAHSLD began by identifying the wide variety of service roles performed by health sciences libraries:

access to information,
reference services,
education services (i.e., information skills instruction),
curriculum support,
the library as a learning environment,
health science libraries as resources in the national information community,
retrospective collections,
special collections,
consultation (i.e., more in-depth reference/research services),
customized information services (e.g., selective dissemination of informtion),
patient education, and
community health information service.

For each role, AAHSLD identified one or more goals. The goal for resource sharing, for example, is to make library collections available through national interlibrary services to both institutional and individual borrowers. Fore each goal, there is a set of objectives. A resource sharing objective is to achieve a 75% fill rate and fill 85% of received requests within 4 calendar days. For each objective, one or more performance measures are recommended. In this case, DOCLINE fill rates and turnaround time in filling OCLC ILL requests would be appropriate. In addition, for many objectives, other alternative performance measures are suggested, even though there may be little consensus as yet on methodologies for collecting requisite data.

The major strengths of AAHSLD performance measures are being role-based and relating roles, goals, and objectives to performance measures. Their most conspicuous weakness is the absence of attention to standardizing data collection procedures.

[11] Contact Martha Kyrillidou at the Association of Research Libraries, 21 Dupont Circle, Washington, DC 20036, voice (202) 296–2296, fax (202) 872–0884, Internet martha@cni.org.

Comparative data on these performance measures are included in AAH-SLD's *Annual Statistics of Medical School Libraries in the United States and Canada.*[12]

III. Cost Analysis

Alas, there is very little comparative data on the costs incurred by academic libraries. Cost analyses are done frequently, but they vary markedly in their methodologies, their results are rarely reported widely, and there are no regular compilations or summaries of data on costs as there are for other aspects of academic library operation. A standout exception to this trend is the recent *ARL/RLG Interlibrary Loan Cost Study.*[13]

One of the greatest issues facing academic library managers is the financing of document delivery. ARL and the Research Libraries Group (RLG) joined forces to establish solid baseline data on the fiscal ramifications of interlibrary lending (e.g., ILL costs vs the costs of commercial document delivery, serial cancellations).

Categories of costs included were:

staff,
networking, telecommunications, photocopying, and delivery;
software, supplies, equipment, and other rental and maintenance;
direct and indirect charges for borrowing from other suppliers; and
costs recovered from borrowing and lending activities.

Of course, the greatest challenge faced in trying to collect comparable data on costs is having all participants analyze the same costs using the same set of categories. Some aspects of interlibrary borrowing and lending extend beyond a librry's own budget, and budget categories can vary greatly from library to library. This study sought to avoid such problems by distinguishing clearly between subsidized and cost-recovered/reimbursed services, explaining each cost category in detail, and providing separate step-by-step instructions and worksheets to facilitate data collection.

The strengths of this study are its scope, detail, and utility.

Seventy-six of ARL's 119 member libraries participated in the study, making it the most inclusive such study ever conducted.

The detailed definitions, instructions, and worksheets provided to participants are also unparalleled and provide excellent models for anyone conducting an ILL cost analysis.

[12] See previous note for AAHSLD contact information.
[13] Contact C. Brigid Welch at ARL. See previous note for contact information.

Using the results, each library can assess its ILL costs by category, comparing those figures to the averages and ranges for peer institutions.

The most glaring weaknesses of this study are its failures to train respondents, to report library-by-library results, and to provide for regular replications.

In the Colorado study for which this approach to cost analysis was first developed and applied, respondents received in-depth, hands-on training.[14] Participants in the ARL/RLG study had to rely exclusively on printed instructions and definitions.

Institutional anonymity was the price of obtaining such a high level of participation in the study. While the reluctance of academic library directors to publicize ILL transaction costs is understandable, it inhibits the conduct of such research and minimizes the utility of its results.

This study was conducted in 1991 and published in 1993. Although this study provides an excellent model on which to base replications, there are neither plans nor funding for a regular schedule of such studies.

IV. Topical Issues

In addition to general statistics and performance measures and cost analysis data, academic library managers frequently need timely data on specific topical issues. Five such issues which arise frequently are:

automated systems and networks,
buildings,
electronic access to information,
prices and inflation, and
salaries.

A. Automated Systems and Networks

Academic library managers who are shopping for automated systems can obtain substantial amounts of information from vendors of such systems. In addition, there is at least one regular overview of this important market which encompasses all of the major players. Each April, *Library Journal* publishes a new installment in its series, "Automated System Marketplace." This annual update identifies the major automated systems and contains the following data:

---

[14] V. Boucher and S. Fayad (1988). *Library Resource Sharing in Colorado*, Colorado State Library, Denver. The cost analysis model developed and implemented in this study was promulgated more broadly in S. Dickson and V. Boucher (1989). *Research Access through New Technology*. AMS, New York.

leading vendors by library sector (e.g., academic),
new and total system installations, and
total minicomputer and microcomputer installations by vendor and library
    sector.

In addition, the article contains complete contact information for each
vendor (noting moves, mergers, and name changes that occurred during the
year) and a paragraph about each vendor's status in the automated system
market.

The October 1, 1993 issue of *Library Journal* includes an article entitled
"LJ's Statewide Networks Survey." In addition to the developmental status
of such networks, it reports:

numbers and types of participating libraries,
network functions (e.g., circulation, acquisitions, serials control, ILL, cata-
    loging),
availability of document delivery systems,
Internet and e-mail support,
common hardware and software,
funding levels,
reasons for establishing a statewide network, and
advantages seen since developing a statewide network.

B. Buildings

When academic library managers must address institutional needs for new
library facilities, much of the detailed information needed can best be obtained
from colleagues who have recently dealt with such issues, their architects, or
consultants. For a broader, more preliminary perspective, however, managers
can turn to at least one regular overview of academic library construction
projects. In it architectural issue each December, *Library Journal* publishes a
lengthy article in its long-running "Library Buildings" series. This annual
update identifies academic library buildings under construction and being
planned.

For new facilities as well as additions and renovations, several useful
statistics are provided. They include:

project cost,
gross square feet,
cost per square foot,
construction cost,
equipment cost, and
shelving and seating capacity.

In addition, the interested reader will find contact information for each project's architect. For projects still in the planning stages, progress is reported using a checklist of standard milestones.

C. Electronic Access to Information

There is little available data on electronic access to information via academic libraries. What little exists comes from specific items in the IPEDS and ARL surveys described earlier.

Since at least 1990, the IPEDS survey has included a few input items relating to electronic information, such as expenditures on database access and numbers of computer files in the collection. In 1996, this survey may ask about the availability of selected electronic services, such as access to local and remote online public access catalogs (OPACs), client/server interfaces (e.g., Mosaic, WWW), and instruction on access to networked information.

In 1991, ARL conducted an Inventory of Library Access: Facilities and Services. It requested several figures relating to the automation infrastructure, such as numbers of OPAC terminals, printers, and access ports for remote users. It also asked about types of access services provided, such as: OPAC integration into campus local area networks, access to OPACs of other libraries, on-campus document delivery, and reference services via e-mail.

By 1993–1994, several electronic information items were included in ARL's supplementary statistics questionnaire. Categories of expenditures include computer files and search services, document delivery/interlibrary loan, computer hardware and software, and bibliographic utilities, networks, and consortia. Counts relating to electronic access include number of electronic databases available on institutional computers (via the library OPAC), number of records of locally owned materials in the local OPAC, and the percentage of cataloged library holdings represented by OPAC records.

Apart from these IPEDS and ARL exceptions, there is virtually no available data on electronic access to information. While there has been a great deal of discussion of this problem at conferences and in the library press, little progress seems to be being made. Martin Dillon of OCLC is the author of a discussion paper, "Measuring the Impact of Technology on Libraries," written for a September 1993 library statistics forum sponsored by the National Commission on Libraries and Information Science. It is by far the best available statement of this problem and the questions that need answers.

Dillon's questions fall in several major categories:

the extent of automation in libraries,
the size of the library automation market,
interlibrary lending and borrowing traffic,
the database infrastructure and access services,

the role of scanned text in document delivery,
electronic document creation, and
the role of the Internet.

He points to several potential sources of data to answer these questions: traditional statistics (e.g., IPEDS, ARL), unit cost measures (e.g., ARL/RLG ILL study), transaction log analysis, and vendor analyses of trends in electronic services (e.g., an unpublished OCLC market research and analysis document, *Trends in Library Services Survey Report*).

An issue which Dillon does not address is the lack of comparability in management information available from automated systems. At this writing, there is no consensus—among libraries or vendors, let alone both—about how to standardize such information. And, even if there was such a consensus, there is no obvious vehicle for academic library managers to use to bring such a consensus to bear on the automated system market. As no vendor is addressing this problem seriously, libraries cannot threaten to defect from systems that offer inadequate management information; most vendors are under no pressure to step into this breach. There is nothing on the horizon to suggest that this issure will be addressed in a revolutionary fashion. Evidently, progress on this front is going to be evolutionary—slow and incremental. The growing literature on transaction log analysis indicates some progress in a productive direction; although, the limitations of such analysis in a networked environment may be its downfall. We can only hope that this data need will not suffer the fate of the need for cost analysis data, remaining unstandardized and, for the most part, inaccessible.

D. Prices and Inflation

The Academic Library Price Index (ALPI) is an invaluable tool for tracking average prices paid by academic libraries for selected goods and services and the impact of inflation on such prices. This index is published annually in *Inflation Measures for Schools, Colleges, and Libraries.*[15] It reports relative year-to-year prices of goods and services paid by college and university libraries to support their current operations. It measures inflation by determining additional funding libraries need to buy the equivalent of last year's purchases.

The ALPI has three major components:

personnel compensation, the subcomponents of which are salaries and wages and fringe benefits;
acquisitions, the subcomponents of which are books and periodicals and other materials; and

[15] Contact Kent Halstead of Research Associates of Washington, 2605 Klingle Road, N.W., Washington, DC 20008, voice (202) 966–3326.

contracted services, supplies, and materials, the subcomponents of which are binding, contracted services, supplies and materials, and equipment.

The acquisition subcomponents provide even greater pricing detail. The books and periodicals subcomponent includes separate subindexes for U.S. college books, North American academic books, foreign books, U.S. periodicals for academic libraries, and foreign periodicals. The other materials subcomponent includes separate subindexes for microfilm, 16-mm film, video cassettes, filmstrips, cassette tapes, and CD-ROMs.

The three major components and their subcomponents are weighted according to national averages to generate the overall ALPI. This figure may be used as is or tailored to fit the composition of an individual institution's budget.

Strengths of the ALPI are its superiority to the Consumer Price Index (CPI) as a measure of inflation's impact on academic libraries and the step-by-step instructions for customizing it. Its major weakness is its reliance on 1982–1983 figures in establishing its national weighting structure. (Although this deficiency is mitigated in large part by the index's flexibility to reflect local budgets.) Another weakness, which it shares with most price indexes, is its inability to estimate additional funding libraries need to keep pace with rapidly evolving information technologies.

E. Salaries

Salary data are collected and reported by several associations which count academic librarians among their members.

1. ALA

Each year, the American Library Association's Office for Research and Statistics and Office for Library Personnel Resources publish the *ALA Survey of Librarian Salaries*.[16] Each April, over 1000 academic and public libraries are selected to be part of a stratified random sample. This sample is stratified by size and type of library and region of the country. Academic library groups included are 2-year colleges, 4-year colleges, and universities. Geographic regions are North Atlantic, Great Lakes and Plains, Southeast, and West and Southwest. Academic libraries are surveyed about the salaries paid for five positions:

director,
deputy/associated/assistant director,

[16] Contact Mary Jo Lynch at the ALA Office for Research and Statistics, 50 E. Huron Street, Chicago, Il 60611–2795, voice (800) 545–2433 x4273, fax (312) 440–9374, Internet mary.jo.lynch@ala.org.

department/branch head,
reference/information librarian, and
cataloger/classifer.

Results appear in the just-mentioned report and are summarized in an article
in *American Libraries*. Key statistics reported by library type and region are
the range, mean (average), first quartile, median (i.e., the middle or second
quartile), and third quartile.

This project has several strengths:

The publication is usually completed within 6 months of the survey.
Data are collected and published annually.
Salaries are reported for full-time librarians with master's degrees from gradu-
   ate programs accredited by ALA.
The survey has a high response rate (76% in the latest edition).
The number of cases reporting is noted for each position, giving the reader
   some idea of the reliability of the results.
A clear example is given of how to use the data.
Appended to the annual publication is an excellent annotated bibliography
   of print sources of salary and other compensation data.

The ALA salary statistics have only two noticeable weaknesses:

Gender and average years of experience are not taken into account as explana-
   tions of salary differences.
In at least one table, salaries are averaged across types of libraries.

In one table, salaries for the five positions listed earlier are averaged together
for academic and public libraries. While it can be useful to consider the salary
market across library types, as these figures are presented in the *American
Libraries* article, they may appear lower than expected for academic libraries alone.

2. ARL

Each year, the Association of Research Libraries publishes the *ARL Annual
Salary Survey*, reporting the results of its survey of the 100+ largest academic
and research libraries in North America. In addition to major U.S. and
Canadian university libraries, this survey includes nonuniversity research libraries, medical school libraries, and law school libraries. Salary figures are
collected for director, associate director, assistant director, department/
branch head, and subject and functional specialists. Data include beginning,
median, and average professional salaries by institution, in rank order, and
by group over 10 years.

This report has several unique features:

It includes comparisons of professional beginning and median salaries for the last 10 years.
There is also a comparison of purchasing power which charts changes in salaries versus changes in the Consumer Price Index (CPI).
Numbers of ethnic minority staff in U.S. libraries are tracked.
Salaries for each position are broken down by gender and years of experience (from less than 5 years to 15 years or more).

Strengths of this report are that it covers 8000 professional staff salaries, reports differences by gender and years of experience, and includes separate summaries for law and medical school libraries. Its weaknesses are all sins of omission: leaving institutions to interpret what "professional" means and not including salaries and wages for support staff and student assistants. The latter information is especially useful in addressing personnel budgets.[17]

3. MLA

The Medical Library Association publishes the *MLA Salary Survey*.[18] During the 1980s, this survey was conducted every 3 years; but, during the 1900s, it is being conducted every 2 years. Similar in design to the SLA salary survey, this one reports four statistics: lowest 10%, median, highest 10%, and average (mean). Salaries are grouped by geographic region, primary area of responsibility, type of library (e.g., academic medical center, college, or university), type of position (e.g., faculty vs. nonfaculty status), number of staff supervised, type of degree, years of experience, age, and gender.

Strengths of this survey are an excellent overview summarizing major findings and survey-to survey trends, tables that report salary statistics meaningfully and concisely, crosstabulations of key variables (e.g., salaries by region and type of library), data on fringe benefits, and reports of numbers of respondents. Its major weaknesses are an uneven response rate from survey to survey and a lack of clarity about what the labels "lowest 10%" and "highest 10%" mean. (Are these figures averages or percentiles?).

4. AALL

The *Private Law Libraries Survey of Compensation* is a biennial project of the American Association of Law Libraries' Private Law Libraries/Special Interest

[17] *Library Mosaics*, a monthly periodical for library paraprofessionals, conducts a biennial survey of support staff salaries. The results usually appear in a late summer issue. Contact *Library Mosaics* at P.O. Box 5171, Culver City, CA 90231, voice (310) 410–1573.

[18] Contact the Medical Library Association at 6 N. Michigan Avenue, Suite 300, Chicago, IL 60602, voice (312) 419–9094, fax (312) 419–8950.

Section (PLL/SIS) which is conducted by the Special Libraries Association
(SLA). While salaries paid by law school libraries are covered by ARL's survey
and those paid by government and nonprofit agencies by SLA's survey, this
project focuses on salaries paid by private and corporate law firms. Thus, it
may be of interest to academic library managers seeking to determine prevailing salaries for librarians with this specialty. Salaries are sought for seven
positions: director/chief librarian, branch chief, supervisory librarian, librarian, library assistant/technician, and library clerk. In summarizing salary patterns, SLA groups the results in many of the same ways used in its own salary
survey: years of experience, level of education, gender, geographical area, and
size of firm.

   The strengths of this project are its inclusion of all metropolitan areas
with at least 20 AALL/PLL-SIS members, the averaging of the top and
bottom 10% separately (to avoid skewing), and SLA's administration of the
survey and analysis of the results in the same manner as its own survey.

   Its major weakness is its poor response rate (48% in 1991). Other drawbacks are the inclusion of cash bonuses in reported salaries and problematic
handling of part-time salaries.

5. SLA

The Special Libraries Association conducts a biennial salary survey of its over
10,000 members.[19] The report, the *SLA Biennial Salary Survey*, summarizes
the results based on a wide variety of criteria, including:

regional and metropolitan area location;
type of organization and type of library
job title, library budget, and different levels and areas of responsibility;
academic background, previous experience, and years with present em-
     ployer; and
gender, race/ethnicity, and age.

   In addition to this dizzying array of tabulations, another major strength
of this survey is its off-year update, based on a 25% sample of the SLA
membership, which appears in the fall issue of *Special Libraries*.

   The two greatest weaknesses of this survey are its poor response rate
(45% in 1993) and the misleading date in its title. Data in the edition dated
1993 (the year of publication) were collected as of April 1, 1992.

   Academic library managers are blessed with an abundance of available
data to inform their decision-making. General surveys provide a wide variety
of statistics that measure the resources and services of college and university
libraries. While many of the figures collected in such surveys are becoming

---

[19] Contact the Special Libraries Association at 1700 18th St., N.W., Washington, DC 20009.

dated as meaningful indicators, most remain useful, and steps are being taken, albeit slowly, to address the revolution being wrought by electronic access to information. Benchmarks and performance measures are new and often problematic in their development, but, with the participation of academic library managers, can be made into useful indicators of productivity and efficiency. Cost analysis data have been elusive until now. But, with some consensus about how to do it beginning to form, there is hope for more and better data of this type. Finally, there are several sources of data on specific topics of keen interest to academic library managers (e.g., automated systems, buildings, prices, salaries). These sources should not be overlooked.

It is always tempting to launch a new survey to meet one's specific data needs, but since surveys are expensive and time-consuming for the researcher as well as for the subject, they should not be a first resort. Before making such a substantial investment, consider sources of available data, such as those reviewed here, and exploit them fully. If they meet your needs—even in part—it will be worth it.

Cooperative Efforts in New Methods of Information Delivery: The Michigan Experience

William A. Gosling, Margo Crist, Brenda Johnson, Wendy P. Lougee, and Beth Forrest Warner
The University of Michigan Library
Ann Arbor, Michigan 48109-1205

I. Introduction

Cooperative initiatives have developed in a variety of ways during the past decade. In the mid 1980s, the University of Michigan's cooperative institutional culture was one of each unit being responsible for its own operations. Support from other units on campus was purchased or negotiated with the result being very much a we/they culture and a strong sense of mistrust. In the 1990s, this culture has evolved into an environment where interunit and interinstitutional cooperation has become valued, and efforts toward greater collaboration have been realized.

This chapter chronicles this changing culture as it relates specifically to Michigans's library and information technology organizations and more broadly to the campus information environment. It also documents multiple approaches to cooperation that have simultaneously emerged and coalesced into more formal partnerships.

II. Background

During the mid-1980s, early efforts at joint activities were rooted in the development of the university library's automation program, the selection, and the ordering of its first fully integrated library system. Negotiations were handled through the provost's office for the hardware, a shared campus mainframe rather than a wholly dedicated library machine, on which to operate the library's on-line system. This computing hardware was provided by the Information Technology Division (ITD), a centralized service provider

ADVANCES IN LIBRARIANSHIP, VOL. 19
Copyright © 1995 by Academic Press, Inc.

of mainframe computer support for most units on the campus. While the hardware was centrally funded, the library was asked to fund a systems programmer position and an operator position in ITD, in addition to the staff in the Library Systems Office. The hardware and mainframe operating system software would be maintained by the ITD staff, while CICS system and software and the NOTIS applications software would be maintained by the library systems staff. Communication across units was difficult at times, and some matters required extensive negotiation to resolve turf issues.

During the succeeding 10 years, a number of institutional, organizational, and technological forces have fostered new ways of approaching the development and support of information access activities. The campus has witnessed a move to team-based, cross-functional approaches to problem solving through adoption of total quality management techniques. At the same time, the deployment of a distributed computing infrastructure has prompted the campus to reconsider the configuration of support for information technology services. From a culture of distrust and competition, an environment enabling cooperation has emerged, and partnerships have been established formally between the staff of the library and ITD and, more recently, with the School of Information and Library Studies. In addition, other partnerships on campus have been established or strengthened, including joint projects with the University Press, the College of Engineering, and various other colleges and library units.

III. The Institutional Environment

A number of factors in the institutional and broader higher education communities are clearly shaping the environment in which research libraries such as Michigan are planning. The changing *institutional* landscape at the University of Michigan includes:

- more pronounced financial constraints,
- greater flexibility of budgets, particularly at the school and college level,
- increased emphasis on interdisciplinary programs,
- increased use of information technology in all sectors,
- increased emphasis on cooperation and sharing of resources,
- increased emphasis on international initiatives and undergraduate education, and
- the changing nature of information itself.

More recently, these factors have coalesced in a changing budget structure called value centered management which provides schools and colleges with local accountability for their income (including tuition) and a responsibility to support central services. This shift, together with the constraints of revenue and the opportunities of technology for distance-independent programs, has put increasing emphasis on expanding the definition of the university community. Consequently, the future is far more likely to emphasize distance learning and services to share information and other resources outside of the university in addition to supporting on-campus user needs. Maximizing institutional resources through collaborative programs becomes critical in a time of static or shrinking fiscal bases while needing to expand and enhance information services.

IV. Information Technology Environment

The changes in the information technology sector have been similarly dramatic. While most institutions are grappling with the transition to distributed computing infrastructures and the implementation of client/server models, Michigan, perhaps, has been unique in the dimensions of these challenges. Michigan was an early leader in deployment of computing with the development of its Michigan Terminal System (MTS) operating system and set of mainframe services in the 1960s. The level of integration MTS achieved in teaching, research, and the business of the university increased the difficulty of moving this large campus to distributed systems.

In 1992, to realize this transition, Michigan launched a 2-year effort to migrate to a distributed computing model and phase out its MTS systems. Known as the Future Computing Environment (FCE) project, considerable staff time and resources were directed toward putting in place the infrastructure for key services such as electronic mail, file systems, storage, statistical computation, and database systems. What is notable about this migration effort is that it was coupled with a necessary movement on the part of the campus ITD to be more collaborative and to develop partnerships for specific areas of development.

The FCE process was enabled by dramatic growth in the campus computing infrastructure. Provost allocations were made to units to assist in establishing ethernet connectivity for all buildings. Through grant and internal support, many units moved more aggressively to install workstations capable of exploiting the new network capability. There has also been a similarly dramatic rise in units building on this infrastructure and contributing to the networked information environment with applications such as gopher and World Wide Web services.

Early Cooperative Projects

Several themes have emerged from the types of cooperative activity with a service focus the library has pursued. These include:

- cooperation that has evolved from the partnerships that have traditionally existed between the library and academic departments
- cooperation that has evolved among staff as they have sought to harness the new technologies to accomplish outreach objectives
- cooperation that has emerged in response to shifts in physical facilities
- cooperation that results from the partnerships and obligations with organizations outside the university.

Development of information technology applications has been a catalyst for these efforts, but it has been vital to keep as a central reality that the technology is a tool not the goal. For many of these developments, technology truly has been overlaid onto cooperation that already existed or had another framework in addition to the technology application.

While libraries have been accustomed to dealing with access models based on an index approach (i.e., citation or bibliographic-based systems), the emerging models increasingly are based on access to the complete documents or the primary information source itself. Gopher and web browsers have brought about a new linkage among information identification, description, and document retrieval. These factors have provided both opportunities and challenges to traditional notions of access.

V. Information Delivery Efforts with Academic Units

Applications of new technological methods of information delivery have occurred most often in arenas where partnerships have formed a continuing element in the relationships between the library and the discipline. Where there were already strong connections between a subject selector and faculty, there has emerged real synergy with exciting results. The catalyst seems to be created by recognition of the potential for use of technology jointly by the librarian and by selected faculty that means direct and strong impact on research and instruction in the disciplines. Typically, these partnerships capture both the skills of a motivated librarian, who can harness the technology for the particular use in a discipline, and the input and shaping by a faculty member who brings a specific research application to bear. Examples of these collaborations exist in several projects.

VI. The UMLibText Project

The UMLibText Project evolved in the late 1980s, based on the carefully established liaison between the English language and literature subject selector and the appropriate faculty. The understanding on the part of that selector of research needs in the field led to the acquisition, not just of the Old English corpus, the Oxford English Dictionary (OED), and a set of Middle English texts in digital format, but also to experimentation with and ultimate acquisition of software allowing for textual analysis and manipulation. This development was a joint effort but was led by the librarian who saw the opportunities the technology offered.

Search and display software, PAT and Lector (Open Text Systems, Inc.), was acquired and installed on equipment loaned to the library by the ITD. Together, these packages provide a powerful search and display system capable of handling large amounts of structured text. System development was carried out by library staff with participation by a number of users from various humanities disciplines who used the system, gave feedback, and generally helped the library understand the functions needed.

The holdings of the UMLibText system currently total over 5000 items, including the following major text collections in addition to the original acquisitions: the first installments of the Chadwyck-Healey Patrologia Latina and pre-1900 English poetry text collections; a copy of translations of the Bible and of the Koran; the first folios and the early quartos of Shakespeare; and a large collection of modern English texts that include both literary and philosophical works. The principal source of these texts has been a select number of electronic text vendors, including Chadwyck-Healey, the Oxford Text Archive, and InteLex. For the Oxford Text Archive materials, some SGML (Standard Generalized Markup Language) encoding was done by staff in the Graduate Library.

The opportunity to use UMLibText is available to all faculty, staff, and students affiliated with the University of Michigan's Ann Arbor campus. Continued publicity and presentation of the system as a production service has brought UMLibText a high level of visibility on campus. The diversity of resources contained within UMLibText has ensured that the system is used by not only literary and linguistic scholars, but also faculty, staff, and students from other humanities and social science departments, as well as from the Medical School and from Electrical Engineering and Computer Science.

VII. The Papyrology Imaging Project

The Papyrology Imaging Project is a similar partnership, developed in 1991, in the use of the outstanding collection of papyri at the University of Michigan. The library holds the largest collection of papyri in the western hemisphere. Efforts to make papyri more available for research, as well as for those not allowed to handle the originals, have led to a very active imaging effort jointly pursued by the library and a lead faculty member in papyrological studies. The building of an image database of the papyri is an important means of harnessing the technology in ways that address both access and preservation needs.

Preservation of and access to these materials are of primary concern to the scholars involved in their use. Previous methods involving photographs and microfilm now are being replaced by the use of digital images. In addition to offering a good method of preservation, access to the materials is greatly enhanced by the ease of sharing and displaying these images for research and teaching purposes. Research activity is notably facilitated by the possibilities of enlarging, darkening, or lightening the images to better decipher and translate them! The pilot project has involved scanning individual papyri and creating a database of descriptive records. Currently, 3000 images have been created, most at 300 dpi. In addition to the images, a database containing detailed information on each document has been created. These databases contain information about physical location, excavation labels, existence of negatives and plates, and detailed information about publication and publication rights for each papyrus.

VIII. Gopher Development

With the development of gopher software by the University of Minnesota, campuses across the nation saw an almost overnight proliferation of gopher servers, and Michigan was no exception. For some time, the University Library and ITD worked in parallel, developing gopher services for the campus. In 1992, a joint working group was appointed to coordinate the activity of these two central gophers. Fortunately, the two services had evolved with fairly distinct purposes—the library's gopher (ULibrary) focused on academic resources available on the internet, whereas ITD's Gopher Blue sought to provide a platform for campus information resources to be disseminated. The working group arrived at common protocols for the clients and servers and also worked with campus information providers to establish guidelines for formatting and identifying resources.

The ULibrary gopher began with little else than the Clarinet news service and rapidly expanded to include resources such as full text journals, guides, reference tools, library on-line catalogs, indexes and abstracts, and statistical documents. Although many of the resources were identified and added to ULibrary on the singular initiation of a librarian and may have a more "popular" audience, large sections of the gopher are strongly linked to academic programs.

The health and biological sciences areas are exceedingly rich with examples of collaborative development with academic units. Some examples of resources that are of high value to campus include: Human Genome Project reports and newsletters, which facilitate communication among genome researchers; Genbank, a database of all published nucleic acid sequences; PROSITE, a compilation of sites and patterns found in protein sequences; CancerNet from the National Cancer Institute; and International AIDS resources.

The Government Documents and Political Science sections have been vigorously enhanced and maintained with resources such as LEGI-SLATE for text of bills and the Federal Register, Congressional Committee assignments, and historical documents from the Articles of the Confederation to Constitutional Amendments. A number of unique resources also have been created by the documents staff, including heavily used congressional directories.

IX. TULIP

The University LIcensing Program (TULIP) developed from Elsevier Science publishers' interest in discovering more about the potential of electronic publishing and its impact on the readers of their journals. In 1992, they approached a group of academic libraries and asked them to submit proposals describing how they would offer electronic versions of a select group of journals. A community of nine universities, some with related consortia, were selected to test these potentials in the identified area of materials science. The topic was chosen because of its fairly focused area and identifiable user community.

Upon notification of being chosen as one of the participants in the TULIP study, the team proceeded to make available the image versions of approximately 40 material science journals; these were made available through a locally developed search and display system called Desktop Information Resources and Collaboration Tool (DIReCT) developed by the College of Engineering information technology staff with initial support from the Digital Equipment Corporation (DEC). The DIReCT software allows users to browse or search for journal articles of interest, display them on their desktop workstation, and print articles at printers located throughout the campus. DIReCT also allows users to "profile" their interests and to have abstracts of articles which match that profile automatically delivered by e-mail.

The second component of the display mechanism was to use the library's NOTIS system and mount these citations and abstracts as an MDAS citation file available through the campus OPAC. The library citation file enabled searchers to identify citations of interest and either connect to the print holdings described in the library's OPAC or to request, through a set of prompts, that articles be printed at any 1 of 10 identified campus printing sites.

The TULIP team was composed of staff from the ITD, three people from the University Library, and technologists from the College of Engineering. The project was developed and brought into production through a contributed effort on the part of the several units represented on the team. As needed, resources were identified within the respective units to provide space or programmer support or telecommunications connectivity to enable the project to operate as envisioned. Again, there were no separate budget allocations or staff hired specifically to work on this project. Respective skills were claimed from existing staff within the library, ITD, and the College of Engineering. The success of the project is a direct result of the cooperative spirit exemplified by this group of people working to bring the TULIP project very successfully into production.

X. Outreach beyond Library Facilities and the Campus

At times in the development of cooperative endeavors, the technology products have become the basis for outreach to occur and to create new connections and collaboration. There has been an ongoing thrust toward outreach into the campus community so that librarians could operate more directly in the user's space. Learning or pursuing research in the library's physical spaces is not as natural or as productive for many users as is the ability to interact with staff and library resources from a student or faculty office/study space. Outreach efforts that previously were being pursued now can be built on a new technology base and products, resulting in wholly new connections and interactions for both librarian and user.

The new integrated Science Library on the Michigan campus offers a new and interdisciplinary sense of place for the library. A complement to these facilities will be the substantially enhanced and increased document and information delivery approach. Efforts will be focused on faculty and students being able to retrieve more information directly at the desktop (see description of examples of projects under Digital Library Program), as well as more traditional paper-based delivery via RLG's Ariel, fax, and courier services. Science librarians will be "on the road," avoiding any perception that they are captives of the new Science Library facility. They will be targeting departments and individual faculty for the kind of support efforts that have been in place in departmental libraries. This type of "personal" service will be essential to the success of the endeavor. In a similar fashion, the university will open in early 1996 the Integrated Technology Instruction Center (ITIC), an experiment in collaborative instruction, research, and learning. Again, the library space will be a "place," but library service will reach out to those outside the facility, and the resources will become increasingly digital and ubiquitous.

On a state-wide level, the University of Michigan Library deals increasingly with "virtual patrons," notably in such projects as MLink which connects the library to over 300 public libraries throughout the state. Staff provide on-line reference services and information access through the M-Link gopher. Another example is ComNet, a special network under development for Detroit social service agencies. In both cases, the ability of the library to provide resources electronically and to provide support that has a human face are vital combinations. Cooperative approaches are evident with these two projects as MLink coordinates with the Library of Michigan and the Public Library Cooperatives of the State, and ComNet is pursued under the leadership of the university's School of Social Work.

The projects just noted reflect a successful track record for cooperation, each harnessing information technologies as a tool and each forging new relationships between the library and other units. These projects also began to accumulate a variety of electronic information resources on the campus network. Increasingly, it was becoming clear, however, that the pace of development on the internet and the rapid move on campus to distributed resources required a more formal management model to ensure a more cohesive campus environment.

XI. The Administrative Management Model

The Michigan administrative management model has evolved toward the form of a complementary partnership with no one unit being selected over another to coordinate the campus initiatives. On some campuses, the university librarian has been asked to assume responsibility for campus computing facilities, especially academic computing. On other campuses, the university library has reported to the head of the computing services for information technology operations. Since 1993, several of these mergers subsequently have been terminated with the reestablishment of the independent library or the administratively separate computing center. The partnership model at Michigan has offered the opportunity to build programs on the strengths each unit has to contribute while avoiding some of the shortcomings associated with one unit assigned an overall management role.

One of the factors promoting this development at the University of Michigan has been the recognition that of the several parties needed to create a successful service on the campus, each has valuable expertise to offer. No one unit could hope to address the range of issues which electronic information access activities require. Even collectively they are challenged by the rapidly overwhelming rate of change in the formats in which information is being produced and in the ever-escalating pace of change in technology by which that information is made available.

Recognition of the benefits of complementary resources and expertise versus overlapping and competing ones also pointed toward the need for greater joint ventures. The first steps toward enhanced cooperation grew out of an information symposium held in 1991. That year-long effort involved three faculty committees in discussions surrounding electronic information; groups focused on user needs, funding, and collection issues related to electronic information. Following that committee process, a smaller task force was chaired by a former UM president and the Dean of the School of Information and Library Studies (members of the task force included the Dean of the Library, the Vice-Provost for Information Technology, the Associate Dean for Engineering, and a faculty member). That task force arrived at several specific recommendations for future action:

- the campus should identify a strategy to blend the complementary vision and expertise of the library and computing communities;
- the campus should build for the future through specific projects which address not only "quality of life" issues for the community, but also contribute nationally to the evolving digital information environment; and
- policies are needed that preserve the connectivity so essential to an academic community requiring the development of open electronic access policies for information resources.

Those recommendations, in essence, focused on issues that are now commonly shared in the popular press discussions of the "information superhighway"— that is, as the networks grow and access to computer resources becomes ever more distributed, how do individuals find and use appropriate electronic information resources. Their recommendations also conveyed a sense of urgency in moving forward with a project-based approach toward digital information.

This symposium report became an agenda for action, which senior managers from ITD and the University Library used to identify projects on which they could work jointly in an effort to move this campus information agenda forward. The process began with a series of managers' meetings. At first, these quarterly sessions were reporting mechanisms used primarily to educate senior managers as to the major programs and needs of the other units. In October 1992, senior managers charged a joint library/ITD working group to coordinate gopher services between the two organizations. Based on the experiences of this working group, the senior managers group focused on the need for a campus wide information service and in February 1993 charged a collaborative resource team to draft a working document outlining the conceptual requirements and organizational responsibilities for such a service. These discussions quickly led to the realization that there was a broader agenda to be discussed. Drawing on recommendations in the CWIS document and the fact that the organizations had not been able to get any other major projects underway, the Vice-Provost for Information Technology and the Dean of the Library, joined by the Dean of the School of Information and Library Studies, determined that the process would benefit from a single, dedicated position to provide leadership and to create focus on a substantial core of projects to meet the informational needs of the campus. This collaborative effort resulted in the formation of the Digital Library Program (DLP) and the appointment of a DLP director in 1993.

The program director, selected from the library, was appointed to meet regularly and coordinate operations closely with the three directors: the Dean of the Library, the Vice-Provost for Information Technology, and the Dean of the School of Information and Library Studies, resulting in a successful bridging of programs among these organizations.

Early in the development of the DLP, three overarching goals were identified which helped drive the projects undertaking. First, the notion of a campus digital library is defined *comprehensively*, i.e., as inclusive of traditional library information resources as well as administrative, unit, and individual information. Second, the program seeks to bring *coherence* to the environment, i.e., creating a logical organization for the network information resources much like libraries have sought to bring a logical organization to collections of print volumes. Finally, there is a goal of creating a *coordinated* environment, i.e., employing standards and common systems which promote easy and effective access to information.

These three "Cs" have guided the selection of projects. In addition, an attempt has been made to identify projects which will put in place a foundation for particular types of information and, simultaneously, add significant content to the available information resources on the local network.

As the program evolved, the partners also engaged in discussions to help shape the roles of the partner organizations. Discussions among the senior management of the organizations focused on defining the core competencies of each and on the delineation of the responsibilities which derive from those areas of expertise. As illustrated in Fig. 1, these competencies also helped guide the selection process in creating project teams.

Seizing upon the earlier recommendation that the collaboration focus on *doing*, a project-based approach has been utilized from the beginning of the program. Projects have been pursued which

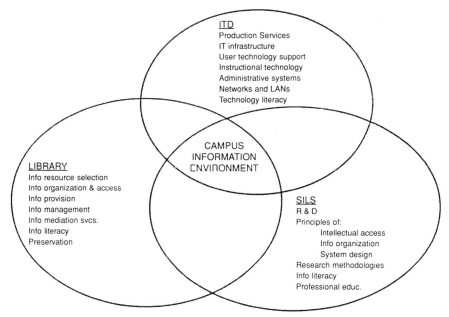

Fig. 1 Expertise/core competencies of the partner organizations.

- create and/or acquire new digital information resources,
- develop the necessary functional components for the campus digital library,
- create mechanisms to involve other campus information providers/creators in the evolving campus wide efforts, and
- provide integration and coordination of information resources.

An underlying strategy has been to identify projects which fall into two domains. First, there has been a focused effort to identify and organize campus networked information resources. Second, projects have been launched which deal with specific formats of information in order to address the unique issues of structure, retrieval, and storage appropriate for that information type. A schematic of this format-driven approach is represented in Fig. 2.

The descriptions of a few selected projects undertaken within the digital library program umbrella highlight these two categories of activity.

XII. Information Gateway

A joint working group has developed a single portal for accessing and browsing the networked information available from campus units. Called the "UM

- UM Information Gateway
  - Identify resources
  - Organize information for access

- Context/Tool Projects

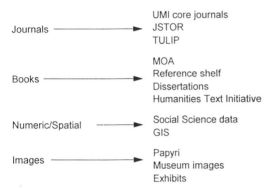

Fig. 2   Digital library strategies.

Information Gateway," the project has created a taxonomy for describing all types of resources on campus and has developed an interface, using a web browser homepage, which allows users to identify and connect with networked resources. For example, a user can look at topical headings for resources (much like a catalog) and identify unit and individual resources. The development of the gateway was coupled with a university community census to identify campus resources and capture sufficient information to develop descriptive entries.

The working group which developed the gateway consisted of staff from the Information Technology Division and the School of Information and Library Studies, a library cataloger, a graphic designer, and a representative from the University Relations Office (to assist in developing the appropriate policies for defining the campus "collection" of information resources). Chaired by the head of the campus Undergraduate Library, the group's perspective was user-driven and attempted to promote a flexible yet structured system of campus resources.

As the gateway moves to a production service, a similar team of technologists and librarians will be involved in further development of the access structures and will work with units to develop local resources.

XIII. Core Journals

A collaborative project with University Microfilms International (UMI) has created a substantial networked collection of journals. Beginning in November 1994, bit-mapped images of articles from early 600 journals were made available on-line, providing access for authorized campus users to general and core titles in several disciplines, especially the social sciences. This project has allowed users to print articles from journals such as *Nature*, the *Journal of the American Statistical Association*, the *International Labour Review*, *Time*, or the *NYT Magazine* any time, day or night. The response has been overwhelming; within 4 months, the number of pages printed from the service averaged over 85,500 pages per month or about 11,000 articles, averaging 7.98 pages/article.

The service takes journal article images provided by UMI and links them with the Wilson journal citation indexes found in the library's on-line catalog system, MIRLYN. If an image exists for an article and/or a print item is owned by the library, the user is prompted to display library print holdings or request a print from the image files of the article. The user provides identification (the service is licensed for the campus community only) and selects the print site from which to retrieve the printed article.

The early phase of this service has focused on putting distributed printing functions in place. The next phase will focus on viewing capabilities and linkages with the campus accounting and billing service to handle royalty and printing payments.

XIV. JSTOR and Making of America

Two projects funded by the Mellon Foundation will add considerable historical content to the digital library. Under the Journal STORage Project, or JSTOR, staff will oversee conversion of the entire run, up to 1990, of 10 core journals in economics and history to digital form. Titles such as the *American Economic Review*, *American Historical Review*, and the *William and Mary Quarterly* will be scanned and made available using the DIReCT interface developed for the TULIP project.

This archive of journals will be made accessible to five colleges at three sites: the Tri-College consortium (Bryn Mawr, Swarthmore, and Haverford), Denison, and Williams and also to the University of Michigan community. Mellon's goals include an assessment of user behavior related to print vs electronic access and an evaluation of the economic implications of digital vs physical collections.

The collaborative components of JSTOR span on- and off-campus groups. On campus, staff in the College of Engineering and ITD will provide hardware and client support, whereas librarians will assist in developing access structures and providing user support. Contacts within the libraries at each remote site have been established to codevelop training programs for users in those communities and formally to channel inquiries about the system and its performance. The deployment teams plan to use traditional electronic communication and potentially interactive communication technologies.

Mellon also funded the Making of America Project (MOA) in which the University of Michigan and Cornell University will collaborate. The goal for this undertaking is to build a significant image collection of books dealing with the development of the United States. Books published between 1860 and 1960 will be scanned, stored, and made accessible via the network.

In the first phase, launched in 1995, 5000 volumes from these two institutions will be converted to digital images. Ultimately, the project will expand to include other institutions. MOA will result in the development of a digital library of thematically related primary sources on the history of America— an aggregate collection which will represent a resource richer than the sum of the individual holdings of each participating institution.

MOA involves interinstitutional development of all phases of the digital library. Technical staff from both institutions will work on access systems and client development. Preservation staff will address issues surrounding image capture and conversion quality control. Selector/bibliographers will work on selection criteria for the collection, and user support librarians will assess and develop programs to ensure effective use of the resources. Faculty also will be involved in the selection and evaluation components. Finally, an advisory panel will include librarians and technologists from a number of other institutions. A primary goal of the undertaking will be to establish the infrastructure for multi-institutional collaboration of this sort.

XV. Humanities Text Initiative

The library, the School of Information and Library Studies, the University Press, and the College of Literature, Science, and Arts joined forces to launch the Humanities Text Initiative, providing both financial support and an organizational coalition for this endeavor. The initiative includes a librarian coordinator for the program and, with additional funding from the Vice President for Research, a production suite of hardware and software to support the creation and conversion of texts and related media.

The Humanities Text Initiative provides a program focus for instruction and research related to electronic text and related systems for wider practical access to text in the humanities. Guided by faculty leadership, the program will serve as a catalyst for interdisciplinary scholarship. The initiative librarian has primary responsibility for the development and management of text resources, working with library and campus units to develop projects which enhance the archive.

The initiative builds on UMLibText, the existing archive of encoded texts in the humanities noted earlier. In addition to an active program of text conversion, commercial products in SGML have been added, e.g., *Information Please Almanac, McGraw-Hill Encylopedia of Science and Technology*, and *American Heritage Dictionary*.

To support emerging campus interests in publishing and the creation of text, the librarian works with scholars and the University Press to develop systems and services in support of creation and wider distribution of text. Within SILS, the librarian is involved in exploratory systems development and teaching related to text structure and analysis.

More recently, the initiative has received additional support through a competitive proposal process sponsored by the office of the president. This presidential initiative will fund faculty fellows to work in the area of text creation, research and librarian assistants, and a physical center for collaborative activity.

XVI. Social Science Data Sets

Sophisticated users of statistical information have become used to the cumbersome process of loading data tapes and using difficult analysis software. A project geared toward making these data more accessible to the general user has developed a graphic interface to data sets using a web browser such as Mosaic which allows even the inexperienced user to identify variables of interest and retrieve statistical and numeric information. The forms and menu button capabilities of a web browser are used as input to a modified HTTP server and the capability developed to write SAS code files and submit SAS jobs. In addition, the project integrates the complementary code books for datasets with the data themselves. Currently, the following datasets are available: National Health Interview Survey, General Social Survey, American National Election Study, and the Current Population Survey.

Other pilot project efforts have been developed under the library/ITD/ SILS digital library program umbrella, including explorations of electronic reserve reading services, proposals to convert engineering technical reports to image files for network access, a project to make a video encyclopedia available on the campus broadband network, the Museum Educational Site

License Project (Getty Art History Program), UMI-based dissertation delivery program, and collaborative work with geographic information systems.

As the just-mentioned descriptions suggest, the several projects to deliver electronic resources to the campus are highly collaborative, involving not only collaboration between librarians and technologists, but with other campus units, such as academic departments and the University Press, vendors, and publishers as well. Such collaboration has become increasingly important as the challenges of creating and managing collections change. It is also increasingly clear that the emerging digital information landscape has a great many unknowns—not the least of which is how to fund and create a smooth integration of paper-based and digial libraries.

With the decision to hire a central coordinator in 1993 to facilitate identification of and planning for delivery of the emerging electronic information resources, a critical step was taken to enhance the cooperative model and solidify a partnership between key organizations on campus. This base has greatly reduced the time to develop a project as compared with efforts through traditional methods. The result is a rapidly developing campus network information environment.

XVII. Regional Cooperation

In addition to the campus and state out-reach efforts, the University of Michigan has been involved in two major state and regional cooperative programs as well.

A. Michigan Research Libraries Triangle

The Michigan Research Libraries Triangle (MRLT) is a cooperative effort between the three ARL libraries in the state: the University of Michigan, Michigan State University, and Wayne State University. MRLT is a voluntary consortium based on the recognized need to make better use of existing library resources through cooperative efforts. The combined resources of the three libraries provide access to approximately 12 million volumes, 122,000 journal titles, and a number of citation databases. Thanks to earlier grants from the W.K. Kellogg Foundation, virtually all materials are bibliographically accessible through each library's on-line catalog. While patrons at each university have had access to the collections of the other schools, access has not always been easy. Recognizing the need for improvement, the three libraries sought funding to link more closely their on-line systems through a Department of Education Title II-A grant in 1993. The major objectives were to

- allow patrons to identify materials held at any one of the three libraries through a seamless interconnection from any authorized OPAC terminal
- allow patrons to request materials found in the other libraries from an on-line interlibrary loan request screen and to expedite delivery of these materials
- enable the three libraries to mount cooperatively and access citation databases in addition to the on-line catalog
- enable the three libraries to expand and facilitate cooperative collection management strategies in a time of shrinking budgets and journal cancellations
- enable the libraries to more effectively coordinate preservation decisions
- use the project as a building block toward the creation of a linked library network of local library systems at the state, regional, and national level.

Following the award of the DoE grant in October 1993, the MRLT libraries purchased Z39.50 intersystem protocol software [PACLink from NOTIS Systems, Inc. (Ameritech Library Services)] to enable linking the three on-line catalogs. The linked OPACs became available to patrons in June 1994.

Phase two of the project involves providing an online mechanism to request materials for interlibrary loan through the local OPAC. Building on the PACLink software in place to provide search capabilities, the MRLT libraries are installing PACLoan to provide patrons with the on-line request mechanism and to provide staff with ILL management software. Managing the anticipated increased document delivery activity will require use of the latest technology and increased demands on staffing. In addition to the enhanced ILL request mechanism, the MRLT libraries also are pursuing joint licensing agreements for on-line citation files linked to their on-line catalogs. Databases such as the MLA Bibliography, Current Contents Search, and Agricola will be mounted at one of the institutions but will be available to patrons at all three sites. This cooperative approach to licensing and access will allow the MRLT libraries to make the best use of acquisitions budgets, computing resources, and staff time while increasing the availability of information resources for patrons.

B. Committee on Institutional Cooperation

In a parallel regional effort, the University of Michigan has been a long-time participant in the Committee on Institutional Cooperation (CIC), an academic consortium of 13 major teaching and research universities[1] in the Midwest, established in 1958. The CIC is founded on three guiding principles:

[1] The CIC institutions are University of Chicago, University of Illinois and University of Illinois-Chicago, Indiana University, University of Iowa, University of Michigan, Michigan State University, University of Minnesota, Northwestern University, The Ohio State University, Pennsylvania State University, Purdue University, and University of Wisconsin-Madison.

- no single institution can or should attempt to be all things to all people
- interinstitutional cooperation permits educational experimentation and progress on a scale beyond the capability of any single institution acting alone
- voluntary cooperation fosters effective, concerted action while preserving institutional autonomy and diversity.[2]

Historically, the CIC libraries have a long list of cooperative activities, including the CIC Resource Sharing Agreement, growing cooperative collection development efforts, several major preservation microfilming projects, and the work of the CIC Task Force on Mass Deacidification. However, decreasing library budgets at a time when information resources were increasing exponentially required even greater cooperative efforts. Beginning in late 1992, a strategic plan was developed by the CIC library directors which has as its focus a vision of the CIC information resources as a seamless whole, regardless of location or ownership. Implementation of this strategic plan was given impetus in 1993 by the award of a 3-year, $1.2 million grant from the Department of Education (Title II-A) to create a virtual electronic library for the CIC institutions. The grant helps establish the necessary technological infrastructure to support seamless interconnections, based on the Z39.50 protocol, among the existing on-line systems. Although the first phase of the project, Z39.50 search protocol implementation, has been similar to the MRLT project, the CIC libraries do not all use the same on-line system and have pushed the boundaries of the existing standard by linking NOTIS and non-NOTIS systems.

Phase II of the project, beginning late spring of 1995, will test the use of PACLoan for interlibrary loan among three CIC NOTIS sites. The rest of 1995 will be spent expanding the use of PACLoan and developing a comparable patron-initiated loan mechanism for the non-NOTIS libraries. As with the MRLT project, managing the anticipated increased document delivery activity will require use of the latest technology and increased staffing.

In addition to the enhanced ILL request mechanism, the CIC libraries also are pursuing joint licensing agreements for on-line citation databases. Databases, such as Beilstein and ERIC, will be mounted at one of the institutions but will be available to patrons at other participating sites. This cooperative approach to licensing and access will allow the CIC libraries also to make the best use of acquisitions budgets, computing resources, and staff time.

In a complementary project, CIC library directors charged the Task Force on the CIC Electronic Collection to examine the issues involved and to develop policy statements for the acquisition, access, and preservation of electronic journals. Working with CICNet, over 700 journals have been made available through a gopher server. In addition to providing gopher access, a

[2] *1993–1994 Annual Report*, Committee on Institutional Cooperation, 1994, p 1.

subset of electronical journals has been selected, with several of the libraries providing cooperative cataloging of the electronic journals in order to provide access via OCLC and CIC on-line catalogs.

XVIII. User Communities

Last, but not least, we have witnessed an enormous rise in expectations among the library's users. They have become accustomed to network access to information, anytime, anyplace, and justifiably are interested in seeing library resources available in this way. The rise in importance of remote access has provided challenges for user support. The Michigan response to these challenges has irrevocably altered the traditional service relationship and notion of libraries as facility-based services.

Nothing in the shifts at the University of Michigan Library toward more cooperative, collaborative arrangements across library units, across campus units, and outside the traditional campus itself suggests, however, an abandonment of the role of library as place and the role of librarian as navigator and partner. These roles are being changed and transformed but not diminished. The library remains a vital place where the entire array of information sources and formats can be combined and integrated in ways of the user's choosing. The librarian remains a central figure who can facilitate creation, discovery, and integration of sources in methods that truly lead to knowledge. The new approaches and combinations only affirm the central place of the library and librarians in the future of the knowledge enterprise.

Quality Improvement in Libraries: Total Quality Management and Related Approaches

Joanne H. Boelke
Library Services and Information Technology
Mankato State University
Mankato, Minnesota 56002

I. Introduction

Change has been a way of organizational life for libraries for several decades. The growing dimensions and rapidly increasing pace of change that libraries now face, however, are readily apparent in current library professional publications. It is also obvious from the literature that quality improvement looms large as one of the many topics of concern for today's libraries.

In 1987, Shaughnessy noted that "the challenge of raising the quality of library services is perhaps one of the most serious, yet least talked about issues in the profession" (p. 9). Clearly, the present situation is different. The attention now given to quality improvement in libraries and its attendant organizational change is evident in the proliferation of articles on quality issues, both theoretical and practical. It is also evident in library and professional association activities and in the considerable amount of discussion related to quality improvement topics in general.

At this point, library quality improvement efforts focus largely on the total quality management (TQM) approach or on processes using TQM principles under different names. It is, however, a topic that is not without controversy.

Because TQM is the process that now receives the most attention in the library field as well as in other sectors, the approach, in its varied forms, is the focus of this overview of current quality improvement activities in libraries. (Brockman's 1992 paper provides an excellent survey of the development of the library and information science quality movement as it has evolved from quality control, to quality assurance, and now to total quality management.)

This chapter covers the general characteristics of TQM and related approaches, highlights background publications and bibliographies, and analyzes the various elements of TQM as they are discussed in the library literature. Because virtually all of the publications on the topic focus on academic and special libraries, the article concentrates on specific TQM applications and outcomes in these types of libraries. Although the literature on TQM in public and school libraries is sparse, applications in these libraries are covered briefly, and some of the controversies related to TQM that libraries are encountering are also considered. In addition, perspectives from selected countries outside the United States, activities in professional library associations, training opportunities, and electronic resources for TQM discussion and information are summarized to a limited extent. Finally, the relationship of TQM to current library organizational issues and trends is discussed throughout this review of quality improvement in libraries.

II. TQM in General

A. Historical Perspectives

Although the quality movement of this century began in the United States in the 1920s with the work of Walter Shewhart and others at the Bell Laboratory, it took off dramatically in post-war Japan. The roots of the strong Japanese quality revolution, however, are American.

In an effort to rebuild Japan's economy and to improve the quality of its products after World War II, W. Edwards Deming, an American pioneer quality consultant, lectured in Japan on statistical quality control methods. His work, the training that Joseph M. Juran provided on the managerial aspects of quality control systems, and the work of Philip Crosby were the impetus for the enthusiastic Japanese adoption of quality control principles.

By the 1980s, however, many American companies, feeling the Japanese challenge sharply, moved to quality improvement processes. During this period of competition the U.S. Navy established the term commonly used today, "total quality management" (Riggs, 1992c). Following its solid establishment in the corporate and industrial sectors, TQM is now being embraced by the nonprofit world, including a significant number of libraries.

B. TQM Defined

The essence of a TQM-based organization is a customer-centered culture which emphasizes continuous, incremental improvement of products and services through employee involvement and participative management. Other key principles of a TQM organization are a focus on employee training; the breaking down of internal barriers between service areas and external barriers between the institution and its outside contacts; the elimination of the fear of reprisal; the use of problem-solving teams; the application of statistical methods; long-range planning; and a "recognition that it is the system, not the employees, that is responsible for most inefficiencies" (Jurow and Barnard, 1993c, p. 3).

TQM also emphasizes the need for top management commitment to quality improvement, a reduction in processes and procedures, and the elimination of rework by doing the work right the first time. These characteristics of TQM as an approach to quality improvement, although phrased differently and with disparities in some of the concepts, are found in Deming's 14 points, Crosby's 4 "absolutes," and Juran's 10 steps (Riggs, 1992b, pp. 96–99).

Many of those writing in the library field see the need for a strategic plan to be in place as well, along with its underlying mission and vision statements (Riggs, 1992b). It is also generally agreed that this formal, systematic approach to continuous improvement is a gradual, multiyear process, not a quick fix. It is unquestionably an approach that requires significant resources, especially for training.

In a cogent analysis of the status of TQM in libraries, Dougherty (1992) discusses questions being raised about the emphasis TQM places on customer satisfaction through the continuous improvement of organizational processes and procedures, given the present critical economic situation for most libraries. He concludes that the business world shows that "it's continual improvement or loss of market share" (p. 3). He supports this conclusion when he states that

> we could view our current financial straits as providing us with the perfect opportunity to re-think our service objectives, delivery mechanisms, and internal systems. Exigency has required many organizations to take a new, hard look at what it is they want to accomplish and how they can be successful at doing it. . . . TQM could prove to be just another management fad. Or it could be the catalyst that causes librarians to examine issues such as leadership, staff empowerment, incentive programs, work simplification, innovation, and performance evaluation. (p. 3)

C. TQM: Pros and Cons

1. Possibilities and Proponents

The level of interest in TQM and its various processes in the library field is indicated in several ways. The rapid growth of the library-focused TQM electronic discussion list, TQMLIB, with 317 members by Fall 1994, is one sign of the attention the process is receiving. Although the numbers were not large, the fact that 18 of the 30 respondents to a survey conducted by the Library Administration and Management Association (LAMA) Total

Quality Management for Libraries Discussion Group use a TQM process indicates that these activities are beginning to appear in libraries (Bell, 1994a). The number of library professional association programs devoted to aspects of TQM and the recent rapid growth of TQM-related articles in the library professional literature also illustrate the interest in the process.

Undoubtedly, a large number of libraries today are at least contemplating, if not actually implementing, this new customer-oriented, teamwork-based process for continuous quality improvement. As proponents point out, few service institutions seem more appropriate for TQM than libraries, with their long-established focus on users and the delivery of quality services.

2. Barriers, Potential Problems, and Opponents

A survey of member libraries of the Association of Research Libraries (ARL) shows, however, that TQM has a long way to go, especially in academic libraries. Of the 91 ARL libraries responding to the survey, only 15 indicated that they currently had a formal quality improvement program [Association of Research Libraries (ARL), 1993].

A number of barriers to the implementation of TQM have been encountered in all types of organizations, including libraries. The problems that surface are discussed to a certain extent in the library literature, without reference to specific institutions (Jurow and Barnard, 1993c; Pearson, 1993; Stuart and Drake, 1993). They range from the view that this is only another management fad of the day, to management's fear of the loss control, to employee reluctance to recommend changes because of fear of the management, to the concern that the business and industrial background of TQM might not lend itself to the nonprofit sector, including libraries. Questions about the vocabulary and TQM jargon are examples of this last problem. Terms like "customers" are still associated primarily with business and industry, which is problematic for some members in fields such as librarianship.

Another barrier is the fact that TQM is not a quick fix but requires a long-term investment of time over several years as processes are analyzed and an organization's culture is changed. This can cause resistance and other difficulties in these days of increasing financial and other pressures.

Still another fact to be faced is that the more professionalized the organization is, the harder it seems to be for some in the field to accept the customer focus of the approach. If TQM is interpreted as not just customer-driven but customer-controlled and not led by professional expertise, many professionals find the approach difficult to accept. Unquestionably, academics often resist the idea of students as customers. These same academics may also fear that TQM could threaten the autonomy of faculty members because of their traditionally varied teaching methods (O'Neil, Harwood, and Osif, 1993, p.

248). As Jurow and Barnard (1993c) note, it is also interesting that in the health care field, where TQM has had real imapct, it is usually the physicians who are more resistant to the process. It is easy to see librarians reacting with this same mind-set.

The author of a provocative article that discusses the place and perception of librarians in academia also sees problems with the relationship between professionalism and TQM (Veaner, 1994). In a strongly stated view of the appropriate role for academic librarians, Veaner stresses the need to maintain the intellectual character and leadership function of librarians if they are to retain their status as professionals with programmatic responsibilities in the academic environment. This means that he vigorously opposes management methods like TQM that promote less hierarchy in libraries.

More lessons learned from less than successful applications of the TQM process are well-covered by Pearson (1993). Problems can exist in establishing a good relationship between management control and promoting employee empowerment. This has resulted in the need for established standards of service which are understood and accepted by all concerned. Moreover, organizations should consider the overall context of their operation when setting their standards for quality, avoiding an unrealistic perfectionism. Another problem encountered is related to TQM statistical tools, which can focus too heavily on zero defects. An inappropriate emphasis on these tools in complex service organizations such as libraries may result in TQM and its goals being regarded as unattainable. This may also lead to the view that TQM is unrealistic manipulation. Pearson (1993) points out that

> the challenge of TQM, like any other organizational program, is to assure that its full systemic outcomes—its effects on the organization at large, organizational stakeholders, and the organizational context—are considered. . . . Before initiating TQM, managers must fully consider and understand the likely effects that the program will have on employees and the tasks they perform. TQM should be implemented only after there is reasonable understanding of the impact that it may have on stakeholders—work groups, throughout the organization, and outside the organization. TQM should be an effort implemented not for its own sake, but to enhance the learning capability of the organization. (p. 149)

There appears to be an essential fact that underlies all of the basic TQM elements as well as the caveats related to them. Given the demands of TQM, it seems apparent that the libraries adopting the process must be basically healthy institutions, not faced with severe management, staff, professional identity, or resource problems. As a library administrator who is deeply involved in implementing TQM in an academic library states, "a library contemplating using TQM will want to think of what it will give up in immediate staff productivity in order to accomplish the long-range changes" (Butcher, 1993, p. 55).

D. Background Publications

A number of publications, both library-related and general, are available to libraries that are considering the TQM process. A good overview of TQM in libraries is provided in *Integrating Total Quality Management in the Library Setting* (Jurow and Barnard, 1993a), also published as an issue of the *Journal of Library Administration* (Jurow and Barnard, 1993b). This volume includes articles on applications in specific libraries, an overview and model for implementing the process, a discussion of tools and techniques, and a description of the use of TQM in other nonprofit sectors. For applications from the special library perspective, the Summer 1993 issue of *Special Libraries* (St. Clair, 1993a) is highly recommended.

In addition, several articles offer good, if briefer, introductions to TQM in libraries. Mackey and Mackey (1992) provide an excellent analysis of Deming's 14 points as they might apply to libraries. They also include a flow chart (a specific TQM technique) and an example of the use of a customer survey to analyze problems with the reference process. Riggs (1993) provides a clear, concise overview of the process, along with practical advice on successfully using the approach in a library setting.

The literature appearing in library publications is not sufficient, however, for libraries considering the process. Library managers will find it necessary to consult publications included in several excellent bibliographies that list key works on TQM in general. These same bibliographies usually also include publications on the application of the process in various fields. It is only by consulting the works of the early quality gurus themselves (i.e., Crosby, 1979; Deming, 1986; Juran and Gryna, 1988) as well as important works on TQM in fields like higher education that a thorough understanding of TQM principles will be gained. It is also important to consult standard titles such as Scholtes's *Team Handbook: How to Use Teams to Improve Quality* (1988) for guidance on implementing the approach.

A good article, designed to bring readers "up to light speed on the topic" (O'Neil, et al., 1993, p. 250), includes references to a number of publications on TQM from various perspectives. Other good bibliographies listing key works on TQM in various sectors are available in the library literature (Liu, 1992; St. Clair, 1993b; Sears, 1993; Zabel and Avery, 1992). Bibliographies appearing in electronic discussion lists such as TQMLIB (Bell, 1994b; Lessin, 1994c) and LIBADMIN (Doering, 1994) are also sources for references to important TQM literature.

Another excellent source of information is the SPEC Kit and Flyer 196, *Quality Improvement in Libraries* (ARL, 1993), compiled by Jack Siggins and Maureen Sullivan as part of the Office of Management Services Collaborative Research/Writing Program. Following the flyer that provides an overview of quality improvement in ARL libraries, information on some 10 library programs and on training sessions are provided through the standard SPEC Kit survey and review process. Selected readings on quality improvement are also listed.

A column first appearing in the Winter 1994 issue of *Library Administration & Management* (O'Neil, Harwood, and Orsif, 1994) also provides background information. This column is designed to keep the library profession informed about TQM activities through discussion of the topic, references to recommended books and articles, and announcements of educational and professional opportunities.

Total Quality Management: A Sourcebook (O'Neil, 1994) is an excellent resource that combines library-related TQM information with an introduction to the process in general. The major portion of the book includes reprints of several key articles from the library literature on TQM. An annotated bibliography of additional articles from the library perspective is also included along with appendixes that list general TQM books and other resources in the field.

III. The TQM Process: Key Elements

Barnard (1993) presents a systematic and useful model for implementing TQM in research libraries. As such, it is an excellent starting point for identifying the "various issues, elements and processes . . . that comprise a comprehensive TQM-based transition" (p. 58) to an institution that focuses on quality and the customer.

As the definition in Section II,B indicates, among the requirements for a TQM organization are the need for at least most of the following: strong top management support; a systems approach and strategic planning; a customer focus; an emphasis on employee teamwork, empowerment, and training; the use of measurement and analysis techniques to determine problems and evaluate improvement; and a commitment to continuous improvement (Barnard, 1993; Brown, 1994; Loney and Bellefontaine, 1993; Warnken, Young, and Ahuja, 1992). Realistically, it is unlikely that all of these elements will be present when a library initially undertakes TQM. The fact that they invariably appear as key aspects when the process is discussed, however, indicates that most, if not all, of the elements will be incorporated as a library becomes a TQM-based institution.

Barnard (1993) makes a good point in noting that unlike the manufacturing and corporate sectors, where TQM often requires "sudden, holistic change" (p. 58), many of the elements of TQM are already in place in libraries.

They are simply ready for expansion and improvement while other new approaches are being introduced.

A. Top Management Support

A process that involves a lengthy period of initiation, training, and implementation before results can be realized unquestionably requires top management support. Moreover, the focus on employee empowerment, which looks for improvement recommendations from those doing the work and is "predicated on the belief that those who do the work are best able to manage it" (Butcher, 1993, p. 55), could not exist without top management commitment to employee teamwork and involvement.

Although acknowledging that internal activity can begin elsewhere in the library, Barnard's (1993) implementation model for research libraries strongly supports the essential role of top management commitment, especially if support is not provided by the university or other parent institution. As phase one (called First Steps) in the model, she emphasizes the importance of library managers gathering information about TQM and thoroughly analyzing its potential role in the library (pp. 59–60). Although Barnard and others acknowledge that leadership at the university or state level can be useful for academic libraries, if this does not exist a library with strong top management commitment can start alone. When taking this approach, the library may even serve as an institutional example.

With a primary focus on customer service in quality improvement, a strong role for top management also is articulated by St. Clair (1993c). In his view, although recognizing the importance of staff involvement and teamwork, he states that the definition of quality service is a management responsibility and that "nothing will happen if management does not [lead the way and] directly encourage and endorse an attitude of service build around customer service" (p. 126).

B. Systems Approach and Strategic Planning

Deming consistently pointed out that in his view at least 80% (and sometimes more) of an organization's problems are due to the system, not the employees. In concisely defining TQM, one writer in the library field observes that

> the quality managment approach focuses . . . on finding and reducing the causes of variation that occur in the systems used to produce the results [i.e., products or services]. . . . The most useful way to . . . [eliminate] problems is to address directly the production systems and determine if the system has flaws that routinely lead to poor quality in the end. (Younger, 1991, pp. 82–83)

The focus on the system points to an obvious and important relationship among strategic planning, organizational development, and TQM. This is a connection that is advocated and discussed by many library professionals concerned with these processes (Clack, 1993; Loney and Bellefontaine, 1993; Riggs, 1992b; Warnken et al., 1992).

In a discussion of five important TQM concepts, it is observed that "the 'system' [should deliver] what the customer wants. . . . [In essence,] a systems approach looks at the individual departments in the context of the entire library" (Warnken et al., 1992, p. 401).

Riggs (1992b) strongly advocates combining the approaches of strategic planning and TQM and states that "all services and products provided by the library should come under the scrutiny of TQM" (p. 99). He indicates, however, that "ideally, before a library begins rolling out TQM, a strategic plan is in place. [This is important because] the principles of TQM frequently refer back to the library's mission and vision statements, goals, objectives, and strategies" (Riggs, 1992c, p. 481). In combining the two processes, Riggs (1992a) sees a means of ensuring the improvement of the "working culture of libraries, and offering refinement in services provided to students and faculty" (p. 34).

Deming's opposition to individual performance ratings is also in line with the focus on the system and not on the individual employee. As Aluri and Reichel (1994) point out in their analysis of performance evaluations in light of TQM, "academic libraries [wishing to implement the method successfully] should pay attention to Deming's ideas on performance evaluation" (p. 153). In the authors' view, when management takes the traditional approach to performance evaluation, with its focus on the employee, it is forgetting that the system as a whole needs to be evaluated and improved. Thus, they see TQM as a major paradigm shift which should force "library managers and employees to examine the fundamental objectives of their organizations and the extent to which their organization meets those objectives" (p. 153).

C. Customer Focus

Customer service and satisfaction lie at the heart of TQM, as those familiar with the process well know. Although in the library setting the tendency is to automatically think of the external customers (the users), staff members themselves are also customers when they depend on the services of staff in other library departments in order to provide service to the public.

When the definition of quality as it is viewed from the quality improvement perspective is understood, it is easy to understand the focus on the customer. As this has been explained, "quality is defined as the goodness of the results, whether products or services, as judged by the customer" (Younger, 1991, p. 82).

Sirkin (1993), a consultant and librarian, makes excellent points when she defines customer satisfaction as including the following: "repeat customers, referrals or endorsements, meeting (or exceeding) customer expectations, [and] the creation of a service-oriented environment" (p. 72). To the public, good quality service often means such basic aspects as "courtesy, [a good] attitude, helpfulness, and [the customer] being treated with respect" (p. 73).

In a review of the variety of customer-service training programs that are receiving increasing attention today, Arthur (1994) ties this to quality improvement efforts. Arthur proposes that front-line training can "lay a foundation of service standards and customer concern on which to base future [quality-service] issues" (p. 222). Among the recommendations made for a good training program are a focus on enhancing customer-service skills, such as nondefensive communication and problem handling. The program also should be designed for the service requirements of the specific library.

Although librarians writing on this aspect of TQM (e.g., Warnken et al., 1992) are careful to point out that it may not always be possible to satisfy all customer needs, the library should be making decisions based on understanding those needs. It is equally important, however, that customers understand what the library can provide and what limitations exist. As those in the field well know, this is an unusually difficult period for libraries, a time when "greater productivity . . . [and expanded services are] expected with fewer resources" (Riggs, 1992b, p. 94). This makes communication with the customer essential, and a number of successful efforts to do just this are reported in the literature.

1. Determining Customer Needs: Focus Groups

A preliminary communication technique that seems to be gaining more and more favor in the service sector in general, including academic institutions and libraries, is the use of the focus group. As one of today's more common forms of market research, this qualitative research approach is used to determine perceptions and attitudes about a product or service. For a library, this means determining how it is perceived by its customers and what they identify as their needs.

A typical focus group usually consists of a small homogeneous group discussing a topic, led by a nondirective moderator. In academic libraries, where active advisory committees are common, using the committee as a focus group can be a logical choice. Other good choices for these libraries are groups that consist of students at the same level or in the same discipline.

Informality that leads to less inhibition, the unexpected ideas and insights that often materialize, and the synergism of a group process are some of the benefits of this approach. A description of the use of focus groups by Xavier

University Library is available (Warnken et al., 1992), and Young (1993) also provides a guide to the process and Xavier library's experiences with it.

2. Determining Customer Needs: Surveys

Frequently, focus groups are followed by a common quantitative research technique, the survey or questionnaire. A brief description of the process for a library-developed survey is included in the report of Xavier University Library's approach to determining customer needs (Warnken et al., 1992). In-depth information and guidance on library evaluation and surveys are also available in a number of well-known works (e.g., Hernon and McClure, 1990; Lancaster, 1993).

Another useful and less time-consuming approach is to use a standard, published survey. One such example is Van House, Weil, and McClure's *Measuring Academic Library Performance: A Practical Approach* (1990). This manual includes a number of tested and validated surveys on various aspects of library use. Directions for conducting the surveys and a software package for analyzing the data collected are also provided.

3. Determining Customer Needs: Suggestion Systems

A well-known but often neglected communication device for libraries, the suggestion box or notebook, should not be overlooked. Hearing and responding to customer suggestions, complaints, and compliments can make a difference. "Often the simple fact that library staff listen and explain what the situation is . . . will keep customers" (Sirkin, 1993, p. 78).

D. Employee Teamwork, Empowerment, and Training

1. Employment Teamwork and Empowerment

The concepts of a team approach and employee empowerment are probably the TQM elements that rise to the forefront most frequently when the process is discussed and debated. Certainly this is true in the library field.

The involvement of the entire organization in the improvement and maintenance of quality products and services is central to Deming's philosophy. To accomplish this, with a focus on "breaking down barriers" between units and "driving out fear," he emphasized the use of work groups or teams to decentralize decision-making through "problem-solving on topics close to their interests" (Besemer, Dorsey, Kittle, and Niles, 1993, p. 70). To put it another way, this means "giving responsibility and authority to those doing the tasks for the evaluation and improvement of the areas where they work" (Sirkin, 1993, p. 80).

These aspects of TQM are very similar to those outlined in an article on job satisfaction and performance (Siggins, 1992). As the article points out, an organizational philosophy with these characteristics may result in increased job satisfaction and performance with a committed staff "working at or near their full potential" (p. 309). In Siggins' view, a well-functioning organization includes

> collaborative team efforts, integration of purpose, initiative, acceptance of responsibility, concern about the whole of the organization, active problem solving, acceptance of unit and library-wide goals, and a focus on quality service and performance. Staff who are satisfied with their jobs tend not to wait for the department head to notice a problem with service, methods of operation, . . . or other functions. They assume responsiblity themselves for the unit's success and take the initiative to deal with problems and meet objectives. . . . (p. 309)

For those familiar with the managment literature in general, the works of well-known organizational behavior theorists also come to mind. Certainly the landmark philosophies of McGregor (1960), the father of the Theory X and Y view of organizational management; Herzberg (1987), with his view of extrinsic and intrinsic employee motivation; and the expectancy theory of motivation (Vroom, 1964) have a number of elements in common with current thinking on quality improvement and employee involvement in the libraries in which they work.

This philosophy is also clearly in line with the advocation of participative management that has appeared in the library literature for a number of years (e.g., Martell, 1987; Webb, 1988). The literature also discusses the movement beyond participative mangement to actual team management (Besemer et al., 1993; Hawkins, 1990; Lowell and Sullivan, 1990; Sullivan, 1991). A view expressed on quality in libraries states that "the heart and soul of quality improvement in an academic library is the empowerment of employees and the increased level of participation garnered through team management" (Miller and Stearns, 1994, p. 408). These writers view team management as evolutionary rather revolutionary, although the structure does require a change in the traditional organization's culture.

Although many view these trends as flattening the organization (Riggs, 1992c, p. 482), other voices are also heard. From another perspective, "TQM has [not] flattened the library organization. It has moved leadership further down into the organization to the team level which[,] in time, will free up middle managers for more planning and less time putting out brush fires" (Butcher, 1993, p. 54).

Finally, there are some writing in the field of academic librarianship who, although seeing management approaches like TQM as resulting in a flatter organization, vigorously oppose this result (see Section II,B,2). If this view is espoused, a team-centered approach and staff empowerment that results in moving away from a stratified structure is seen as actually having a detrimental effect on the position of librarians as professionals and equal to the faculty (Veaner, 1994).

Whatever the view of the effect on the organization's structure, those who are most familiar with TQM tend to agree that the process "will require library managers to move away from expertise in the technical toward that in people and team building skills, like coaching, listening, creatively soliciting, question asking, and trust building . . ." (Lubans, 1992, p. 40).

2. Training Needs for Teamwork

It is generally recognized in the TQM literature that "training is a key component" (Jurow and Barnard, 1993c, p. 8). Moreover, it is a component that is required at each stage of implementing the system and for all levels of the staff.

According to Loney and Bellefontaine (1993), initial training for senior managers should focus on "knowledge of team stages, mechanics of meetings, interpersonal skills, valuing [individual] differences, and basic problem-solving skills" (pp. 90–91). They also see this as the time for quality and customer-service awareness training, in-depth exposure to various TQM versions, and training in "vision development and strategic planning" for senior managers (p. 91). These authors see all managers and supervisors as needing training in team building, leadership, and the quality effort.

Loney and Bellefontaine (1993) also recommend that all employees receive training on quality and customer satisfaction, on the organization's strategy and vision, and on team and quality tools skills. The tools include "basic problem solving, voting techniques, brainstorming, flow charting and fishbone techniques" (p. 92). Front line employees and support staff will also need special training on how to carry out customer-service goals. This training should concentrate on improving skills in client relations, listening, questioning, and communications.

A staff that is able to think analytically, recognize and solve problems, and use measurement as an improvement tool is central to the success of TQM (Jurow and Barnard, 1993c, pp.8–9). A particularly useful discussion of TQM training is Towler's (1993) description of training for team problem-solving. The problem-solving team training program that Towler presents has seven components and takes 18 hours. As Towler points out, however, employees should then be equipped to solve problems so that they will not recur. In other words, this type of training is essential for achieving one of the key TQM elements, eliminating rework by doing the work right the first time.

3. A Team Model and Pilot Projects

A first step in implementing the team approach to problem solving is to identify and select processes for pilot projects. Key considerations in Barnard's

(1993) view are the "importance of the process to the primary customers; whether the process is experiencing difficulty . . . ; and the likelihood of eliminating waste" (p. 67). According to Barnard (1993) and others, it is also important to "pick fruit that is closest to the ground." In other words, the pilot projects not only should be important but also have a good chance of succeeding.

Some with TQM experience recommend that the management should select the pilot projects, using the results of subcommittee work which identifies and prioritizes external and internal needs (Barnard, 1993). Others see the teams themselves as identifying problem areas (Miller and Stearns, 1994).

It is generally agreed that the team should include members from all parts of the organization affected by the problem and be composed of no more than 6 to 10 members. It is also agreed that various levels of the organization should be included: "the manager and/or supervisor of the group, the individuals who actually perform the work . . . , and/or those who are affected by the process" (Towler, 1993, p. 99). In a large organization, Barnard's (1993) model seems appropriate. This team model includes a sponsor (not part of the team but the highest level of manager to approve the steps recommended by the team), a facilitator (someone from another department who is expert in TQM), the team leader (the supervisor responsible for the process under consideration), and the team members (anyone who works on any part of the process). Again, others who have implemented the process took a different approach and had each team select its own leader and determine its own agenda and schedule (Miller and Stearns, 1994).

Whether or not the teams themselves identify the problems, most models have the teams performing the following functions:

> gathering and analyzing objective data, developing alternative solutions and proposing changes to policies and procedures to improve library services to internal and external constituencies. Their proposals generally are made to an administrative council within the libraries, the members of which are responsible for the implementation of new [or improved] services or policies. (Miller and Stearns, 1994, p. 409)

E. Measurement and Analysis Techniques

The use of measurement and analysis techniques to determine problems and evaluate improvement is still another important element of TQM. With the continued improvement of products, processes, and services as one of the main purposes of a TQM organization, "data gathering and analysis must be in place to provide meaningful information to managers, administrators, and those acutally engaged in doing the work" (Jurow, 1993, p. 114).

1. The Need for Measurement

Many voices from the library field focus on the need for systematic and quantitative measures if the quality improvement process is to be implemented. An award for library quality modeled on the Malcolm Baldrige National Quality Award, established in 1987 for the U.S. industrial and corporate sector, has been suggested. W. David Penniman (1993), former president of the Council on Library Resources (CLR), finds that the user-based definition of quality that is inherent in TQM makes the "establishment of new measures of quality . . . compelling" (p. 129).

In Penniman's (1993) view, the establishment of a Baldrige-type award for libraries would result in procedures which emphasize processes, customers, and continual improvement. "[This should enable] libraries of all types . . . [to] benefit from each other's experiences" (p. 129). Penniman's suggestion for a library quality award is strongly reinforced by a library-related discussion of the Westinghouse Electric Corporation's 12 Conditions of Excellence, which were adapted to become the Baldrige Award criteria (Spiegleman, 1992).

As Penniman (1992) has observed,

> we must change the way we measure success for our information service providers. With the correct measures, we will encourage them to consider the drastic reengineering of their enterprise that must occur and prepare them to rethink how their current dollars are spent. . . . (p. 42)

Penniman (1992) concludes that

> the cost and value of information services must be understood. Quantitative analyses are essential to the responsible management of libraries now and in the future. Many of the tools and techniques used in "total quality management" programs currently receiving major attention in U.S. industry are appropriate for the redesign of information services. We need to understand more fully how these tools can be applied in the information service arena. (p. 44)

2. The Measurement Tools

Because the TQM approach emphasizes determining problems with the processes not the employees, a special set of measurement tools is used. Both Jurow (1993) and Shaughnessy (1993) point out that most of the data that librarians collect does not provide information on the quality of the processes or services of the library. In contrast, TQM tools provide a means of measuring the performance of the system, an important asset during this period in which the profession is experiencing an increasing emphasis on accountability because of budgetary problems. As Lubans (1994) points out, "TQM tools, easily learned and used, are a valuable methodology for uncovering a mess [i.e., an indication of a problem] and defining the underlying problem" (p. 146).

Jurow and Shaughnessy each provide good definitions and descriptions of TQM data-gathering tools which, as Shaughnessy (1993) states, "are useful in displaying data, identifying trendlines and generally assisting staff in understanding the quality improvement process" (p. 11). These tools include the use of flow charts, check sheets, fishbone (cause and effect) diagrams, run and control charts, histograms, and scatter diagrams. Jurow (1993) provides a good illustration of where these tools fall within the stages of the Shewart Cycle, known as the Plan, Do, Check, and Act cycle in the quality improvement process. She also provides references to several books that clearly describe these tools and how to use them.

Detailed guides to the TQM measurement process are also included in the *Library Benchmarking Notebooks Series* by Holly J. Muir (1993a,b). These publications will be especially useful to special libraries as practical sources on TQM measurement.

3. Benchmarking

Benchmarking has assumed a key role in TQM measurement processes. This "process . . . establishes an external standard to which internal operations can be compared . . . by contributing information about what other organizations are able to accomplish in the same or similar operations" (Jurow, 1993, p. 120).

Muir (1993a,b) and Jurow (1993) both outline specific benchmarking steps based on TQM measurement techniques that a library would take in comparing a practice with the same operation in another institution. In writing on the topic, Shaughnessy (1993), however, makes the following observation:

> Since it is not known which libraries, within the major types of libraries, provide the best service (and therefore are able to serve as benchmarks), the benchmarking process needs to begin at the local intraorganizational level. Libraries need to begin collecting data on the patron/library interface so that internal progress toward improvement might be measured. Those libraries that are able both to collect reliable data and demonstrate high-quality service based on the data collected may, at some point, serve as true benchmarks for the library profession. (p. 10)

Another useful source to inform libraries considering benchmarking is Allan's (1993) article on the role that an information specialist or special librarian who is part of a larger organization can play in the organization's general benchmarking process. Although describing benchmarking in a national research laboratory (Sandia National Laboratories), the steps outlined in Allan's article and in an article on the same process by Trujillo (1994) provide useful persectives for librarians considering the approach for their own libraries. The results of the last benchmark survey by the National Association of College and University Business Officers, which include library benchmarks, may also be a useful resource for academic libraries (Force, 1994).

F. Commitment to Continuous Improvement

The use of TQM measurement and analysis techniques to determine problems and evaluate improvement should feed nicely into another key element of TQM, "continuously improving the system in order to achieve the best results" (Younger, 1991, p. 83). The final integration of a quality improvement process, with its focus on continuous improvement, is well-outlined by Barnard in her model for implementing TQM in research libraries (Barnard, 1993, pp. 68–70). In this model, phase four (called Evaluation and Expansion), the quality improvement approach is integrated into all library operations and is understood by all library staff. Pilot projects are evaluated, and improvements to be made in the problem-solving processes and in team building are identified. Following this, other quality improvement projects are initiated, involving new teams and more staff.

At the phase four stage, Barnard (1993) also sees senior management creating a 3- to 5-year strategic plan, starting with a 1-year plan for projects needing immediate attention. The remainder of the plan will involve adapting TQM at all organizational levels on a library-wide basis.

In tying the customer-based aspect of quality improvement to a continuous effort, Leonard (1992) calls for basing aspirations more on "users' stated needs and expectations than on our traditional interpretations of quality service" (pp. 304–305). This focus will undoubtedly require ongoing assessment of user-perceived needs.

Continuous improvement is also in line with those who see that "a strength of the TQM approach is that it is designed to promote improvement as part of a comprehensive (systems) approach [that continues to evolve]" (Loney and Bellefontaine, 1993, p. 94). With views and models such as these, a focus on incremental continuous improvement ("kaizen," to use the Japanese term) should be inherent in any library undertaking TQM or a similar quality improvement process.

IV. The TQM Process in Practice

Two surveys point out that libraries undertaking TQM are in a variety of stages and are using a wide range of approaches. These are the survey conducted for the LAMA Total Quality Management for Libraries Discussion Group, using the TQMLIB electronic discussion list (Bell, 1994a), and the 1993 survey conducted by the Association of Research Library's Office of Management Services for its SPEC Kit and Flyer on quality improvement programs in ARL libraries (ARL, 1993).

The fact that TQM is a recent undertaking for most libraries using this quality improvement approach is shown clearly in the LAMA survey. Of the 30 libraries responding to the survey, 18 were implementing TQM. Eight had used the process for less than 1 year, 5 for 1 to 2 years, and 5 for 3 to 4 years. Of 30 libraries, 19 were academic, 7 were military, 2 were governmental, 1 was public, and 1 was special. Twenty-three of the libraries had 50 or fewer employees, whereas 3 had 51 to 100, 3 had 151 to 200, and 1 had 101 to 150.

Training varied a great deal in the LAMA survey as far as the time allotted and the sources. In some libraries it was solely vendor supplied, in others it was provided by in-house staff, and in still others it was a combination of both or a university course. The most common types of courses were on quality awareness or orientation and team building, followed closely by courses on the continuous improvement process and implementing quality improvement approaches. Statistical process control was offered the least number of times (3). Surprisingly, although 18 libraries were implementing TQM, only 13 had given at least introductory training to more than 20% of its staff. Seven libraries, however, had reached between 81 and 100% of the staff.

Of the libraries using teams, projects have been conducted in a wide variety of areas, including "barcoding, strategic planning, inventory control, reshelving, training, bindery, circulation, reference, acquisitions, automation, technical services, and serials" (Bell, 1994a). Comments on TQM came from respondents who were reading up on the process, from those who were trying to introduce or had already implemented the team approach, and from those who work in libraries that have no interest in TQM.

The ARL survey shows the same pattern of varying stages and approaches in the 15 of the 91 responding libraries that indicated that they have a quality improvement program (ARL, 1993). Fourteen of the 15 ARL libraries with programs were in institutions where programs were also found in other departments or were institution-wide, whereas 1 library was the only department in its institution with a program. Only 1 of the 91 libraries indicated that an academic department in its university had a quality improvement program, an interesting example of the apparent lack of interest in such programs by most academic departments.

Six of the 15 ARL libraries had library-wide programs. In the 9 libraries where only selected departments were involved, serials and administration each were the focus in 4 libraries, closely followed by a variety of other departments (except reference and branch libraries, which had no such programs). Like the LAMA survey, the variety of projects was wide, with most focused on team building, customer awareness, continuous improvement, or the statistical control process.

Again like the LAMA survey, the percentage of each library's total staff involved in the program varied considerably. In 12 libraries, staff participation was 50% or less, whereas at the other end of the spectrum 3 libraries had between 76 and 100% of the staff involved. Also, like the LAMA survey, the approaches and the attention given to training were quite varied. Although it was part of the library's quality improvement program in all but 1 of the

15 libraries, the use of training ranged from great (7 libraries) to small (4 libraries). There was wide variety in the types of training, which was also in line with the LAMA survey. In addition to an introduction to TQM and team leader and team member training, workshops on TQM training for administrators, communication, handling customer complaints, brainstorming to improve customer service, and time management were reported.

Although some issues reported in the ARL survey, such as the presence or absence of a written policy for quality improvement programs and staff guidance, were not addressed in the LAMA survey, the similarities in the results of the two surveys are striking. In both surveys, a relatively small number of libraries were actively involved in formal quality programs. The SPEC Flyer indicates, however, that

> it is clear that those who have turned to quality improvement programs have done so eagerly and with a strong sense of commitment. The fact that they recognize the value of a philosophy that emphasizes quality of service to library users first is indicated by the wide variety of library functions in which they are currently applying quality improvement techniques. The number of members adopting quality improvement programs should increase rapidly in the next few years as those members currently considering a commitment to such a program make their decisions and others hear about the success of their fellow member libraries. (ARL, 1993)

The same statement seems to apply to the libraries responding to the LAMA survey. Given the similarities of many of the experiences with TQM and other quality improvement programs reflected in the two surveys, the ARL prediction should hold true for the LAMA libraries as well.

A. Academic Libraries

The ARL (1993) Spec Kit provides a good deal of information on quality improvement programs in specific academic libraries. The vision statements from Duke University, the University of Minnesota, and the State University of New York at Buffalo, which are presented in the kit, should be particularly useful as models for libraries. Detailed outlines of program plans and structures, schedules, and sample reports from specific libraries should also be useful to other libraries contemplating the implementation of a quality improvement process. Finally, the section on training that outlines in some detail the various approaches to this important aspect of the quality process will be helpful to any library undertaking the process. Descriptions of training programs at the Harvard College, University of Michigan, Wayne State, and Pennsylvania State libraries as well as the ARL OMS workshops are included.

The detailed discussions of specific quality improvement programs that are found to a limited extent in the library professional literature provide, however, the clearest picture of how various libraries have approached the process and what some of the outcomes have been. The approaches range from a formal step-by-step process using pilot projects, to a focus on organizational development, to library reorganization, to undertaking the process in just one of the library's wide range of services.

1. Academic Libraries: Library-wide Quality Improvement

a. Oregon State University Library. One of the more specific accounts of a library-wide undertaking is the article describing the Oregon State University Library's experience (Butcher, 1993). This library, whose university was implementing an institution-wide continuous improvement process, proceeded to consider and undertake TQM on a step-by-step basis, much in line with the model suggested by Barnard (1993) (see Section III,D,3).

After attending a 3-day TQM training program, the library administration and the library division heads decided to undertake the process for several reasons. These included the potential for greater efficiency, improved service, and better utilization of resources as well as political reasons. Like many other universities and colleges, the academic units on campus were reluctant to enter an organizational change process which has its foundation in the business world. Thus, the library, as the first academic unit to undertake the process, saw an opportunity to be on the cutting edge, which could result in increased visibility on campus.

After pros and cons were weighed, including the time investment and the potential for staff fearing that jobs would be eliminated, the decision was made to try two pilot projects: examining the reshelving process and the flow of government publications.

A detailed account of the TQM model used is presented in the article, and some of the lessons learned about the team experience are discussed. These include the advisability of starting with small teams and not crossing too many departmental lines in forming the teams. A good deal was also learned about survey methodology.

Both teams turned in their final recommendations to the Assistant University Librarian for Research and Public Services, and the teams then proceeded to implement them. These included acquiring better signs for the government publications unit, conducting training sessions for library staff on government publications, and improving a number of shelving procedures and arrangements.

As time-consuming as the training and meetings were, the benefits of participation and decision making by those doing the work were realized. At Oregon State University Library, "TQM is slowly creating a culture which looks at customer service and quality improvement in almost every undertaking. . . . TQM is seen by library staff and faculty as an impartial problem-solving tool and one which anyone can use" (Butcher, 1993, pp. 55-56).

b. Georgia Tech Library. Georgia Tech Library is another example of a library undertaking the process as part of an institution-wide TQM effort. The library, however, has developed its own model of CQI (continuous quality improvement). The action plan developed by a team of five library staff members includes the following key elements: "1. involve everyone on the staff; 2. identify internal and external customers; 3. improve customer satisfaction; 4. increase opportunities for customer interaction and feedback; 5. provide value-added services; 6. encourage innovation and efficiency; 7. communicate openly; [and] 8. identify staff training, education, and development opportunities" (Stuart and Drake, 1993, p. 133).

With a focus on customer satisfaction, the library started its program using techniques based on those of Milliken & Company, winner of the first annual Baldrige National Quality Award. Techniques also came from the TQM literature and from the library staff. Those techniques included "opportunity for improvement" forms used to elicit suggestions from library staff, the use of brainstorming as a tool, staff development efforts, and training workshops. Topics covered in the workshops included the Internet, handling customers, and managing multiple priorities. A distinguished service award and celebrations for the entire staff are also part of the library's approach.

The Georgia Tech Library is now moving toward giving work groups composed of the individuals most responsible for delivering the services the authority for determining their programs. A good example is assigning work groups in the general reference departments the responsibility for determining the nature of information service. Focus groups with university stakeholders and a suggestion box on the Georgia Tech Electronic Library are also part of the library's quality improvement efforts.

Unlike some libraries reporting on their quality improvement efforts in the professional literature, Georgia Tech concludes that "statistical quality control is difficult to apply to the quality of an information transaction or transfer, because information is intangible and its value is often elusive" (Stuart and Drake, 1993, p. 135). Stuart and Drake (1993) also conclude that "with CQI, benchmarks and other measures do not have to be precise. Anecdotal evidence of success or failure is as valid in a CQI setting as is the complaint level" (p. 135).

The quality improvement experience at Georgia Tech has also revealed the importance of recruiting the right type of librarian to work in the CQI environment. The library finds that such an environment requires a staff comfortable with empowerment and interested in contributing to the problem-solving and decision-making aspects of the organization's operations. In line with Oregon State's conclusion, the Georgia Tech Library sees that "while modes of service will vary, the imperative for quality will persist" (Stuart and Drake, 1993, p. 136).

Although some academic libraries undertaking TQM or CQI as a library-wide effort address established library procedures on a step-by-step basis, others take a broader and more far-reaching approach as far as impact on the library as an organization. Three good examples are the quality improvement activities at the Harvard College Library (HCL), Perkins Library at Duke University, and Davis Library at Sampson University.

c. Harvard College Library. The complex task that HCL started in 1990 with the institution of a strategic planning process is a long, intense, and extensive organizational change effort with a variety of specific strategies used. As Lee (1993) points out, although the development of the strategic plan itself was accomplished in 1 intense year, the 1990 strategic planning process at HCL was the start "of an effort to redefine our organization both for now and for the future. The articulation of a revised mission, and, more critically, the development of a vision statement were the beginning of a continual struggle for redefinition" (p. 226).

Key to the strategic planning process were eight success factors:

> support from the University Library, ARL . . . and CLR, strong executive leadership, a focus on organizational development, careful composition of the taskforces, creation of staff focus groups, a time frame for the process and the plan, a recognition of concurrent changes, and the development of a new generation of managerial staff. (Lee, 1993, p. 225)

The establishment of a "cohesive staff and organizational development program [that] is now an HCL priority . . ." (Lee, 1993, p. 228) is an important outgrowth of the strategic planning process. A steering committee on staff and organizational development and the position of a staff/organizational development officer were established in 1991 to continue this work. Focusing on developing programs to improve the effectiveness of the staff, emphasis is given to "team building and facilitation, problem solving, communication and collaboration, negotiation, and conflict resolution" (Lee, 1993, p. 228).

According to Clack (1993), the steering committee has the ongoing responsibility to support staff and organizational development and also to consider aspects of TQM that could be applied in academic libraries. The agenda of the committee also includes studying benchmarking in other organizations for applications to libraries, attending Harvard Quality Process problem-solving training sessions, and developing a library-wide communication program.

The steering committee planned to begin a workshop on organizational change for library staff in the fall of 1992, to collaborate with trainers in the Harvard Quality Process on training design, and to serve as a resource for members of the cataloging services department. Because the cataloging department was being reorganized into a team structure at the time Clack's article was written, with staff members examining and reconsidering work processes, it was logical for this department to be the first to receive training in TQM tools and process management.

As HCL's staff development officer observes, "in a process of organizational development and planned change, the principles of TQM, including participation in planning and examining and improving work processes, are useful and relevant" (Clack, 1993, pp. 40–41). Moreover, HCL finds that TQM is also in line with the service objectives that are central for all libraries, as many writers on the topic note. Clack (1993) also points out that the support of the library's leadership is critical, and that

> if this ongoing process of personal and organizational renewal continues to be supported, we will reshape our organizational culture. . . . The training process [based on TQM] will be one of the factors which will lead the library to develop a collective sense of identity and purpose and staff commitment to fulfilling the library's mission in times of uncertainty and change. (p. 41)

TQM principles clearly will be and have already been playing a key role in Harvard College's major organizational change effort. The major strengths of this approach that HCL has identified are the aspects that are commonly pointed out and used by other proponents of TQM for library quality improvement. These include an emphasis on broad-based participation, a commitment to the group process, and good communication with the entire staff.

d. Perkins Library (Duke University). Perkins Library began its quest for reorganization through a continuous improvement (CI) process in 1986 when it moved to a team-based approach in technical services. With a vision statement and guiding principles in place, teams were formed for implementation planning, communication, futures, staff education, and continuous improvement recognition (ARL, 1993, pp. 41–49). Several "quick start" teams were also launched to address issues like shelf failure, document delivery, and branch libraries.

According to J. Lubans (personal communication, 1994), these efforts evolved into a reorganization of the library, with a movement from the traditional hierarchy to a more team-based structure. This means that former departments are now self-managed home teams (also called quality circles), with the former department heads usually serving as team leaders. Although a leadership group still exists, consisting of the executive group and members from each home team, the budget is decentralized to the home teams, each team is looking at restructuring positions when vacancies occur, and performance evaluation consists of team assessment. TQM tools such as control charts along with the nominal group technique, which involves voting, have been employed. Staff training is emphasized, each team is in the process of learning group dynamics, and the teams are at various stages of adopting the self-management concept.

In discussing the Perkins Library experience, Lubans also indicated that the library has already "picked its low-hanging fruit" and is ready for something more sophisticated and for more advanced training (personal communication, 1994). This is a comment also heard from other libraries that have implemented TQM or CQI (Shapiro, 1994). Like many libraries in universities that are attempting to undertake TQM on an institution-wide basis, Perkins Library, through its own efforts and initiative, is actually something of a quality improvement pocket at Duke.

e. Davis Library (Sampson University).

At the other end of spectrum as far as size but not as far as effect on the organization is Davis Library's use of TQM principles in its reorganization effort at Sampson University. Facing a situation of understaffing in one department and overstaffing in another, procedures developed around personalities, and a demoralized staff, Samford University's Davis Library reorganized completely in the space of a year. This major effort was accomplished using quality tools and methods (Thomason, 1993).

A planning committee of four librarians started the process by interviewing the staff of 10 professional librarians and 19 support staff members. Given the widespread negative feelings revealed by the interviews, the planning committee immediately implemented some of the projects recommended by the staff to demonstrate that it was possible to change (Fitch, Thomason, and Wells, 1993, p. 294). Following this initial approach, the planning committee turned over the idea of reorganization of the library to a team of librarians. Eventually this group included both professional and support staff.

Relying on the TQM methods of brainstorming, continuous improvement teams, tools like affinity charts and fishbone diagrams, and placing emphasis on data rather than assumptions, the librarians determined specific objectives. One of the first of these was to determine which library functions were necessary and who should perform them.

The entire staff also was asked to suggest how the organization should be reshaped (Fitch et al., 1993). A plan generated by the group was selected through a vote. A key feature of this plan is a circular organizational structure, which produces a much flatter organization that eliminates an entire layer of administration. The director in the new structure now handles external matters, and the associate director deals with internal issues when requested to do so by unit coordinators. Department heads were replaced with coordinators who focus on facilitating work, communication, and acquiring resources for their units.

Staffing patterns were also evaluated and new job descriptions were written. Then another radical step was taken. All positions except the director's were declared vacant and the staff members were allowed to request three position choices in the new organization, with the director making the final choice. The result, with virtually everyone getting their first choice, meant that two-thirds of the staff moved into new or revised positions.

According to this account of reorganization, Davis Library has increased service and improved processes. These improvements include more professional hours at the reference desk and more support staff time at the circulation desk. Finally, the library sees that two major projects were facilitated by the new organizational structure: the automation of the library and a building expansion. Given this experience, the library concludes that through the use of a TQM process which empowers all staff, a "library can be turned upside down and land on its feet" (Fitch et al., 1993, p. 298).

2. Academic Libraries: Quality Improvement in Specific Services

a. Reference Services. Quality improvement in reference service has been a topic of professional concern and discussion for a number of years. As Bicknell (1994) indicates, however, the focus has been on measuring the accuracy of answers to questions, along with the tabulation of the number of questions received. Although not limited to academic or special libraries, two articles provide good theoretical discussions of evaluating reference service using quality improvement methods.

Bicknell combines some assessment components found in the library literature with a definition of quality from the business service sector. She finds several aspects of service interaction which, in her view, should be considered in assessing the quality of reference work. In offering specific suggestions for addressing them, Bicknell concludes that "every quality reference program should focus on meeting user needs and expectations by enhancing staff behaviors and communication skills, by providing a user friendly reference environment, and by ensuring suitable levels of staff morale and workload" (p. 80).

Aluri (1993) also takes the broader quality improvement perspective in addressing the improvement of reference service. Critical of reference evaluation studies that have been based on a win–lose situation (e.g., studies undertaken by outsiders which do not include those actively involved in providing the service), Aluri suggests an alternative. The method that he recommends is based on the principles of teamwork and incorporates a long-term perspective, a systems view, and the use of well-known quality improvement tools. This involves identifying key measures for determining the quality of reference service, collecting data using check sheets, plotting and interpreting the data on control charts, and using cause and effect diagrams to identify and determine the root causes of problems. Pareto charts, which "illustrate the degree to which each factor [of a process] contributes to the overall problem" (Jurow, 1993, p. 119), are also used.

The account of Wichita State Library's efforts to improve reference service is a specific example of the use of quality concepts for the process (Brown, 1994). The approach involved four projects. The use of a problem log that recorded complaints as well as solutions provided a good means for reference librarians to communicate with each other, and a suggestion box was an effective way to elicit feedback about the service. An effort was also made to evaluate how well reference questions were answered, the characteristics of the customer, and how well customer needs were met. This was accomplished through the use of an obtrusive survey instrument, the Wisconsin–Ohio Reference Evaluation Program. Finally, in an effort to empower and improve the work of the librarians, a reference automation quality circle was established to plan for several automation procedures and techniques to be undertaken. Ideas are presented for future efforts, and the reference department concludes that it has "addressed what is perhaps the most important quality improvement activity—making improvement a continuous process" (p. 219).

b. Access Services. An article describing how some of the basic principles of quality service have been integrated into the access services department at Texas Tech University Libraries provides another good specific example of the quality improvement approach in academic libraries (Chang, 1992). Through process evaluation and with a goal of achieving "patron centeredness," the Texas Tech University Libraries access services department has established an article delivery service without increasing costs. Emphasizing top management support and mobilizing the staff for quality and user-centered service required several well-known quality improvement techniques. These included emphasizing job security and satisfaction, providing training programs and opportunities for continuous learning, encouraging staff creativity and autonomy, and building teamwork through trust. Chang (1992) concludes that the experience at Texas Tech University Libraries shows that a quality services philosophy can become "a foundation concept of a library's service ethic and unite the efforts of various units" (p. 75).

c. Technical Services. An interesting perspective on quality improvement in technical services has been presented in a paper by Arnold Hirshon (1994). Although Hirshon considers reengineering as supplanting TQM, others writing in the field regard it as another aspect of TQM (Manning, 1994). Briefly stated, reengineering is based on a strong customer orientation, the elimination of hierarchies, and the use of teams for "radical changes in the whole process . . . to bring significant organizational improvements" (Hirshon, 1994, p. 14).

In the radical change that Hirshon considers necessary for the survival of technical services, he recommends for the near-term adapting strategies such as outsourcing (i.e., contracting technical services work to vendors). For the long term, however, he sees the need to adapt to the major changes in accessing networked information that are occurring. In Hirshon's view, the "future of technical services should be to design and implement 'bibliographically correct' information storage and retrieval systems that are tailor-made for the client-server-based national information infrastructure" (p. 19). Whether his vision is one version of TQM or a step beyond, Hirshon clearly sees the need for dramatic quality improvement and change in technical services.

B. Special Libraries

Quality improvement efforts have a longer history in special libraries than in other types of libraries, as the professional liberature indicates. Because quality assurance processes have been well-established in the health care field for some time, some of the earliest library quality improvement efforts are seen in medical and hospial libraries. Quality efforts in libraries in the corporate sector, however, are not far behind.

1. Medical and Hospital Libraries

An excellent account of a hospital library's quality assurance program, which started in 1980, is provided by Fredenburg (1988). In this useful article, the author describes the Shephard-Pratt Hospital's program model, with its emphasis on planning, proactivity, improvement, problem solving, and evaluating with factual data. The role of library staff at all levels and others in the organization, recordkeeping, and integrating the library program with the larger organization's quality program are clearly described. They also provide good suggestions for other libraries starting a quality assurance program.

Other articles of special interest to libraries in the health care field include the survey by the Alliant Health System Library at Norton Hospital and Kosair Children's Hospital in Louiville, Kentucky. The purpose of the survey was "to establish TQM benchmarks and to examine the significance of . . . [the library's] role in clinical care" (Fischer and Reel, 1992, p. 347). Another useful article describes the evaluation of user satisfaction based on a widely distributed survey, which resulted in a number of promotion ideas and awareness services (Henry, 1993).

Still another interesting involvement in a hospital's quality assurance program is described in the role one hospital library takes in occurrence screening (a QA process in which adverse occurrences or unexpected outcomes are identified and examined). As part of the process, the medical librarian prepares educational packages which include articles that address practice patterns or state-of-the-art articles to anticipate or diminish future problems (Howell and Jones, 1993).

An extensive manual for medical library continuous quality improvement, published by the Educational Research Corporation, should also be a useful guide (Stanley, Stanley, and Trivedi, 1994). The manual provides a plan and the tools that can be used to assist the staff of a medical library department in improving their CQI program. Among other key resources for libraries in the health care field is *The Health Care Manager's Guide to Continuous Quality Improvement* (Leebov and Ersoz, 1991).

2. Corporate Libraries

Given the business and industrial focus of TQM initially, it is not surprising that a number of accounts of library quality improvement efforts that have used the approach come from corporate libraries. One classic example of the application of TQM in corporate America is the adoption of the approach by Florida Power and Light (FPL) in 1981.

Efforts paid off in 1989 when FPL became the first American corporation to win the coveted Deming Prize, awarded by the Union of Japanese Scientists and Engineers for outstanding company-wide quality. Thus, it is not surprising that FPL's library soon became involved in the process. Walton's classic *Deming Management at Work* (1990) includes a description of the library's quality improvement efforts. These included improvement in the ordering process, working with the accounting department to streamline the invoice payment process, and charting and improving the online search services in relation to the quality of searches and document delivery time (pp. 55–56). They also included the provision of library and information services to a newly established FLP branch in 1982. A cross-functional team of library staff and customers developed a highly successful satellite library at the branch which could serve as a model for other FPL branches (pp. 72–73).

Another good example from the corporate sector is the CQI effort at Boeing Technical Libraries, which was begun in 1988 when the library was faced with growing demands and inadequate staff to meet the needs. Campbell (1992, 1994) describes the initial efforts in using a time-consuming departmental task analysis (DTA). As part of the process, the library's mission and responsibilities were defined, customer requirements were identified through surveys, work activities were analyzed, suppliers were informed of the library's requirements, issues that inhibited the delivery of high quality service were studied, and mechanisms to obtain customer feedback were developed.

The measurement of performance began with the prioritizing of issues and inhibitors and with the identification of the areas where quality improvement was most needed. Since then library process improvement teams at Boeing have identified and implemented improvements through flowcharting and customer surveys. Although still service oriented, looking "at everything in terms of the process involved and value added" is one of the major results (Campbell, 1994, p. 12). Cost savings, becoming team players, and adapting to and initiating change are the rewarding results of this library's quality improvement efforts.

The mission of 3M's Information Services is "to be the primary, global technology and business information resource of all 3M personnel (3Mers)" (Peterson, 1994, p. 14). The corporation's U.S. business library organization is a network of over a dozen U.S.-based libraries and information functions that serves 3Mers worldwide.

To meet the challenges of the 1990s, Information Services revitalized their strategic planning effort. Extensive use was made of customer and staff input and knowledge of peer operations, using the total quality process which is called Q90s at 3M. In what could be considered reengineering by many because it involved the total Information Services operation, use of the typical TQM tools along with a new strategic plan were "integrated into a single management process" (Peterson, 1994, p. 15).

When faced with increased demands and limited resources, Information Services used surveys, focus groups, consultation with top management, and informal benchmarking to identify their "key success requirements" and to develop a long-range plan. Among the strategies identified for implementation were to devote more time to providing information and less to the network and to cluster resources in fewer facilities. Another strategy adopted was more reliance on electronic systems for information access and delivery. Providing information support in a different way and a reliance on TQM processes to identify how to accomplish this has resulted in significant improvement in staff morale and customer support.

Reengineering also occurred at the AT&T Information Research Center (IRC). Although TQM was already in place in the IRC, which provides information to all AT&T employees, it was recognized that the entire information service needed to be changed. Making process improvements was not adequate as a means of meeting the competition of external information providers. In the space of 6 months, five managers devoted themselves to making recommendations (Strub, 1994). A new structure of self-managed work teams, a strategy team, and a set of core services evolved. A new technology platform also became available to provide just-in-time desktop delivery services. Because of productivity improvements, revenue trends increased despite decreased staff in the IRC and AT&T as a whole.

According to Strub (1994), lessons learned from the undertaking were the need for resilient managers who can deal with change and a recognition that too much time was devoted to technological improvements. Not enough attention was given to the people involved who needed training to move to a self-managed structure.

In addition, although maintaining the TQM focus, the IRC adopted results driven quality (RDQ) to counteract the slow process aspects of TQM. "RDQ embraces TQM's long-term vision . . . while helping managers make immediate tangible improvements" (Strub, 1994, p. 19).

3. The Government Sector

Applying TQM to the federal government, with its enormous civilian work-force and millions of military personnel, obviously has been and continues to be a formidable task. Beginning in the 1970s with productivity efforts in the Department of Defense which evolved into a TQM approach in the 1980s, the goal of the government-wide effort is "to break down the rigidity and excess structure" (Frank, 1993, p. 173). It is also intended to improve productivity, cost savings, and staff morale.

In 1988 a full TQM effort was launched, and the Federal Quality Institute (FQI) was formed. Among the services the FQI offers is an information network on TQM applications, including a database on the approach (Frank, 1993, p. 176). Other services offered by the FQI are an electronic bulletin board on TQM, basic information packages on the process, training sessions, and staff to assist agencies in establishing their own TQM information centers.

Because of the many challenges faced in applying TQM to governmental functions (including a lack of long-range planning, little top administrative support, a rigid personnel system resistant to participative management, and no incentive to save money), most of the successful applications of TQM come from the grass roots (Frank, 1993, p. 181). A good example is found in an article describing TQM efforts at one Department of Defense laboratory.

In describing the TQM efforts of the Air Force's Phillips Laboratory (PL), which replaced several laboratories, Duffek and Harding (1993) discuss the effects on the PL research library. Changes in the laboratory itself forced the research library to focus on customer relations, more aggressive market-ing, and improving online searching to keep costs low. Thus, the research library discovered that "no part of a [governmental] organization is so insular or small that it will escape the effect of change"(Duffek and Harding, 1993, p. 140).

C. Public and School Libraries

Although the literature on quality improvement in public or school libraries is not prevalent, there is good evidence that these libraries are also undertaking quality efforts. The approaches vary, of course, just as they do in other types of libraries.

In public libraries, current efforts that are taking a TQM approach are often, but not always, part of a city-wide quality improvement initiative. A good example is the Austin Public Library, winner of the 1993 Gale Research/ *Library Journal* Library of the Year Award. The library creates very close ties with the Texas city's government in numerous ways, including playing a major role in the city's TQM activities, the BASICS Program. The library director serves as the coordinator of the city TQM program, and a quality resource center is maintained at one branch to serve the BASICS Program. Logically, the "tools and processes [of the BASICS Program] are [also] part of the library routine now" (Berry, 1993, p. 31). (A good account of the library's application of TQM is given in Soy's 1993 case study.) The fruits of these efforts are seen in the financial support the library receives, with a budget that is a bit better than budgets for most urban public libraries in the financially strained state. A bond issue was also passed in 1992 and a building program is underway.

The St. Paul Public Library is another library that is undertaking quality improvement as part of a city-wide effort. Currently, three quality teams and several other committees are working on projects, making use of TQM principles (D. Willms, e-mail message, November 28, 1994).

The 1994 winner of the Gale Research/*Library Journal* Library of the Year Award, the Brown County Library (located in Green Bay, Wisconsin), also makes use of TQM techniques. The library's movement to team management and greater staff involvement has enhanced a partnership and bonding with the community. This includes the maintenance of the Community Quality Center for resources and the establishment of a number of programs, which has resulted in a contribution of $30,000 from the Northeast Wisconsin Quality Improvement Network (Berry, 1994).

Evidence of other quality efforts in public libraries is seen in accounts of the use of quality circles in libraries, including some Chicago Public Library branches, the Duluth Public Library, and the East Brunswick Public Library in New Jersey (Mourey and Mansfield, 1984; Segal and Trejo-Meehan, 1990; Stone, 1987).

TQM efforts for school libraries often are part of the movement in education toward what some in the field call "total quality education." This has involved changing the management structure to provide educators, including school library media specialists, with the opportunity to become active participants in site-based management. This means empowering them "to make local decisions on curriculum as well as management" (Barron, 1994, p. 49). The sources for information on the TQM movement in education are numerous, including entire issues of some journals being devoted to the topic. The impact of the movement on the school library media center is considered specifically in some discussions, as it is in Barron's (1994) article.

V. Quality Improvement in Selected Countries outside the United States

Some of the more theoretical and thought-provoking articles on quality improvement in libraries and information services have appeared in publications from outside the United States. These include discussions by Brockman (1992), Bryne (1993), and Johannsen (1992b).

In the United Kingdom, quality assurance is addressed through the British Standard Institution's BS5750 standard, which outlines the requirements of a quality system and is used for government accreditation. The international equivalent is the ISO9000 standard, which was developed along the lines of BS5750. As Byrne (1993) indicates when he defines BS5750,

> quality assurance looks at the creation of a product or service as if it was a system with procedures set down in writing. . . . As such [it] is focussed on how well the system is producing an end product or a service is preforming. BS5750 is not concerned with establishing and maintaining quality standards and does not recognize the need for a continuous improvement process. (p. 69)

Brockman (1992) states that 20 organizations in the United Kingdom have full BS5750 government accreditation. Although Byrne finds few published accounts of BS5750 related to library and information services, he suspects that there are more than the literature would suggest because many information services are part of organizations which have obtained BS5750/ISO9000 certification. Both Byrne and Brockman turn their attention to the choice between BS5750 certification, with its concern for how well a system has performed, or embarking on full-scale TQM, with its call for cultural change.

Although surveys of U.K. companies show a growing awareness of TQM, many hindrances are acknowledged. Change in this situation, however, may be in sight. Indications of this are seen in the spring 1993 conference of the European Association of Information Services which "produced a draft work program aimed at achieving a set of guidelines for implementing TQM . . . within the information sector" (Byrne, 1993, p. 71). Other international conferences and seminars are discussed by Byrne, and Brockman mentions the introduction of TQM into British Civil Service courses. The worldwide attention that TQM in libraries is receiving is evident in the number of articles on the topic that are appearing from countries such as Australia, Denmark, and Germany, to name just a few (Armstrong, 1991; Johannsen, 1992a; Poll, 1993).

An interesting scholarly article by a Danish library school faculty member analyzes the problems related to the implementation of TQM (Johannsen, 1992b). The author concludes that the practitioners of TQM are ahead of theorists of information science and calls for the "development of an adequate theoretical and methodological framework with relevance for quality control implementation within information science" (p. 274).

In looking at the international scene, Canadian medical libraries appear to be well-entrenched in quality assurance. An excellent collection of articles discussing the topic in the Canadian health care field is presented in *Quality Assurance in Libraries: The Health Care Sector* (Taylor and Wilson, 1990). Since the 1950s, standards for libraries have been included in North American accreditation standards through the efforts of the Joint Commission on the Accreditation of Hospitals in the United States and the Canadian Council for Hospital Accreditation. Beginning in 1967, medical staff library services have been a prerequisite under the Canadian Council for Hospital Accreditation plan (Eagleton, 1988).

VI. Professional Activities and Other Resources

The continued level of activity related to quality improvement efforts is reflected not only in current library professional publications but also in the activities of professional associations, in other conferences, and in training and workshop opportunities. It is also evident in the information and communications that are available in electronic forms such as discussion lists and gopher sites.

A. Professional Association and Related Activities

A look at the activities of the American Library Association (ALA) alone shows a high level of interest in quality improvement. As an example, two ALA discussion groups are devoted to TQM, LAMA's Total Quality Management for Libraries Discussion Group (ALA, 1994, p. 61) and the Public Library Association's discussion group on the same topic (ALA, 1994, p. 74).

At the ALA summer of 1994 conference many other groups in the organization presented programs and discussions on the subject as well, just as they had at previous conferences and midwinter meetings. The LAMA TQM discussion group focused on considering its recent survey (see Section IV) (Bell, 1994a). During the same conference, however, two LAMA and Reference and Adult Services committees cosponsored a program on "Focusing on the Customer: Applying Lessons from the Corporate Sector" (Brewer, 1994), and LAMA's Middle Management Discussion Group presented a program on "Successful Teambuilding: Managing to Survive the Challenging 90s" (Jackson, 1994).

A major conference cosponsored by the Association of Research Libraries' Office of Management Services and Wayne State University Libraries, with major support from the Council on Library Resources, was held in April 1994 in Washington, D.C. Titled "Total Quality Management Programs in Academic Libraries: Initial Implementation Efforts," participants came from around the world, and the speakers included several luminaries in the field (Lessin, 1994a).

One of the early conferences on the topic, which was sponsored by the Wayne State University Library System (1992), was "Meeting and Exceeding Customer Expectations: Total Quality Management, Higher Education and the Academic Library," held in November 1992. During the same year, papers on aspects of quality improvement were presented at the Sixth National Conference of the Association of College and Research Libraries (Kirk, 1992).

B. Training and Workshop Opportunities

Training and workshop opportunities have also been numerous. As an example, in October 1994, OMS presented one of its 4-day workshops in Boston on "Implementing Continuous Improvement in Libraries" (Haws, 1994). Other workshops include the Special Libraries Middle Management Institute on Human Resources, which was held in 1994 [Special Libraries Association (SLA), 1994], and the Michigan Library Association's Management and Administration Division's workshop on TQM in 1993. The 3-day SLA Education Conference/Middle Management Institute, "Total Quality: A Vision for the Future," held in Los Angeles in January 1993, is also typical of these efforts (SLA, 1992).

During the summers of 1993 and 1994, the School of Information Studies at Syracuse University offered an intensive course on quality improvement as part of its Summer Institute on Leadership and Change in Libraries (Information Studies, 1994; Schaper, 1993). Presented by Louise Schaper, the course focused on the basic TQM philosophy and factors related to TQM success. Another excellent introductory workshop, which has been conducted numerous times by Holly Shipp Buchanan, is "The Quality Imperative: An Introduction to Total Quality Management for Information Professionals," cosponsored by SLA and the Council on Library Resources (Buchanan, 1992).

Finally, as academic libraries describing the quality improvement experience in the literature indicate, the training resources on their own campuses often provide good opportunities for their staff. The assistance provided by the Harvard University resource personnel who are training the university's staff in the Harvard Quality Process seems to be especially notable (Clack, 1993, p. 33).

C. Electronic Resources

A number of electronic discussion lists (listservs) are now available for those interested in quality improvement in libraries. The discussion list Total Quality Management for Libraries (TQMLIB) is, of course, especially relevant. The Library Administration and Management list (LIBADMIN) often also includes topics related to TQM.

To receive the addresses of listservs that have the term "quality" in the description, an e-mail request may be sent to a list such as LISTSERV@BIT NIC.EDUCOM.EDU. In the text, the message should read: list global/ quality (Bell, 1994b). At least 18 discussion lists on various aspects of quality will be provided, covering fields ranging from education to the service sector.

There are also a number of other Internet resources related to quality issues. One of the newest is maintained at Clemson University (Lessin, 1994b). Access is http://deming.eng.clemson.edu or gopher to deming.eng.clemson.edu:70. In the same e-mail message, Lessin forwards information on accessing two other existing gopher sites on quality, one at Babson College and the other on the Malcolm Baldrige award.

VII. Conclusion

In this review of the current status of quality improvement activities in libraries, it is evident that total quality management or closely related approaches are not just "flavors of the month" or "fads of the day." The economic threat to libraries is clearly a reality for most institutions. At the same time, the pressures to advance technologically and to provide service to users who have increasingly high expectations are growing at an unprecedented rate. It is apparent that library administrators also find that most library staff members now expect and are ready for greater participation in organizational problem solving and decision making.

Given the nature of these major, often daunting challenges and compelling calls for change, it is unlikely that most libraries are in a position to ignore quality improvement efforts. It also seems logical that these programs focus on continuous improvement in products and services, the elimination of rework, teamwork, a flattened organizational structure with greater employee involvement, and an increased emphasis on customer needs. The fact that these are key components of TQM and related approaches seems to indicate that for many libraries such a process is the quality improvement effort of choice.

The experiences of those libraries that have undertaken quality improvement efforts, however, have much to tell the profession. These are programs that can be approached in a variety of ways. An improvement process can be implemented in single departments, adopted as an organization-wide effort, or serve as the impetus for a complete reorganization of the library.

Several factors appear to work in favor of success for the quality improvement undertaking. These include the presence of newer staff, the choice of pilot projects which are significant and also promise confidence-building success, a clear recognition that this is a time-consuming and long-term effort, and the existence of strong support from top management.

Although today's quality improvement efforts have been successful for a number of libraries, there are also cautionary signals not to be overlooked. Libraries well underway with the process now are calling for more sophisticated applications and for better training that goes beyond the basics. At the same time, the many demands inherent in the process perhaps indicate that the libraries best able to succeed are basically healthy institutions that are ready for change in their organizational culture and have the resources necessary to accomplish an undertaking of this magnitude. Indeed, this approach does not appear to be the answer for a library severely strained as an organization. A library in this situation may require a different renewal process, tailored to its unique situation, before it undertakes a comprehensive and demanding TQM or CQI program.

Implementing quality improvement in many libraries may very well be a matter of judicious selection (i.e., picking and choosing). The varying approaches and experiences of those libraries that have adopted the process and the questions being raised by some members of the library profession point to this conclusion.

Although TQM may hold much promise in general, various specific aspects may work better in some libraries than in others, just as the overall approach to undertaking the process is not and realistically should not be standardized. Like many of the organizational innovations that have arisen in the past, individual libraries may be well-advised to choose what is needed for their own quality improvement situation, to adapt as needed, and even to ignore some aspects altogether. The review of current quality improvement efforts indicates some strong support for this view.

The quality improvement process appears to be a necessity, however, in whatever guise it assumes. The realities of the current library situation indicate that quality improvement is essential not only for survival but for facing the major changes and growth required for the libraries of today and tomorrow.

References

Allan, F. C. (1993). Benchmarking: Practical aspects for information professionals. *Special Libraries* **84**, 123–128.

Aluri, R. (1993). Improving reference service: The case for using a continuous quality improvement method. *RQ* **33**, 220–236.

Aluri, R., and Reichel, M. (1994). Performance evaluation: A deadly disease? *Journal of Academic Librarianship* **20**, 145–155.

American Library Association (ALA) (1994). *ALA Handbook of Organization, 1994/1995 and Membership Directory*. American Library Association, Chicago.

Armstrong, B. (1991). Libraries around Australia: Introducing total quality management to Telecom's National Resource Centre. *The Australian Library Journal* **40**, 349–354.

Arthur, G. (1994). Customer-service training in academic libraries. *Journal of Academic Librarianship* **20**, 219–222.

Association of Research Libraries (ARL), Office of Management Services (1993). *Quality Improvement Programs in ARL Libraries* (SPEC Kit 196). Association of Research Libraries, Washington, D.C.

Barnard, S. B. (1993). Implementing total quality management: A model for research libraries. *Journal of Library Administration* **18**(1/2), 57–70.

Barron, D. D. (1994). Site-based management: Background, research and implications for school library media specialists. *School Library Media Activities Monthly* **10**(6), 48–50.

Bell, P. (1994a). Electronic message on TQMLIB (TQMLIB@CMS.CC.WAYNE.EDU) dated 30 June.

Bell, P. (1994b). Electronic message on TQMLIB (TQMLIB@CMS.CC.WAYNE.EDU) dated 30 June.

Berry, J. (1993). Austin Public Library : Library of the year 1993. *Library Journal* **118**(11), 30–33.

Berry, J. (1994). Brown County Library, Green Bay, Wisconsin: Library of the year 1994. *Library Journal* **119**(11), 30–33.

Besemer, S. P., Dorsey, S. B., Kittle, B. L., and Niles, C. M. (1993). Managing the academic library through teamwork: A case study. *Journal of Library Administration* **18**(3/4), 69–89.

Bicknell, T. (1994). Focusing on quality reference service. *Journal of Academic Librarianship* **20**, 77–81.

Brewer, J. (1994). Electronic message on LIBADMIN (LIBADMIN%UMAB.bitnet@KSUV-M.KSU.EDU) dated 21 June.

Brockman, J. R. (1992). Just another management fad? The implications of TQM for library and information services. In *Aslib Proceedings*, Vol. 44, pp. 283–288. Aslib, London.

Brown, J. D. (1994). Using quality concepts to improve reference services. *College & Research Libraries* **55**, 211–219.

Buchanan, H. S. (1992). *The Quality Imperative: An Introduction to Total Quality Management for Information Professionals—Course Syllabus*, 2nd ed. Author, Louisville, KY.

Butcher, K. S. (1993). Total quality management: The Oregon State University Library's experience. *Journal of Library Administration* **18**(1/2), 45–56.

Byrne, D. (1993). Quality management in library and information services. *The Law Librarian* **24**, 69–74.

Campbell, C. A. (1992). Information services at Boeing: Adding value by measuring and improving quality. In *Online '92 CD-ROM Conference Proceedings*, pp. 43–47. Eight Bit Books, Wilton, CT.

Campbell, C. A. (1994). Continuous quality improvement in the Boeing Technical Libraries. *Bulletin of the American Society for Information Science,* **20**(April/May), 10–12.

Chang, A. (1992). Quality access services: Maximizing and managing. *Collection Management* **17**(1/2), 63–75.

Clack, M. E. (1993). Organizational development and TQM: The Harvard College Library's experience. *Journal of Library Administration* **17**(1/2), 29–43.

Crosby, P. B. (1979). *Quality Is Free: The Art of Making Quality Certain.* McGraw-Hill, New York.

Deming, W. E. (1986). *Out of the Crisis.* Massachusetts Institute of Technology, Center for Advanced Engineering Study, Cambridge.

Doering, D. (1994). Electronic message on LIBADMIN (LIBADMIN%UMAB.bitnet@KSUV-M.KSU.EDU) dated 16 March.

Dougherty, R. M. (1992). TQM: Is it the real thing? *Journal of Academic Librarianship* **18**, 3.

Duffek, E., and Harding, W. (1993). Quality management in the military: An overview and case study. *Special Libraries* **84**, 137–141.

Eagleton, K. M. (1988). Quality assurance in Canadian hospital libraries: The challenge of the eighties. *Health Libraries Review* **5**, 145–159.

Fischer, W. W., and Reel, L. B. (1992). Total quality management (TQM) in a hospital library: Identifying service benchmarks. *Bulletin of the Medical Library Association* **80**, 347–352.

Fitch, D. K., Thomason, J., and Wells, E. C. (1993). Turning the library upside down: Reorganization using total quality management principles. *Journal of Academic Librarianship* **19**, 294–299.

Force, R. (1994). Electronic message on LIBADMIN (LIBADMIN%UMAB.bitnet@KSU-VM.KSU.EDU) dated 9 November.

Frank, R. C. (1993). Total quality management: The federal government experience. *Journal of Library Administration* **18**(1/2), 171–182.

Fredenburg, A. M. (1988). Quality assurance: Establishing a program for special libraries. *Special Libraries* **79**, 277–284.

Hawkins, K. W. (1990). Implementing team management in the modern library. *Library Administration & Management* **4**, 11–15.

Haws, G. (1994). Electronic message on TQMLIB (TQMLIB@CMS.CC.WAYNE.EDU) dated 2 September.

Henry, B. J. (1993). Continuous quality improvement in the hospital library. *Bulletin of the Medical Library Association* **81**, 437–439.

Hernon, P., and McClure, C. R. (1990). *Evaluation and Library Decision Making.* Ablex, Norwood, NJ.

Herzberg, F. (1987). One more time: How do you motivate employees? *Harvard Business Review* **65**(5), 109–120.

Hirshon, A. (1994). The lobster quadrille: The future of technical services in a re-engineering world. In *The Future is Now: The Changing Face of Technical Services: Proceedings of the OCLC Symposium, ALA Midwinter Conference,* pp. 14–20. OCLC Online Computer Library Center, Inc., Dublin, OH.

Howell, P. B., and Jones, C. J. (1993). A focus on quality—the library's role in occurrence screening. *Medical Reference Services Quarterly* **12**(2), 83–89.

Information Studies (1994). Electronic message on TQMLIB (TQMLIB@CMS.CC.WAYNE.EDU) dated 24 June.

Jackson, R. (1994). Electronic message on TQMLIB (TQMLIB@CMS.CC.WAYNE.EDU) dated 16 March.

Johannsen, C. G. (1992a). Danish experiences of TQM in the library world. *New Library World* **93**(1104), 4–9.

Johannsen, C. G. (1992b). The use of quality control principles and methods in library and information science theory and practice. *Libri* **42**, 283–295.

Juran, J. M., and Gryna, F. M., eds. (1988). *Juran's Quality Control Handbook*, 4th Ed. McGraw-Hill, New York.

Jurow, S. (1993). Tools for measuring and improving performance. *Journal of Library Administration* **18**(1/2), 113–126.

Jurow, S., and Barnard, S., eds. (1993a). *Integrating Total Quality Management in a Library Setting.* Haworth, Binghamton, NY.

Jurow, S., and Barnard, S., eds. (1993b). Integrating total quality management in a library setting [special issue]. *Journal of Library Administration* **18**(1/2).

Jurow, S., and Barnard, S. (1993c). Introduction: TQM fundamentals and overview of contents. *Journal of Library Adminsitration* **18**(1/2), 1–3.

Kirk, T., ed. (1992). *Academic Libraries: Achieving Excellence in Higher Education: Proceedings of the Sixth National Conference of the Association of College and Research Libraries.* Association of College and Research Libraries, Chicago.

Lancaster, F. W. (1993). *If You Want to Evaluate Your Library*, 2nd Ed. University of Illinois, Graduate School of Library and Information Science, Champaign.

Lee, S. (1993). Organizational change in the Harvard College Library: A continued struggle for redefinition and renewal. *Journal of Academic Librarianship* **19**, 225–230.

Leebov, W., and Ersoz, C. J. (1991). *The Health Care Manager's Guide to Continuous Quality Improvement.* American Hospital Publishing, Chicago.

Leonard, P. (1992). On my mind: This too shall pass, or we will. *Journal of Academic Librarianship* **18**, 304–305.

Lessin, B. (1994a). Electronic message on TQMLIB (TQMLIB@CMS.CC.WAYNE.EDU) dated 30 March.

Lessin, B. (1994b). Electronic message on TQMLIB (TQMLIB@CMS.CC.WAYNE.EDU) dated 30 March.

Lessin, B. (1994c). Electronic message on TQMLIB (TQMLIB@CMS.CC.WAYNE.EDU) dated 6 May.

Liu, M. (1992). Selective guide to literature on quality assurance. *Science & Technology Libraries* **13**(2), 3–35.

Loney, T., and Bellefontaine, A. (1993). TQM training: The library service challenge. *Journal of Library Administration* **18**(1/2), 85–96.

Lowell, G. R., and Sullivan, M. (1990). Self-management in technical services: The Yale experience. *Library Administration & Management* **4**, 20–23.

Lubans, J. (1992). Productivity in libraries? Managers step aside. *Journal of Library Administration* **17**(3), 23–42.

Lubans, J. (1994). Sherlock's dog, or managers and mess finding. *Library Administration & Management* **8**, 139–149.

Mackey, T., and Mackey, K. (1992). Think quality! The Deming approach does work in libraries. *Library Journal* **117**(9), 57–61.

Manning, H. (1994). Total quality management: Not just another flavor of the month! *Bulletin of the American Society for Information Science* **20**(April/May), 9.

Martell, C. (1987). The nature of authority and employee participation in the management of academic libraries. *College & Research Libraries* **48**, 110–122.

McGregor, D. (1960). *The Human Side of Enterprise.* McGraw-Hill, New York.

Miller, R. G., and Stearns, B. (1994). Quality management for today's academic library. *College & Research Libraries News* **55**, 406–409, 422.

Mourey, D. A., and Mansfield, J. W. (1984). Quality circles for management decisions: What's in it for libraries? *Special Libraries* **75**(2), 87–94.

Muir, H. J. (1993a). *Identifying Benchmarking Partners: Special Libraries.* Library Benchmarking International, Cincinnati.

Muir, H. J. (1993b). *The Librarian's Guide to Identifying Work Processes and Developing Metrics*. Library Benchmarking International, Cincinnati.

O'Neil, R. M. (1994). *Total Quality Management in Libraries: A Sourcebook*. Libraries Unlimited, Englewood, CO.

O'Neil, R. M., Harwood, R. L., and Osif, B. A. (1993). A total look at total quality management: A TQM perspective from the literature of business, industry, higher education, and librarianship. *Library Administration & Management* **7**, 244–254.

O'Neil, R. M., Harwood, R. L., and Osif, B. A. (1994). A TQM perspective: A busy manager's bookshelf. *Library Adminstration & Management* **8**, 49–52.

Pearson, C. M. (1993). Aligning TQM and organizational learning. *Special Libraries* **84**, 147–150.

Penniman, W. D. (1992). Shaping the future: The Council on Library Resources helps to fund change. *Library Journal* **117**(17), 41–44.

Penniman, W. D. (1993). Quality reward and awards: Quality has its own reward, but an award helps speed the process. *Journal of Library Administration* **18**(1/2), 127–136.

Peterson, B. J. (1994). TQM at 3M: Planning with customer and staff input. *Bulletin of the American Society for Information Science* **20**(April/May), 14–16.

Poll, R. (1993). Quality and performance measurement—a German view. *British Journal of Academic Librarianship* **8**(1), 35–47.

Riggs, D. E. (1992a). Managing academic libraries with fewer resources. *Journal of Higher Education Management* **6**, 27–34.

Riggs, D. E. (1992b). Strategic quality management in libraries. In *Advances in Librarianship*, Vol. 16, pp. 93–105.

Riggs, D. E. (1992c). TQM: Quality improvement in new clothes. *College & Research Libraries* **54**, 481–483.

Riggs, D. E. (1993). Managing quality: TQM in libraries. *Library Administration & Management* **7**, 73–78.

Schaper, L. (1993). Electronic message on LIBADMIN (LIBADMIN%UMAB.bitnet@KSUV-M.KSU.EDU) dated 12 May.

Scholtes, P. R. (1988). *The Team Handbook: How to Use Teams to Improve Quality*. Joiner, Madison, WI.

Sears, D. J. (1993). The "best books" on total quality management: A first review. *RQ* **33**, 85–87.

Segal J. S., and Trejo–Meehan, T. (1990). Quality circles: Some theory and two experiences. *Library Administration & Management* **4**(1), 16–19.

Shapiro, L. (1994). Electronic message on LIBADMIN (LIBADMIN%UMAB.bitnet@KSUV-M.KSU.EDU dated 15 November.

Shaughnessy, T. W. (1987). The search for quality. *Journal of Library Administration* **8**(1), 5–10.

Shaughnessy, T. W. (1993). Benchmarking, total quality management, and libraries. *Library Administration and Management* **7**, 7–12.

Siggins, J. A. (1992). Job satisfaction and performance in a changing environment. *Library Trends* **41**(2), 299–315.

Sirkin, A. F. (1993). Customer service: Another side of TQM. *Journal of Library Administration* **18**(1/2), 71–83.

Soy, S. (1993). Total quality management. In *Against All Odds: Case Studies on Library Financial Management*. (L. F. Crismond, ed.) pp. 187–204. Highsmith Press, Fort Atkinson, WI.

Special Libraries Association (1993). *Total Quality: A Vision for the Future (Winter Education Conference)* [Brochure]. SLA, Washington, D.C.

Special Libraries Association (SLA) (1994). Electronic message on LIBADMIN (LIBAD-MIN%UMAB.bitnet@KSUVM.KSU.EDU) dated 23 August.

Spiegleman, B. M. (1992). Total quality management in libraries: Getting down to the real nitty gritty. *Library Management Quarterly* **15**(3), 12–16.

Stanley, G. L., Stanley, S. J., and Trivedi, A. V. (1994). *Medical Library Interdepartment Continuous Quality Improvement Manual.* Educational Research Corporation, Carbondale, IL.

St. Clair, G., ed. (1993a). Benchmarking, total quality management & the learning organization: New management paradigms for the information environment [special issue]. *Special Libraries* **84.**

St. Clair, G., ed. (1993b). Benchmarking, total quality management and the learning organization: New management paradigms for the information environment—A selected bibliography. *Special Libraries* 84, 155—157.

St. Clair, G. (1993c). *Customer Service in the Information Environment.* Bowker-Saur, London.

Stone, J. R. (1987). Quality circles in the library. *New Jersey Libraries* **20**(3), 13–19.

Strub, M. Z. (1994). Quality at warp speed: Reengineering at AT&T. *Bulletin of the American Society for Information Science* **20**(April/May), 17–19.

Stuart, C., and Drake, M. A. (1993). TQM in research libraries. *Special Libraries* **84,** 131–136.

Sullivan, M. (1991). A new leadership paradigm: Empowering library staff and improving performance. *Journal of Library Administration* **14**(2), 73–85.

Taylor, M. H., and Wilson, T., eds. (1990). *Q.A.: Quality Assurance in Libraries: The Health Care Sector.* Canadian Library Association, Ottawa.

Thomason, J. (1993). Revitalization of library service. *New Directions for Institutional Research* **78,** 49–51.

Towler, C. F. (1993). Problem solving teams in a total quality management environment. *Journal of Library Administration* **18**(1/2), 97–112.

Trujillo, A. A. (1994). Benchmarking at Sandia National Laboratories. *Bulletin of the American Society for Information Science* **20**(April/May), 12–14.

Van House, N. A., Weil, B. T., and McClure, C. R. (1990). *Measuring Academic Library Performance: A Practical Approach.* American Library Association, Chicago.

Veaner, A. (1994). Paradigm lost, paradigm regained? A persistent personnel issue in academic librarianship, II. *College & Research Libraries* **55,** 389–402.

Vroom, V. R. (1964). *Work and Motivation.* Wiley, New York.

Walton, M. (1990). *Deming Management At Work.* Putman, New York.

Warnken, P. N., Young, V. L., and Ahuja, R. (1992). Beyond the survey: Using market research techniques to improve library services and collections. In *Academic Libraries: Achieving Excellence in Higher Education: Proceedings of the Sixth National Conference of the Association of College and Research Libraries.* (T. Kirk, ed.), pp. 401–404. Association of College and Research Libraries, Chicago.

Wayne State University Libraries (1992). *Meeting and Exceeding Customer Expectations: Total Quality Management, Higher Education and the Academic Library* [Brochure]. Wayne State University Libraries, Detroit.

Webb, G. (1988). Preparing staff for participative management. *Wilson Library Bulletin* **62**(9), 50–52.

Young, V. (1993). Focus on focus groups. *College & Research Library News* **54,** 391–394.

Younger, J. (1991). Total quality management: Can we move beyond the jargon? *ALCTS Newsletter* **2,** 81–83.

Zabel, D., and Avery, C. (1992). Total quality management: A primer. *RQ* **32,** 206–216.

A Changing Profession: Central Roles for Academic Librarians

Sheila D. Creth
University of Iowa
Iowa City, Iowa 52242

The scope and the magnitude of change that are occurring in libraries today are both exciting and daunting, particularly when we contemplate how we will manage the many streams of technological innovations pouring into the work environment. Although the new developments in information technology are challenging and, on some days, even overwhelming, the real challenges that we face are not technical in nature but personal. It is the change that will be required of individuals—library professionals, support staff, and the user community—that will present us with the greatest challenges. In order for librarians to influence and shape the future of information services within the highly technological and global information environment, a change in vision as well as activities and operations is required.

I. Implications for Change

There are four major areas in which academic librarians should be exploring new developments and opportunities: roles and responsibilities of library professionals; knowledge, skills, attitudes, and expectations for all staff; organizational structure and culture; and development of partnerships. As library professionals work on a daily basis to cope with the many changes that are occurring in the world of information resources and services, they must also attend to the implications that these changes suggest for the current and future activities of each individual in the library.

A. Changing Roles and Responsibilities

The librarian's role should be characterized by visibility and vitality. Librarians should be highly visible and well integrated into the activities of their

ADVANCES IN LIBRARIANSHIP, VOL. 19

institution and the community they serve. They should be valued as essential to the enterprise or activities of their primary organization or user community. Librarians, not the library building or the collections, should be valued and considered as an integral part of the organization team.

Most importantly, librarians should be seen as part of the solution (i.e., contributing to quality education, assisting with illiteracy in the community) rather than as part of the problem (i.e., escalating costs, inadequacy of undergraduate education).

More generally, librarians need to be bold and imaginative in conceiving of their role and decisive in acting upon it. They should be visionary in conceiving of the present and in imagining the future, and they should be willing to take the risks inherent in translating their vision into action even though many in the user community may be as wedded to tradition and what is comfortable as are many librarians.

Technology is pushing the boundaries and creating opportunities for redefining and expanding the role and activities of librarians in key areas, including strategic planning, information policy development, instruction, knowledge management, and the organization of networked information resources.

1. Strategic Planning

Strategic planning should be a fundamental tenet in library management in order to ensure quality decisions in the allocation of resources. Library professionals need to give greater attention to strategic planning at the organizational and departmental level, and then integrate the plan into the individual's goals and quality of performance. For strategic planning to be worthwhile, staff throughout the organization must be involved in the planning process and will need to understand the importance in relation to the allocation of increasingly scarce resources—human as well as collections, equipment, and the like. In addition, librarians need to be able to respond to the increasing demand for accountability from the user community and from taxpayers for publicly supported institutions. Questions such as why were dollars allocated to a particular service or costly information system and why does an operation cost a specific amount will require that librarians be able to demonstrate the process and quality of decision-making. As Shaughnessy (1992, p. 17) points out, "accountability extends beyond the domain of budgets, fund accounts, and expenditures. It includes all of an organization's assets . . . [including] time on task." He concludes that librarians need to "focus on those activities and programs that are mission critical."

Strategic planning involves assessment and evaluation, cost–benefit analysis, both short- and long-term projection, and innovation. The strategic planning process should involve not only staff throughout the library but individuals from the user community as well as other individuals and groups within the institution that will be instrumental in the success of the strategic plan such as computer professionals.

Some people may view a strategic plan as locking them into a particular direction or decision, thus reducing their ability to be responsive in a changing environment. On the contrary, flexibility does not come from the absence of clear direction and priorities but from that very process. The plan provides the framework within which to respond to opportunities or crises that arise with a clear understanding of what will have to be relinquished or delayed in order to address the unanticipated.

2. Information Policy Development

Another activity requiring immediate attention and leadership from librarians is the development of information policies. There is a range of information policy issues for which immediate and ongoing attention is needed. These issues should be addressed by librarians in a number of forums in order to obtain sufficient views, opinions, and, eventually, consensus. For example, a well-defined policy regarding access to information is needed, with frank attention given to the liability of a "have" and a "have not" information environment that could result if significant costs for access to electronic information and instructional software and hardware are shifted to the end user.

On the broad issue of equal access to information, Douglas Greenberg (1992, p 24), previous vice president of the American Council of Learned Societies, made the following observation related to the democratization potential of information technology:

> Those of us who care about the most fundamental values of our society must work together to ensure that our hard-won struggle for a new kind of humanistic knowledge is not overwhelmed by a powerful impulse to privatize access to that knowledge. If we fail to do our best to make the content of our work coherent, and with access to it, we will have failed not only our intellectual predecessors and descendants, but also the highest ideals of the society in which we live.

Other policy issues that require discussion and redefinition in the information technology environment include censorship, privacy, and intellectual property rights. Librarians should assume a key leadership position in their institutions and communities, and on the national level, in identifying information policy issues and contributing to the definition of coherent and fair policies for the electronic information world.

3. Instruction

The importance of instruction as an essential element in the role for librarians has been emphasized increasingly in the past several years. Librarians need to move beyond the limiting nature of bibliographic instruction to a more comprehensive concept that embraces a much broader role for instruction—the concept of the teaching library.

The teaching library suggests a broader and more integrated role for librarians than the passive nature of reference desk service in which professionals wait for the user to determine if he/she has a question and then decides to ask it. The teaching library goes beyond the idea of tours of the library or instruction of bibliographic sources to a class when a faculty member makes such a request. The teaching construct suggests an outreach mindset, one in which librarians define a range of information needs of the varied user community and design and present instruction in a variety of formats and locations to meet these needs. The teaching library is based on the belief that information knowledge and skills are essential to everyone—student, citizen, and teacher—and that the responsibility of the librarian is to aggressively develop plans and programs to offer diverse ways for individuals to acquire this set of knowledge and skill.

In this environment, librarians need to make full use of information and multimedia technology to support this greatly expanded teaching venture. Librarians should use the Internet, or the local network, as a method for offering interactive instruction, and they should develop hypermedia and expert systems to instruct users on specific tools and information sources and to provide general orientation to library services and policies.

In order to act on a new concept for instruction and outreach, librarians will have to rethink the value to users of the traditional reference and bibliographic instruction services. In order to be successful in implementing a new concept for user instruction and service, considerable staff time will be required. This means that it will not be possible to continue to do everything that has always been done in the past—something will have to be relinquished in order to move into these new endeavors.

4. Knowledge Management Environment

Another direction for libraries and librarians is knowledge management. This concept was developed and implemented at the Johns Hopkins University Welch Medical Library and at the University of California San Francisco Medical Library. Richard Lucier (1993, p. 97) states that a knowledge management environment "embraces the entire information-transfer cycle, from the creation, structuring, and representation of information to its dissemination and use." This moves librarians and libraries beyond the present role of storage, organization, and retrieval into the world of information transfer and creation. The changes occurring because of the networked information environment increase the opportunities for librarians to shift and broaden their involvement in the information and scholarly process.

The most unusual departure in this model is the primary emphasis on collaborative work between librarians and researchers in developing knowledge databases.

As a new enterprise, librarians will have to learn new skills and to set priorities in relation to other more traditional activities in order to have the time and energy to move into the knowledge management enterprise. The work is there, waiting to be done; users, particularly researchers, are open to assistance from librarians as is evident from the experience of Lucier and his colleagues. Librarians with their knowledge of information organization, existing electronic resources, and subject expertise are highly qualified to act as partners in creating this environment.

5. Organization of Networked Information Resources

The final responsibility in which librarians need to step forward to exercise influence is in the organization of networked information resources. The Internet offers a powerful new way to communicate and to gain access to information of all types. "Navigating the Internet" must feel more often than not like entering the Bermuda triangle during hurricane season. In describing the network and software products more generally, Ted Nelson (1993, p. 3) says "what we are seeing out there is a tangled nightmare" and he characterizes the situation as one in which we are increasingly prisoners of clever technologists.

Librarians need to grab the initiative more forcefully in creating better organization and access to what is available on and through the Internet. A virtual library is virtually useless if individuals have no structure from which to search and identify the materials they wish to use.

To accomplish this requires that library professionals broaden their focus on the cataloging of print materials to include electronic resources—both those generated and stored on local networks along with sources on the Internet.

These are only a few of the current and potential responsibilities in which library professionals can exercise a greater presence. Accomplishing this is dependent on a shift in expectations regarding the role and responsibilities appropriate to librarians or information professionals. It is not possible to incorporate a new set of demanding and complex activities without relinquishing or, at the very least, minimizing those activities that have historically been the ones to define the role of librarians.

While we benefit from the past and its distinguished traditions, librarians should not be bound by this past in defining their future. Nelson (1993, p. 2) says that, "tradition becomes truth in mysterious ways that cannot be challenged." We should resist the natural impulse to let the past define the future, to allow tradition to be the framework within which we shape a future role. While librarians should value and respect their history, they need to challenge tradition and traditional ways of providing information services to test whether these services and methods retain their currency and vitality. Indeed, if librarians are to have a future role at all they have to be willing to "rethink everything" as Jerry Campbell urges us to do.

B. Acquiring New Knowledge, Skills, Attitudes, and Expectations

If the scope and the nature of librarians' role in the networked information environment are to be redefined and expanded, then much attention is needed in several aspects of personal and professional development. In an environment of constant change, librarians will have to challenge traditions and assumptions regarding all aspects of library service. A self-critical and evaluative approach to all operations and functions will be essential along with a willingness to make decisions based on facts and user needs instead of on personal feelings or "because we've always done it that way." A reliance on intuitive feelings or past experiences is indefensible as a basis for allocating scarce resources, which is what all decisions regarding operations and services represent. Equally important will be for library professionals to exercise a far greater degree of risk-taking, the willingness to take action when confronting an unfamiliar or unpredictable situation. In a time of rapid change, it will be necessary for decisions to be reached in a timely manner without the luxury of lengthy deliberations.

If fundamental changes in the role and responsibilities of librarians are to occur, then a change in the professional culture of librarianship and in the library organization will need to occur as well. Flexibility on the part of individual professionals is essential, and new ideas need to be considered objectively and not dismissed out of hand even if initially they appear to be unworkable. Indeed, the very process of considering different approaches to operations and services encourages an assessment of what currently exists. Reality within most libraries—constant budget pressures to manage, new technology and information resouces to select and learn, and growing expectations from users for varied and ubiquitous services—requires professionals to reimagine, redefine, and reshape library services and thus themselves.

It is essential that library professionals continuously acquire new knowledge and skill to ensure that they remain a vital part of information services of the future. Librarians are learning a complex range of electronic resources and systems and are addressing complex issues involving information resource selection, cataloging, and copyright while also expanding their instruction of users in new resouces and systems. Librarians also need to design databases for their own use and to assist faculty in such efforts, to develop computer-assisted instructional programs for staff and user learning, and to integrate new technologies into services while assisting users in learning how to apply these same tools to their own work.

There is nothing new in the need for library staff to acquire new knowledge and skills. The pace and scope of learning, though, are quite different than in the past as information technology creates change unlike any experienced before. In this context, the standard approach to teaching and learning for library staff has to be reconsidered to ensure that ongoing, timely, and quality learning is a high priority. Library administrators need to define continuous learning as a part of each individual's job responsibilities and ensure that workloads permit time to be devoted to this activity on a routine basis. Administrators have the responsibility to provide the appropriate infrastructure for staff to learn what is required. This means that funding must be allocated to employ staff to develop internal training programs, to hire external trainers as necessary, and to support staff attending programs outside the library as appropriate. In addition, administrators and managers need to develop a culture in which the process of continuous learning and an acceptance of change by staff is the norm. The library staff needs to be responsible for their own active participation in learning and acceptance of learning and personal development as integral to their performance as any other task or activity.

Beyond knowledge and skills, it is necessary for library staff to accept different expectations regarding their work, their working relationships, and the environment in which they work. They need to develop strategies that allow them to work comfortably and effectively in the turmoil of the academic and information environments. For library professionals, in particular, it will be essential to relinquish what is familiar, traditional, and comfortable.

Professionals need to assess continually what duties and activities would be performed more appropriately by support staff, and then ensure that they have the knowledge, skill, and authority to perform these responsibilities. It would be a mistake simply to shift activities from professional to support staff, thus adding more duties to their assignments. Instead, every library should have a process for ongoing review and analysis of all operations and services. This is necessary in order to identify those tasks or activities that are no longer essential in meeting user needs or ones that are not being performed in the most efficient manner. Staff cannot continue to just add activities and services without relinquishing others; choices will have to be made regarding both the continuation of services and the manner in which tasks are accomplished. These choices should always be centered around an assessment of user needs rather than librarian's perception of user needs or the needs of librarians.

An essential premise in changing expectations for work and working relationships is for library professionals to assume that assignments and responsibilities, along with knowledge and skills, will continually alter and change. Acceptance by professionals that there will not be permanent positions either in regard to specific assignments or duties performed will be necessary. Assignment of staff should be guided by library priorities matched with individual talents and abilities, not limited by labels such as cataloger or reference librarian.

C. Redesigning the Organization

Another significant aspect of information technology is the opportunity it presents in reconsidering the structure and design of the library organization. Most libraries are structured around public and technical services with a reliance on a vertical hierarchical structure. In an environment of rapid and accelerated change, the traditional library organization increasingly is becoming a barrier to quality services. Since the origin of modern organizations emerged in the late 1700s with Adam Smith (1979), it is not surprising that at the end of the 20th century organization principles need to be rethought. The division of labor, or segmenting work into the smallest task, was the most prominent concept to emerge from the early industrial period. The concept rested on a desire to create efficiencies and worker productivity by having individuals perform only one task over and over again. Thus with each worker specializing in one or two simple tasks, time and effort would be more efficiently applied than if each person had to learn and perform multiple tasks and learn different tools and materials. With the development of the assembly line in the early 1900s, the idea of work moving to the workers became another means of generating efficiencies in large operations. In service organizations, these principles not only affected the processing of paper and materials but clients who had to come to the workers as well.

As organizations grew in size, a hierarchical structure based on functional units containing specialized operations developed with management and employees focusing attention and communication almost exclusively within their own organization segment. In this setting, communication and interaction among staff evolved with a vertical orientation, and lines were drawn around working relationships with problem-solving occurring most often in tightly segmented units. Hammer and Champy (1993, p. 66) describe this organizational orientation as creating "functional silos."

There are many examples in libraries that reflect these principles for organizing work. Work is segmented into functional departments to simplify complex work for the staff, although not necessarily for the user. Libraries have multiple processing departments such as acquisitions, cataloging, binding, marking, and shelving. Direct user services require that the client (faculty, student, staff) come to the library facility and often to multiple service points to have questions answered, secure and circulate materials, and participate in group instruction.

The principles and assumptions related to the organization of work proved to be effective in a stable and growth environment. Beginning in the 1980s, though, the reality for organizations across the spectrum of profit and nonprofit, manufacturing, and service began to alter in significant ways. The pace of change was greatly accelerated, economic predictability was no longer possible, competition was intensified, information technology created new opportunities and requirements, customers were more demanding, and employees, particularly professionals, expected to have a greater say about their work and the work environment. The organizational structure that had served so well for so many decades has become increasingly dysfunctional in the turmoil of this new technological, economic, competitive, and cultural environment. These realities, in addition to the vast opportunities for innovative services and products available through the application of technology, suggest that now is the time to challenge these decades-old principles that have shaped organizations, including libraries.

Criticism directed toward large organizations has increased. Descriptions are typified by statements that these organizations are suffering from bureaucratic paralysis and inflexibility, and are sluggish, inefficient, and noncreative. Criticism also focuses on the high overhead costs, in particular the expense of a large management cadre to coordinate the increasingly complex segmented organization. Criticisms that the focus of the organization is too often on activity rather than on results and that there is a lack of responsiveness or responsibility toward the client also exist. Hammer and Champy (1993, p. 66) characterize many organizations as a place where people look inward to their department and upward to their boss but no one looks outward to the client.

Library professionals need to assess their organizations to see if these characteristics apply. Professionals should be less concerned with an organization that reflects order and symmetry, comfort, and familiarity than with encouraging action and decision-making, risk, and innovation throughout the organization. Unless a highly fluid and flexible organization environment is created that permits timely response to changing institutional needs, the role for librarians will decline within higher education; libraries could become the "white elephants" that some have predicted. A vigorous and imaginative response is required to ensure that this scenario does not emerge.

Keen (1991, p. 8) states that the mature organization, with its "long-established norms of stability and security must be replaced with new values such as speed, simplicity, and unparalleled customer service, and a self-

confident, empowered work force." While a fluid, open organizational structure and culture are encouraged, it is necessary to recognize that an organization is not an abstract concept or a piece of paper with boxes and lines
but a living organism, a society comprised of people, feelings, attitudes,
expectations, and needs. A significant change in the organizational structure
may represent a very uncomfortable change for some employees, particularly
as lines blur and responsibilities and authority overlap.

It will be important to keep in mind that the strength of the library is
the staff and that people can be fragile and, therefore, the organization will
exhibit this same fragility. As change is undertaken, staff should be involved
in some manner in the decisions that create major shifts so that they understand the reasons for changes. Staff are more likely to develop a commitment
to required changes in the organization and culture and, by extension, their
own behavior, if they are involved.

Library professionals should explore an organizational design that relies
on small groups or teams as the primary way that work is accomplished,
decisions reached, and service delivered. Employees can no longer be effective
in an insolated and independent mode. Barone (1993, p. 73) states that "complex tasks and rapid change require collaborative effort to succeed. Chaotic
environments require mutual support. The best and most creative and effective answers to problems are the result of synthesizing many ideas and viewpoints."

Teamwork should be central to the library organization, built on individuals grouped together to perform tasks related to a specific process or project.
Keen (1991, p. 8) suggests that organizations in this intense information
environment should shift from "organizing by division of labor to organizing
by division of knowledge." The division of knowledge "captures an obvious
reality of work in an era of rapid change and uncertainty." The concept
of division of knowledge as a principle for organizing has great relevance
for libraries.

Martell (1983, p. 73) in his book, *The Client-Centered Academic Library*,
indicated that the "optimal client-centered design would have the following
characteristics: most librarians in client-centered work groups and these
groups would have a high degree of autonomy, all librarians in the work
groups would be involved in multi-function roles such as reference, collection
development, and advisory services to clients, and a high level of interaction
with clients would exist." By 1993, technology permitting interactive communication from varied locations, distances, and times was available to support
the dynamic client-centered organization envisioned by Martell.

The success of the team approach requires a commitment of all members
to the goals of the team rather than individual goals. The team members also
must have a willingness to share authority and responsibility. This requires

that individuals have respect and trust for one another and their respective talents and abilities.

In addition, creating an effective team environment requires training to assist individuals in learning new skills and behavior for a team-centered organization. Library administrators and managers will need to assume a major responsibility in creating the team-based organization by demonstrating their ability to work as team members, relinquishing power and authority of the traditional manager.

With a shifting organizational environment and culture, managers understandably are uncertain regarding their role. New and clear expectations regarding the role and responsibility of managers are needed to assist individual managers, as well as those they manage, to make the transition into a team-based and collaborative organization. Managers will be key in this transition, including their ability to see their role and responsibilities differently as traditional managerial duties are reshaped for a collaborative and consultative approach rather than one of authority and control. The role for managers should focus on:

coaching and mentoring staff
development of staff
providing advice and assistance in problem-solving and planning new initiatives
developing shared values and vision among staff
encouraging adaptability, initiative accountability, and teamwork
providing resouces within framework of a cost–benefit assessment
taking pride in the accomplishments of others
providing incentives so teams work.

Some individuals will not be well suited to the new managerial construct as "team leaders" and different assignments will be necessary. In any case, a significant commitment from the organization for the development of managers will be required for individuals to learn about and integrate into their management style and philosophy an understanding and respect for collaboration and team work.

Library staff who are struggling to keep up with the demands in today's work environment require, indeed deserve, new ways for accomplishing their work. The redesign of the library organization is imperative if we are to move rapidly and with an entrepreneurial spirit in the delivery of services in the current interactive high-speed communication environment.

In order to make the transition from a structure that has been hierarchical and segmented to one that is fluid and flexible, library professionals need to experiment and explore, to remain open to considering new approaches, and to keep the user as the central focus in any organizational design.

D. Creating New Partnerships

The ability of library professionals to reshape and strengthen information services requires that existing relationships be strengthened and new partnerships be created.

1. Among Libraries

New levels of coordination and cooperation among libraries are required. There is an urgency to move beyond existing cooperation centered largely on interlibrary lending and shared national cataloging databases. New ways to work together need to be imagined in order to improve services and to contain costs by establishing collaborative projects among libraries. Projects might include librarians from different institutions sharing the provision of online reference service. For example, an online reference service might be organized among regional federal depository library staffs to improve access to government information or among several university libraries for users in mathematics or linguistics. The objective would be to expand the availability of information assistance by pooling resources in different libraries with librarians providing so many hours of support for the online service. If information was provided in a timely manner, the user would not care where the information specialist was located or the person's institutional affiliation.

Another possibility for librarians to explore is the sharing of operational activities such as cataloging, acquisitions, and preservation. They should determine the feasibility and cost effectiveness of merging certain operations. Australian academic libraries have been amalgamating technical services since 1988; it is possible to learn something from their experience. The Australian librarians did not initiate this merger. Instead, in the late 1980s the government created a unified system of higher education which merged universities and colleges and their libraries. Before library administrators in this country are mandated to take a similar approach, librarians should explore whether this is a viable approach to cost reduction or containment without a loss of quality service.

2. Information Technologists

Certainly within academic institutions, librarians should be pursuing the opportunities that exist through closer collaboration with colleagues in computing centers. Typically, the relationship between the library and the computing center has been one in which the library has purchased programming and computing support services. The information and technological changes occurring suggest that more than the traditional working relationship between computer professionals and librarians is required. The two need to work together collegially in addressing everything from designing systems to creating tools that ensure easy access to the world of information available on the Internet, and from developing joint user education programs to the developing of institutional information policies.

In his book, *Shared Minds: The New Technologies of Collaboration*, Schrage (1990, p. 4) explored how the expansion of information technology offers a unique opportunity for individuals and organizations to focus on collaboration which he defined as an "act of shared creation and/or shared discovery." The process of collaboration, according to Schrage, requires a different approach and set of expectations, and it is a process between equals.

Both computing and library professionals have to work with limited, and often inadequate, resources in relation to the task before them. Instead of proceeding down similar and parallel paths, the staff of both units should join together as partners in order to meet the escalating demands of the campus community. The role and value of computer and library professionals will be magnified if they pursue a strength in collaborative partnerships. It will not be an easy task either for individuals or for organizations, but it is one that will ensure a creative and exciting future for information professionals into the 21st century.

3. Library Users

The relationship between library professionals and users should shift from librarians being the authorities telling users what they want and what is possible to a partnership. As Donald Langenberg (1993, p. 35), a scholar and university administrator, observed, "institutions that create technology or make policy without a clear understanding and appreciation of the real needs of their clients and constituents risk making serious and expensive blunders. Nowhere is that more evident than in the swift and turbulent currents of information technology."

Greenberg (1992, p. 20) emphasizes the need for more cooperation among working scholars, information technologists, and librarians. Otherwise the technologists and the librarians "will build a better screwdriver when what the scholars really needed is a better hammer."

To create effective working relationships and collaborative partnerships among users, computer professionals, and librarians, new knowledge and skills, behavior, and expectations are required. Library professionals can be successful in shaping this milieu if they pursue the opportunities that exist.

II. Conclusion

Lucier (1993, p. 106) states that in creating the knowledge management environment many unique experiences occur and many important questions on policy, technology, and financing for libraries are raised. The answers to these questions and the future implications for libraries are not always apparent. Rather they emerge and unfold as the work progresses, demanding a high degree of openness and flexibility from all involved.

Will Rogers is credited with saying that you could be on the right train track and still be run over. There is no question that there are many risks in the networked information environment. But the greatest risk is not in falling off the track but in standing still and having the full force of information technology run over us.

It is essential for library professionals to recognize the changes that will and must occur in their roles, and responsibilities. They will need to redefine the requirements for academic librarianship, accept the challenge to reshape the library organization, and establish new partnerships. The goal continues to be quality information service to the academic community; only how it will be accomplished is changing.

References

Barone, C. A. (1993). New interpretations of old rules, or if the ocean is on the right you are headed north. *Cause/Effect* **16,** 1.

Greenberg, D. (1992). You can't always get what you want: Technology, scholarship, and democracy. In *New Technologies and New Directions: Proceedings from the Symposium on Scholarly Communication* (G. R. Boynton and Sheila D. Creth, eds.). Meckler Publishing, Westport, CT.

Hammer, M., and Champy, J. (1993). *Reengineering the Corporation: A Manifesto for Business Revolution.* Harper Collins, New York.

Keen , G. W. (1991). Redesigning the organization through information technology. *Planning Review* **19.**

Langenberg, D. N. (1993). The lonely scholar in a global information environment. In *New Technologies and New Directions: Proceedings from the Symposium on Scholarly Communication* (G. R. Boynton and Sheila D. Creth, eds.). Meckler Publishing, Westport, CT.

Lucier, R. (1993). Knowledge management: Refining roles in scientific communication. In *New Technologies and New Directions: Proceedings from the Symposium on Scholarly Communication* (G. R. Boynton and Sheila D. Creth, eds.). Meckler Publishing, Westport, CT.

Martell, C. (1983). *The Client-Centered Academic Library: An Organizational Model.* Greenwood Press, Westport, CT.

Nelson, T. (1983). Freedom and Power. In *New Technologies and New Directions: Proceedings from the Symposium on Scholarly Communication.* (G. R. Boynton and Sheila D. Creth, eds.). Meckler Publishing, Westport, CT.

Schrage, M. (1990). *Shared Minds: The New Technologies of Collaboration.* Random House, New York.

Shaughnessy, T. (1992). The Library Director as Change Agent. Talk given at University of North Carolina, Chapel Hill, unpublished.

Smith, A. (1979). *An Inquiry into the Nature and Causes of the Wealth of Nations* (Edwin Cannan, ed.), University of Chicago Press, Chicago.

Alternative Conceptualizations of the Information Economy

Sandra Braman
Institute of Communications Research
University of Illinois–Champaign/Urbana
Champaign, Illinois 61820

The economics of information is an emerging field[1] that is developing in response to changes in the nature of the economy driven by the convergence of computing and communication technologies and by growing awareness of the range of problems in dealing with information creation, processing, flows, and use from the neoclassical economic perspective. Issues in the economics of information are critical to the field of librarianship, as to other information industries, because they affect the functioning and survival of libraries as institutions; the more accurately conceptualizations of the information economy map onto realities, the more likely that solutions to economic problems faced by libraries are to be found or developed.

Awareness that the nature of the economy was changing was a feature of the second stage of the information society, datable to the 1960s (Braman, 1993). Since that time, three conceputalizations of the information economy have been put forth, differing in their theoretical framework, validity, response to problems in the economics of information, and utility:

1. This is an information economy because, while the economy operates as it always has, those industries in the information sector have grown in relative importance.

2. This is an information economy because the economy itself has expanded through commodification of forms of information never before commoditized, revealing what has always been deeply contradictory in our economic approach.

[1]Historically, economists have dealt with a few specific types of questions dealing with the economics of information, such as the cost of searching for prices and other transaction costs. These have been narrowly directed questions, however, rather than the far-reaching efforts to understand the economy as a whole that drive current development of the broad field of the economics of information.

3. This is an information economy because harmonized information flows have replaced the market as the key coordinating mechanism of the economy, which now works in qualitatively different ways from how it has operated in the past (the approach of the emerging field of network economics).

Following articulation of the range of problems we face in general and public libraries face in particular in trying to use neoclassical economics in the analysis of information creation, processing, flows, and use, this chapter explores the three approaches to understanding the information economy. It concludes by suggesting that an "enriched" network economies approach may be the most fruitful path to follow.

I. Problems in the Economics of Information

A. The Problem of Creation

From the perspective of neoclassical economics, things are created only in response to demands of the market.

1. Alternative Motivations

While there are those who argue that markets are needed to stimulate information production, at least in the cases of several types of information creation—symbolic, ritual, artistic, and self-expressive—the market is minimally pertinent if at all. We speak to each other in order to build and participate in human relations. We write poetry and fiction out of an internal drive and only hope there may be a market for it; lack of such a market is often completely irrelevant to the continuance of the drive and the creation of text. We express ourselves ritually. We shout in pain, moan when weeping, and sing out of joy because self-expression is critical to our functioning. One of the arguments offered in support of the First Amendment is just this—that freedom of speech needs to be protected because expression as part of our self-actualization processes is a fundamental human right. A policy issue this point raises is the question of a positive mandate for access to communications, in order to support the creation of information that is *not* market-driven and may therefore need economic or other help for survival. Libraries tend to deal with this problem by offering a venue in which community organizations can meet, mounting art exhibits, etc.

2. The Consumer as Producer

A second economic problem in the creation of information is the role of the consumer of information in creating its value; in our historical approaches to economics, the consumer is not considered to be part of the production process. Dallas Smythe's (1981) famous insight that the product being sold in television is the audience—to advertisers who then support the production of programs—offered a first vivid move toward incorporating consumers into the production calculus. This is a problem for libraries as the "canon" disappears and the boundaries of what should and should not be collected become less and less clear.

3. Joint Production

A third problem is raised by the practice of joint production of many information and communication services and goods. Since the relative import of any individual's contribution will be impossible to quantitatively measure, the distribution of the profits and other benefits of the production of those services and goods will always be a political matter. Libraries probably confront this problem most in the area of intellectual property rights.

4. Information Retained by Producer

Some information never enters the market as a commodity because it is retained for use by the information producer. The lack of access to proprietary information is one example of how this problem affects libraries.

B. The Problem of Time

Economists working in the neoclassical tradition are concerned about information only when it enters into and as it affects the market.

1. Simultaneous Production and Consumption

When production and consumption of informational products and processes occur simultaneously, it is difficult to treat economically. Materials of this type generally are *not* held by libraries.

2. Perishability

Information is often said to be quite "perishable" in the persistence of its value; stock market information, for example, rapidly diminishes in value over very brief periods of time. This approach, however, seems to ignore the movement of the locus of perceived value from one category of user—the investor in the stock market or the broker—to another—the historian or economic or cultural analyst. Despite this, information often cannot be stored over time; even when it can, doing so is often not useful. Libraries, of course, face this problem when they face the issue of which material to retain and which to let go as collections expand. The flip side of this problem is the issue of conservation.

3. Provenance

Posner (1986) notes that over time it is increasingly difficult to discern the actual source of information, a problem in the determination of intellectual property rights, an area that again affects libraries.

4. Constant Production

In cyberspace, often works are constantly changing over time as electronic communities together create information, either as specific collaborative texts or as participants in ongoing conversations. In such an environment, at which point is something marked as an identifiable commodity? Similarly, many forms of net art produce multiple manifestations at different points in time; traditional art collectors and dealers are concerned about which is really the piece. The problem this raises for libraries is deciding which version(s) of a text to acquire or retain; many may respond to this problem by offering electronic access to texts rather than the texts themselves.

5. Cumulative and Generative Effects

Information received at different points in time differs in value because it is affected by information received over time. The value of information, that is, is cumulative over time and the reception of each piece of information affects the value of information that is received later. These shifts in value are not treatable with neoclassical economic analytical tools. Boulding (1966) notes, for example, that information about the economic system itself changes the system. Thus information does not only flow within an existing economic structure, but also plays a constitutive role in producing, reproducing, or changing that structure. Boulding describes this problem by calling information a generalized Heisenberg uncertainty principle. This problem confronts libraries as changes in intellectual climate affect acquisition, conservation, and censorship practices.

6. Unpredictability of Use

Economists dealing with other utilities, such as electricity, are able to incorporate statistics regarding habits of usage into their calculations. With information creation and flows, however, it is impossible to determine regular peak periods of usage. This, too, causes problems in economic analysis with predictive intentions. As libraries seek to provide service to citizens, this irregularity provides one more complication to budgeting and personnel decisions.

7. Conversation over Extended Time Periods

Last, it is difficult to know how to mark the time horizons of a particular conversation or information exchange since we continue today to deal with, for example, philosophical problems that have been around for over 2000 years. Rav Nachman of Bratslav, a leading Hasidic figure, commented that we never know to whom we are speaking, for in any given moment of speech, we may be answering someone who asked a question hundreds of years ago. In the library context, design and presentation of reference services are areas where this problem is faced.

C. The Problem of Space

In the 1980s, space as an analytical category began to be important across the social sciences in response to the experience of globalization.

1. Distributed Production

With the growth of trade in services and foreign direct investment, the problem of locating just where informational transactions take place has become increasingly pressing. With data processing, for example, a transnational corporation headquartered in one country may have computers in another that process data from a third country, with the data moving back and forth through telecommunications lines. Does the transaction take place in the country of consumption? In the country of processing? In the home country of the transnational corporation? In the telecommunications lines themselves? Huber (1987) points out that in analysis of telecommunication we habitually examine only the transport of information over space ("tele-communication"), but should also think about transport of information over time ("chrono-communications"). Because this problem affects the pricing and availability of materials, it is something with which librarians must deal.

2. The Disappearance of Space

Space in a sense can be said to disappear as an economic factor in the net environment since services can be distributed globally, across political and geographic borders. While they are distributed globally, however, it can also be said that services are nontransportable—they cannot be carried from one place to another, although they can come into existence across space through the net. The development of international librarianship is in direct response to this problem.

3. The Disappearance of the Customer

Many services can actually be delivered without the customer being present. This too is an abrogation of the notion that both commodities and transactions must be specifiable in space and time. As libraries begin to consider offering their services outside of library buildings, they are confronting this problem.

D. The Problem of Tangibility

1. Embedding the Intangible in the Tangible

One of the most widely recognized problems in the economics of information is the difficulty of distinguishing between the value of information and the value of the materials with which it is associated or in which it is embedded. Babe (1994) claims that because we have almost exclusively dealt with the value of the objects, all of our economic analyses of the information industries have been skewed.

The relationship between the tangible and the intangible can change over time or with bureaucratic circumstance, further confounding economic analysis. The right to use certain portions of the electromagnetic spectrum, for example, is gained from the FCC via a license. Once a station owns a license, however, it may be sold for far greater amounts of money than required for its acquisition—as long as it is sold incident to the sale of a station.

A problem for intellectual property rights comes from the difficulty in identifying products in which particular ideas, capable of many manifestations, are embedded, a problem which inevitably affects libraries. Libraries are also dealing with issues that derive from this problem when they offer training in access to information and access itself rather than texts.

2. Labeling

A second tier of confusion is generated by the labeling on material objects— essentially information about a tangible object that incorporates information. Labeling is a third source of potential value, in addition to the packaging and the information itself. Issues raised by indexing are examples of this type of problem that affect libraries.

3. Information and the Material World

While the physical environment is perceived in terms of the symbolic, the symbolic in turn acts upon and shapes the physical. Thus not only is information often embedded in the physical, but it also shapes the materials which embody it. It is precisely this effect that makes the role of libraries so central to society.

E. The Problem of Intangibility

1. Information as Epiphenomenal

Although information is intangible, it may be called epiphenomenal in that it derives from the organization of the material world. Babe (1994) notes that it is this feature which makes it so difficult to appropriate, for the same material phenomenon may produce different types of information; and different material phenomena may produce the same information: "Different substances, and even human memories, can easily be shaped or formed to convey or hold the "same" information" (p. 32). Librarians confront this issue in the area of collection design.

2. The Embedding of Information in Relations

Many types of information never reach a material form, being embedded instead in relations. Neoclassical economics has no way of dealing with such products and processes. Material of this type is generally not held in libraries, other than as a consequence of providing a venue for community meetings.

3. Information and the Value of Material Goods

It is worth noting that the more information available about a particular material good, the more valuable that material good is. Similarly, the more service available for a particular material good, the more valuable it is. Public libraries acknowledge this by including in their collections material such as repair manuals, magazines such as *Consumer Reports*, and so forth.

F. The Problem of Heterogeneity

1. Heterogeneity of Form

As Porat (1977) pointed out, no one definition can cover all types of information or all of the industries in the information sector. At the same time, single information commodities may have multiple manifestations. These features are difficult for an economic perspective that assumes that all commodities are specifiable in terms of shape that remains stable across space and time, and that can at any given time be precisely located and identifiable. Net art, again, brings this problem to an acute form.

Another aspect of the heterogeneity of form is the constant development that information products and processes are undergoing. While most commodities reach a form that is stable over time, although there may be adaptations and improvements, the innovation pace in the information industries is much, much higher—there does not yet appear to be a moment of product maturation.

Both of these aspects of the heterogeneity of form arise in librarianship in the problem of collection design and acquisition practices.

2. Heterogeneity of Value

Any single information product or process is simultaneously valued differently by different people. This feature is shared with the valuing of material goods, but seems particularly critical in the measurement of the value of information. For information more than for many other types of goods, the value in use may be utterly unrelated to the exchange value. Much of the information provided in newspapers that serves the purpose of providing social coordination, such as information about signing up children for school or infant immunizations, comes cheaply but is invaluable.

For the same person, the same information may hold different value under different conditions: private and public; depending on the speaker; and as constrained by time, place, and manner restrictions.

For libraries, differences in how various types of information are valued become problematic as they seek to maintain and expand budget support. The March 1995 suggestion by the U.S. Congress that the Smithsonian budget, for example, should be decreased because the organization should be getting rid of "old" material is a vivid example of this issue.

3. Heterogeneity of Function

The same informational product or process can simultaneously serve multiple functions in the economy. An accounting system, for example, is a commodity in its own right, a structural device for the production of other commodities, provides coordination within and between organizations, etc. To treat information creation and flows only as commodities denies several critical aspects of information exchange, including the exercise of power. The flatness of access to information in the public library context demonstrates sensitivity to this problem.

G. The Problem of Inextricability

Perceiving information solely as a commodity in neoclassical terms makes invisible many of the most important consequences of information exchange, such as creation of a public space, and the exercise of power. Information is completely dependent on the social, cultural, political, and ecological elements of its context, although these are treated as externalities by neoclassical economics.

There are two possible responses to this problem: one can turn to noneconomic modes of analysis, as Tribe (1985) powerfully argues when he rejects the use of cost–benefit analysis at the level of constitutional analysis. Tribe points out that cost–benefit analyses—the very stuff of economic analysis of communication policy problems—by definition deal with fixed categories and relations within and between categories, whereas the very mission of constitutional adjudication is to reconsider the categories used and activities permitted within and between them. All communication policy issues, Tribe claims, are constitutional issues. A second response to this problem is to try to develop alternative decision-making procedures that can handle types of values not previously incorporated into economic analysis.

In Great Britain in 1995, public libraries are being closed as cost–benefit analyses with a too short time horizon are used to justify their elimination from budgets.

H. The Problem of Inappropriability

Problems in the appropriability of information are at the heart of issues in dealing with information economically, for without appropriation there are no commodities, and without commodities, no markets. The fury of concern over intellectual property rights, the vehicle through which property rights are asserted, reveals how serious a problem this is.

1. Information as a Public Good

Brennan (1990) notes that there is a fundamental contradiction in treating information economically as we have, since the material package in which information is embedded is a private good, whereas the information itself is a public good. There are of course two meanings of the term "public good." The common sense meaning looks at public goods as things that should rightfully be accessible to every member of the public, such as water. A public good in economists' terms refers to something the use of which does not deprive others of its use. In the economists' sense, information is clearly a public good, for knowledge by one person of something does not deny others of that knowledge. Although there may be a difference in their competitive status, as in the case of knowledge of corporations that serves competition in the stock market.) Public debate about information policy often gets confused between the two meanings of the term, for politically many feel that there are many types of information that should be public goods in the sense of available to all.

There is thus a tension for those handling information—while the information or mode of information processing may be easily understood as a public good in the political sense, the desire to generate profit often works against the public interest as individual entities seek exclusive control over informational resources. The movement of a good from the public to the private domain is therefore a means of creating value; exclusivity in the telecommunications network provides an example of this. Clearly the applicability of the economists' sense of the public good to information confounds the effort to appropriate information in a meaningful way as a commodity.

It is precisely the role of public libraries to offer information as a public good to the citizenry.

2. Sale vs Use of Information

While with material goods sale means transfer of an object from seller to buyer, so that the seller no longer has use of what is sold, in the case of information the seller generally retains the information, and its use, even after the sale. This is a radical shift in what is understood to be appropriation. Libraries specifically are designed to take advantage of this by ensuring that there need not be an economic transaction each time a reader seeks access to a text.

3. Leakiness

It is very difficult when transferring information to restrict use of the information to the buyer alone. Information is in this sense said to be "leaky," for it is very easy for nonpurchasers to also use or enjoy the information. As reproduction and transmission costs go down, this problem increases. Again, taking advantage of this is the specialization of libraries.

I. The Problem of Indivisibility

1. Unitizing

It is difficult to identify discrete pieces of information. In the case of a journal article, is it the entire article? a paragraph? a sentence? an idea? the stream of literature in which it is embedded? It is not even clear who has the responsibility of doing the unitizing. In the case of a novel, for example, is the writer, the reader, or the filmmaker responsible for doing the unitizing? In many cases, multiple different types of units may be concurrently applicable; which should be deemed most pertinent for economic purposes? Umberto Eco, in a series of essays on fiction, talks about the problem of time in novels, for example, distinguishing between story time (the fictional time span over which the story being told takes place), discourse time (the time period to which the novel speaks), and reading time (the time it takes to read the book). For libraries, this issue arises in collection design, budgeting, and design of library layout.

2. Partial Information

Partial information is often useless or even damaging, yet it can be difficult to know whether one has complete information or not. It can be hard to know whether what one has received is complete or partial to the degree that it is misinformation or disinformation. As we found in efforts to apply the Fairness Doctrine, which mandated broadcast stations to discuss all sides of controversial issues of public interest, it can even be difficult to know when all sides of an issue have been presented. Again, a critical issue in collection design for public libraries.

3. Satiation

There are many goods for which sales can be made over and over—food, clothing, etc. With information, however, one is often satiated with the first unit of a certain type of information, so that the repeat sales on which many marketing behaviors are predicated are not available. Multiple copies are useless unless they can be sold; hoarding behaviors are meaningless. In this case, libraries are the exception that proves the rule, for it is precisely their function to "hoard," so to speak.

J. The Problem of Subjectivity

The value of information is completely dependent on the individual receiving the information. This subjectivity means that the individual and/or community or reception and use determines value, which is then not knowable to others outside of that community; it is not ascertainable by others. Nor is it the same across potential "consumers," "audiences," "public," or "citizens," even under the same market conditions.

The problem of subjectivity interacts with many of the other types of problems discussed here. With time, for example, what is of value to the stockbroker becomes of value to the historian. Again, a budgeting problem for libraries.

K. The Problem of Self-Reflexivity

There are three forms of the problem of self-reflexivity.

1. Infinite Regress

Both Stiglitz (1985) and Arrow (1962) have pointed to the problem that arises when purchasers attempt to determine the value of an informational product in order to make a buying decision. Stiglitz described this as a problem of infinite regress, for it is impossible to determine whether it is worthwhile to obtain information concerning whether it is worthwhile to obtain information, and so on. Arrow, working within a tradition of research into the costs of acquiring information [Coase (1952) seminally described the firm as an effort to reduce the costs of acquiring information], points out that information's value for the purchaser is not known until she has the information but then she has, in effect, acquired the knowledge itself without cost. This is a problem for libraries that attempt to determine acquisition practices in the present to serve perhaps indeterminable future needs.

2. Self-Reflexivity

Because informational products and processes are constitutive of individuals, communities, and societies, they are constantly interacting with the social, cultural, political, economic, and ecological environments in which they are occurring and to which they refer. Thus in the act of being referential, information flows themselves are changing the reality to which they refer. Again, it is precisely for this reason that access to a wide range of types of information via public libraries is so centrally important to society.

3. Creation through Self-Reflexivity

Informational products and processes themselves generate additional information. Thus, any commodity is at the same a material or agent in the production process, something which is not true of most material goods. This leads to the suggestion that economic arguments for the support of libraries might be developed based on their role in the innovation processes now so central to the economy.

II. Alternative Conceptualizations of the Information Economy

The three different conceptualizations of the information economy differ ideologically and have developed in sequence chronologically.

A. Dominance of the Economy by Information Industries

The first conceptualization of the information economy to appear chronologically, presented in the 1960s by the Japanese (Ito, 1991) and later by the American Daniel Bell (1973), still dominates policy-making. This is the view that the economy works the way it always has, and it is working just fine, but those industries in the information sector of the economy now dominate proportionately. This is an evolutionary view that identifies an information phase as the most recent in the sequence from hunter–gatherer through agriculture to manufacturing; in Bell's terms, this is the postindustrial era.

Machlup (1962), after studying commonalities among a number of different industries, identified what he called "knowledge industries." Porat (1977) operationalized this concept by identifying those categories of work and of industries that are partially or wholly devoted to informational activities or products out of the classification schemes already in use for statistical purposes such as SIC (standard industrial classification) codes that identify every distinct product made commercially. It is this approach that was adopted first by the U.S. Department of Commerce and then by other nations and international entities around the world as the basis of its statistical approach to understanding the informatization of society, and thus it is this approach that is the source of all the statistics we see on the percentage of information work or activity in an economy.

The response of this approach to problems in the application of neoclassical economics to information creation, processing, flows, and use is simply denial that there are any problems at all. In terms of a Kuhnian paradigm change, those who take this position deny altogether the suggestion that there might be difficulties with the currently dominant paradigm. From this position it is possible to promote, for example, the inclusion of trade in services (international information flows) under the General Agreement on Tariffs and Trade (GATT), a set of international rules applying to trade in material goods; the United States has vigorously done so, while many in both developed and developing worlds objected, claiming there were political, social, and cultural effects of information flows as well as the economic effects observable as commodity exchange (Braman, 1990).

This approach has such appeal because of its chronological priority, because it does not require any conceptual adaptation, and, perhaps most importantly, because it can be operationalized using existing statistical and decision-making tools. Certainly, using those methods, the figures we see about the growth of the information economy are striking. Unfortunately, these methods do not validly portray all that is significant about the information economy. Notably, these statistical approaches deal only with material objects, so that the informational relations that are so important today economically do not appear. The disjuncture between this approach and reality has grown so large, however, that a group of corporations has now joined in what is being referred to as the intellectual capital movement, an effort to rethink their accounting systems to more accurately reflect current realities; some academics continue to work variations on the theme in the effort to find a solution still based on this approach (Stewart, 1994).

B. Expansion of the Economy through Commodification of Information

The second approach, emerging in the 1970s out of the critical community, also starts from the position that the economy is working the way it always has—only believes that it has *never* worked. Those who take this position, such as Schiller (1981) and Mosco (1989), claim we can describe this as an information economy because the economy has expanded through commodification of types of information that were never before commodified, from the most private (what is in your thoughts, what is in your urine), to the most public (through commodification of governmental databases, for example). They point to the problems we have in applying neoclassical economics to information and its flows as just further evidence of the deep contradictions that have always existed in the capitalist economy, and their response to these problems and contradictions is to suggest that capitalism be abandoned altogether in favor of an alternative form of economic organization. Schiller, Mosco, and others generally point in the direction of some version of a socialist or communist form of economic organization, whereas Hyde (1983) and others point instead toward a gift economy model. [Michaels (1994) is to my knowledge unique in his understanding of the extremity of the range of approaches to informatized social organization, gained through his work with the Warlpiri aborigines of northern Australia, a people whom he describes as the first information society.] In terms of Kuhnian paradigm change, those who take this perspective are those who acknowledge that there is a need to change and have begun the job of casting about for a new paradigm.

The arguments presented by those who point to commodification of ever more kinds of information and informational relationships are, again, accurate, persuasive, and important, and the evidence supporting those arguments is strong. The expectation that capitalism will be abandoned, however, is unrealistic; the desire for this, however, absorbs the energies that might otherwise have been devoted to developing decision-making procedures and regulations more sensitive to the cultural, social, and political consequences of commodification processes that might not always be desirable. There is a limit, therefore, in the utility of this approach to working policy-makers, although we should take from it the important reminder of some of the potential dangers of what the "informatization" of society.

C. Harmonized Information Flows Replace the Economy

The third approach, emerging in the 1990s, identifies this as an information economy because the nature of the economy itself has qualitatively changed: harmonized information flows have now replaced the market as the key coordinating mechanism of the economy. This is the approach of network economics, an approach based on empirical research into the various forms of organization and types of activities of transnational corporations. The strength of this empirical base; the desire to adapt, not completely discard, the currently dominant conceptual framework for economics; and the increasing utility of this approach in decision-making make this approach most appealing as a basis from which to in fact build the new paradigm in terms of a Kuhnian shift.

Key insights of this perspective include identification of a new unit of analysis, the project, involving multiple interdependent organizations, as more useful than either the industry or the firm for analytical purposes. It is precisely because of the harmonization of information flows among these interdependent firms, called "network" (Antonelli, 1992) or "embedded" (Grabher, 1993) firms, that the role of the market has diminished. (By the early 1990s, about two-thirds of international information flows were *intra*corporate). In the network economy, a combination of cooperation, coordination, and competition replaces sheer competition as the most successful economic strategy. The capacity to innovate, the most valuable capital of all, arises out of networked relations themselves. A lot of time is spent by network economists looking at differences in organizational form; as we have come to understand organizations as systems of information flows, each new information technology makes possible new types of organizational forms.

McLuhan (1964/1994) noted that the content of each medium is another medium, often the medium which just preceded it in dominance. From this perspective, network economics is about the net as medium and the economy as content. This emphasis on information flows is not to deny the continued significance of capital as a motive force and as an operating framework. As Goldstein (1988) points out, new forms of social organization do not drive out earlier forms of organization, they simply form additional layers (with the effect of making social conditions ever more complex). There are multiple types of capital, however; the concept is not a simple one. The task is to understand the nature of capital under current conditions.

Those working in the area of network economics respond to the problems faced in the effort to treat information creation, processing, flows, and use with neoclassical economic tools as evidence of areas where they need to do empirical and theoretical work. Using the language of mainstream economics, network economists are moving the field of economics forward from within as they seek to understand and respond to changing conditions.

Network economists might usefully learn from the insights offered by the other approaches to conceptualizing the information economy. Scazzieri's (1993) seminal work, *A Theory of Production*, offers an original way of conceptualizing the organization of production processes that may be particularly useful as applied to the economics of cyberspace.[2] Scazzieri distinguishes between actual processes (transformative operations) and those that are virtual, that is, not yet existing but conceivable and might exist. Similarly, there are virtual and actual materials. Those of us concerned about the condition of civil society might also add that there are actual and virtual communities in Scazzieri's sense, that is, that we have actual communities as they currently exist, but can also imagine the virtual and work toward them. Elementary

---

[2]Those things that happen in the net, from the doings of the global financial system to the creation of virtual reality environments, are happening in cyberspace.

processes combine into more complex operations. The level of complexity is important to Scazzieri, who defines scale as the number of what he calls elementary processes involved in a production process.

In the information economy, we might think about scale in terms of an information production chain that includes information creation (*de nov*, generation, and collection), processing (cognitive and algorithmic), storage, transportation, distribution, destruction, seeking, and use. Use of this model as an heuristic in research on information policy in a variety of different kinds of arenas has proven useful in bounding the domain and revealed that concepts of such a model implicitly, if not explicitly, drive most thinking, whether judicial, economic, or cultural, about information creation, processing, flows, and use.

We can then understand the activities of transnational corporations as the moves of organizations seeking their appropriate scale in a time when both organizational form and the nature of their activities are changing. Every "information industry" today faces the problem of trying to identify the appropriate scale for each as the institutional forms of activity at each stage of the information production chain reconstitute themselves in the network environment. That is, the questions "What is scholarly publishing in the electronic environment?" or "How can scholarly publishing economically survive in the electronic environment?" are questions about which and how many types of information processing and distribution will continue to be carried out by scholarly publishers; in Scazzieri's terms, these are questions about the scale of these industries. That scale is to a large degree determined by—and determines—the ways corporations are multiply networked with other organizations.

It may be useful in survival terms for libraries to articulate their roles from the enriched network economics perspective. As examples of the kinds of arguments that might be developed, public libraries play a countervailing force to the privatization of information and the socioeconomic inequities to which this process leads. They offer affordable access to information as a public good necessary to the functioning of society. They make available to all the information that is the seed of technological and social innovation, necessary both for economic growth and for adaptation to social change. Much more work needs to be done in this area.

III. Conclusions

Numerous problems confound efforts to apply neoclassical economic thinking to the creation, processing, distribution, and use of information. The three types of responses to these problems that we have seen map onto three different conceptualizations of the information economy that in turn appear to represent the stages of a Kuhnian paradigm shift in our economic thinking. The network economics approach offers the richest avenue for further research and theoretical development for it is valid; articulated within the terms of mainstream economic discourse, so that many can participate in the discourse; and provides a sound base for decision-making, whether public or private. This nascent field, however, has much to learn from those who pursue other approaches to the information economy as well as from those outside the field as narrowly defined, such as Roberto Scazzieri. Thus, it is an enriched network economics approach that is recommended here as a basis for further research and thinking about the information economy in general, and for the organization and survival of librarianship in particular.

References

Antonelli, C. (1992). The economic theory of information networks. In *The Economics of Information Networks* (C. Antonelli, ed.), pp. 5–27. North-Holland, Amsterdam.

Arrow, K. J. (1962). Economic welfare and the allocation of resources for invention. In *Rate and Direction of Inventive Activity: Economic and Social Factors*, pp. 609–626. National Bureau of Economic Research, Princeton, NJ.

Babe, R. E., ed. (1994). *Information and Communication in Economics.* Kluwer Academic Publishers, Amsterdam.

Bell, D. (1976). *The Coming of Post-industrial Society.* Basic Books, New York.

Boulding, K. E. (1966). The economics of knowledge and the knowledge of economics. *American Economic Review* **56**(2), 1–13.

Braman, S. (1990). Trade and information policy. *Media, Culture and Society* **12**, 361–385.

Braman, S. (1993). Harmonization of systems: The third stage of the information society. *Journal of Communication* **43**(3), 133–140.

Brennan, T. (1990). Vertical integration, monopoly, and the First Amendment. *Journal of Media Economics* **3**(1), 57–76.

Coase, R. (1952). The nature of the firm. *Economica* **4**, 386–405.

Goldstein, J. L. (1988). Ideas, institutions, and American trade policy. *International Organization* **42**(1), 179–217.

Grabher, G., ed. (1993). *The Embedded firm: On the Socioeconomics of Industrial Networks.* Routledge, Chapman and Hall, New York.

Huber, P. (1987). *The Geodesic Network.* U.S. Department of Justice, Washington, DC.

Hyde, L. (1983). *The Gift: Imagination and the Erotic Life of Property.* Vintage Books, New York.

Ito, Y. (1991). *Johoka* as a driving force of social change. *KEIO Communication Review* **12**, 33–58.

Machlup, F. (1962). *The Production and Distribution of Knowledge in the United States.* Princeton University Press, Princeton, NJ.

McLuhan, M. (1964/1994). *Understanding Media.* MIT Press, Cambridge, MA.

Michaels, E. (1994). *Bad Aboriginal Art: Tradition, Media, and Technological Horizon.* University of Minnesota Press, Minneapolis, MN.

Mosco, V. (1989). *The Pay-per Society: Computers and Communications in the Information Age.* Garamond Press, Toronto.

Porat, M. U. (1977). *The Information Economy.* U.S. Department of Commerce, Washington, DC.

Posner, R. A. (1986). *Economic Analysis of Law*, 3rd Ed. Little, Brown and Company, Boston.

Scazzieri, R. (1993). *A Theory of Production.* Clarendon, Oxford.

Schiller, H. I. (1981). *Who knows? Information in the Age of the Fortune 500.* Ablex, Norwood, NJ.

Smythe, D. W. (1981). *Dependency Road: Communication, Capitalism, Consciousness, and Canada.* Ablex, Norwood, NJ.

Stewart, T. A. (1994, October 3). Your company's most valuable asset: Intellectual capital. *Fortune,* 68–74.

Stiglitz, J. (1985). Information and economic analysis: A perspective. *Economic Journal* **95,** 21–41.

Tribe, L. H. (1985). Constitutional calculus: Equal justice or economic efficiency? *Harvard Law Review* **98,** 529–621.

Systems, Quo Vadis?

An Examination of the History, Current Status, and Future Role of Regional Library Systems

Sarah Ann Long
North Suburban Library System
Wheeling, Illinois 60090

I. Introduction

After more than a generation of effort, library systems have made major progress in achieving one of their primary goals: extending access to the unserved. The information presented here clearly suggests that as greater emphasis has been placed on the role of libraries through the establishment of systems support organizations, the public has been the beneficiary. One of the most compelling examples is seen in the 25% growth in the number of public libraries from 1960 to 1990,[1] and what can be assumed to be a corresponding increase in the number of persons who now have better access to library services.

The evolutionary process which is shaping library systems today is bringing changes in their mission and the work performed, as seen in the following reports:

Indiana: Consultants recommend that the Area Library Services Authority be disbanded into a single statewide network (*Bloomington Herald-Times*, July 10, 1994, front page).

Vermont: After 14 months of study, Vermonters say that regional libraries should be maintained and adequately funded as there is no potential substitute at this time (*Regional Library Study FY '93*, State of Vermont, Department of Libraries, 1993, Executive Summary, unpaged)

Michigan: Wayne-Oakland Library Federation heals breach with seven members and takes new name, The Library Network.

[1] *The American Library and Book Trade Annual* (1961) reported the existence of 7204 public libraries (excluding branches) for 1960. The Bowker annual, *Library and Book Trade Almanac*, 36th Ed. (1991) reported 9060 public libraries (excluding branches) for 1990.

ADVANCES IN LIBRARIANSHIP, VOL. 19

California: Director of the Peninsula Library System and South Bay Cooperative Library System administers the neighboring Bay Area Library and
Information System via contract.

Illinois: Four regional library systems merge into new Alliance Library System
of 14,000 square miles and 922,532 population, reducing the number of
systems in Illinois from 16 to 12.

The purpose of this chapter is to explore the current status of selected
library systems in the United States and to consider their future evolution.
Because these are recent developments, the author employed an interview
process to gather data. All interviews took place between September 6, 1994
and October 24, 1994. For clarity the interview was based on a set of 10
questions. These appear as Appendix A.

Thirty persons were interviewed. Their names are identified in Appendix
B. The author wishes to acknowledge with thanks the time and consideration
afforded to her by each of the interviewees.

II. Definitions

For the purpose of this chapter, a system is defined as an independent library-
related entity with an autonomous governing board whose responsibilities
include library cooperation and improvement of member libraries. Systems
discussed here may or may not be multitype, that is, serving all types of
libraries—academic, public, school, and special. In this context, systems are
not consolidated entities which offer library services to the public through
directly administered and financed branch libraries. Additionally, this chapter
deliberately did not focus on systems begun with a single purpose, such as
those related to brokering OCLC services, sharing an automated system, or
organizing collection management initiatives.

Other names for systems abound. These include consortium, co-op,
cooperative, federation, and network. Throughout the chapter, the term
"system" is used even though a synonym might be the more common term
in some locales.

Systems as just defined do not exist in every state. Similarly, they vary
greatly from state to state in funding, organization, structure, governance,
and autonomy.

III. System Genesis

Systems grew out of a push for regional public library service and the creation
of larger units of public library service in the 1920s and 1930s. Significant
national trends which contributed to this momentum included:

A "good government" interest in organizing regional services
A national trend toward planning
A concern for persons living in rural areas
A call for federal funding of libraries

Regionalism had its beginnings as part of America's effort to overcome the Great Depression of the 1930s. During this period there was a national emphasis on the improvement of social and economic conditions (*Regional Policies in the United States*, 1980, p. 24). This effort focused in part on conserving natural resources. The establishment of the Tennessee Valley Authority (TVA) is an example. TVA programs included setting up public libraries that were federally funded and crossed jurisdictional lines. Previously the majority of America's public libraries had developed as municipal institutions (Leigh, 1950, p. 227). The TVA public libraries were significant in several respects because they served rural residents, they were federally funded, and they did not conform to municipal boundaries (Shaughnessy, 1975, p. 22).

In 1935, Carleton Bruns Joeckel published a landmark critique of public library organization. *The Government of the American Public Library*. He analyzed the strengths and weaknesses of public library service and proposed a plan for future *regional* library development. It was based on a consolidation of federation of existing units withing a natural region without respect to local municipal or political boundaries (Joeckel, 1935, pp. 351–355).

In the post war period, the American Library Association (ALA) appointed the Committee on Post-War Planning, chaired by Carleton B. Joeckel. The committee report, *A National Plan for Public Library Services*, not only called for larger units of service, but elaborated on this concept and recommended systematic coordination of existing library resources and functions. Specifically, it recommended comprehensive schemes of library coordination with the following essential features:

Direction by a council of library administrators
Definite agreements concerning fields of specialization in library holdings
Reciprocity and circulation of the services to all users of the cooperating
libraries (Joeckel, 1948, p. 155)

These national library recommendations were not limited to public libraries. Joeckel noted that "college libraries and public libraries located in the same community should formulate plans for the effective coordination of resources and services which will mutually strengthen each institution in meeting the needs of its readers" (p. 155) and "cooperation between school libraries and public libraries should be emphasized, especially in small towns and rural areas where population is relatively sparse and tax resources are limited" (p. 155).

Two years later, in 1950, ALA proposed a comprehensive study of public libraries. The project was funded by the Carnegie Corporation of New York. Known as "The Public Library Inquiry," the study resulted in publication of *The Public Library in the United States* (Leigh, 1950).

The study found that a major factor influencing library support was urbanization. It pointed out that American public libraries have developed largely as municipal institutions and that libraries in rural areas were largely nonexistent.

Library leaders were calling for federal aid to libraries as early as the 1920s. In the 1930s they became officially committed to the idea (Leigh, 1950, p. 155). These early proposals in the 1920s were attached to bills for federal school aid. By the 1950s the proposals were for smaller sums and were granted to state libraries for demonstration projects for periods of 4 to 5 years rather than permanent grants for equalization (Leigh, 1950, p. 156).

Two important events took place in 1956. One served as a carrot to promote larger units of library service in the form of the Library Services Act (LSA). The other served as a stick in the form of standards published by the Public Library Division of the ALA (American Library Association, 1956).

The major trends toward regionalism, national planning, and service to rural residents came together in LSA. The act was designed "to promote the further extension by the several states of public library service to rural areas without such service or with inadequate service" (Public Law 597, Section II,2.[a]). It required that each state have a plan for the expenditure of funds. Further federal funds were provided to pay for a share of the planning. A few states already had long range plans, but most did not, and plans were developed. In many states, planning resulted in a rational for the creation of library systems.

The ALA standards represented an official endorsement of the new approach to library organization and service: "Libraries working together, sharing their services and materials can meet the full needs of their users. This cooperative approach on the part of libraries is the single most important recommendation of this document" (American Library Association, 1956, p. 7). In addition, the standards made clear that the new systems were not meant to threaten the local public library: "The development of systems of libraries does not weaken or eliminate the small community library. On the contrary, it offers that library and its users greatly expanded resources and services" (p. 7).

In 1967, systems got a further boost when Title III was added to the Library Services and Construction Act (the successor to the Library Services Act). The new Title III specifically promoted multitype library cooperation and allowed libraries of all types to apply for this funding.

IV. Early System Work and Workers

Even with 30 years of national trends, library community recommendations, federal funding, and industry standards, library systems were not and have not been established in every state of the Union. But by the end of the 1960s, systems were established in a number of states (Nelson Associates, *Public Library Systems in the United States*, 1969, "A Survey of Multi-Jurisdictional Systems" Chicago American Library Association, p. 262).

During the decade from 1960 to 1970, system services evolved in a number of distinct patterns related to the needs of individual member libraries.

Mike O'Brien put it bluntly, "Different systems were different." Don Wright was more specific, "When systems got started in Illinois, the original application required a statement of what was to be accomplished. The idea was to focus systems on the needs of individual members. That meant typewriters in some areas, and book collections in other areas."

Roberta Cade described the New York experience, "There were lots of small libraries in New York and the idea was to get the same service in Ogdensburg as you got in New York City. Systems developed according to the area they were serving."

This emphasis on responding to the needs of the libraries resulted in a multiplicity of services offered by the fledgling systems. From interviews conducted, the author identified 45 services or service modes. These 45 services have been loosely grouped into four categories: library development, economies of scale, resource sharing, and catalyst.

A. Library Development

The trends of the previous years coalesced into a strong force for library development. In this context, library development means not only creating new libraries but enlarging the service area and generally improving existing libraries. "It was a time when people were coming to grips with the idea that a library was not an island. Systems were a way of formalizing cooperative efforts that had already started. It was a way to talk and to undertake formal planning" (Lamont, 1994).

Picking up on another earlier theme, Joe McElroy said, "Systems were developed to serve rural areas." "The major reason for systems in the beginning was equalization of service" (Cade, 1994). "In those days the public library standards recommended systems. The purpose was to equalize services and bring service to everyone" (Trezza, 1994).

The most prevalent system strategy employed to help libraries improve was consultant service. A system staff member would serve as a consultant to a member library whenever it was required. Nancy Bolt described this process as "hand-holding." Carol Morrison said, "Salaries were low and there were simply not people available with master's degrees to work in these libraries, In fact, most of the libraries were run by women who had been 'given the job,' and who were largely unschooled. System staff spent time reassuring public library staff, and they were very grateful for any help." Alice Calabrese said, "The system staff had a high level of expertise. System members could call system staff at any time and get help." "System staff often served as specialists who went out and gave help to libraries beyond the local staff's level of expertise" (Lamont, 1994). "Often this expertise was in the form of a youth consultant. Some system directors worked with trustees" (Cade, 1994). The most poetic response was from Liz Bishoff who said, "I always thought that system staff played the role of aunt—an aunt who came and helped you do things you didn't know how to do, an aunt who was a mentor, a visionary, a trainer and an aunt who was richer and had resources beyond what member libraries had, such as backup reference service and later automated circulation systems."

Continuing education, a common system function, was an extension of the consultative process. In some cases, continuing education was provided by utilizing staff at the largest library in the system.

Development also meant setting up system services to backstop local services. Reference and interlibrary loan services were developed to strengthen existing libraries.

Another development activity was the building of library collections. Collection building in this context could mean that the system purchased books for the local library. In Ohio there were block grants for book purchases to develop collections. In New York, pool collections were established. One library system in Illinois purchased rental books for every system member. On the other side of collection development, system staff helped member staff weed their collections.

Another approach to collection development was the establishment of review centers particularly for children's books. Review copies were received and organized by system staff. Member library staff could visit the review center to make ordering decisions. In some areas, review centers proved to be a service of interest to local school librarians as well.

In some places the emphasis on collection department resulted in a Greenaway plan in which different libraries agreed to collect in certain areas. "Twenty years ago the Suffolk County (NY) Library System implemented a Greenaway plan," Walter Curley explained. "One library got poetry. They didn't like it very much, but they collected poetry diligently. Recently I had occasion to look for some poetry books. I was pleased to see that the library in Suffolk County was the holding library for the poetry book I was seeking— one of three held by libraries in the United States."

The North Suburban Library System in Wheeling, Illinois, also funded a Greenaway plan. It was called the Collection Assistance Project (CAP) and the collections it supported were called CAP collectors. Based on existing subject strengths such as business, health, gardening, and cookbooks, member libraries were given system money to augment their collections. Even today, the same strengths can be seen in member library collections. In some cases the libraries have continued to maintain that strength even though system funds have long since been withdrawn from the program.

Some state library agencies required a resource collection of a certain size within the system. To avoid the task of building up a rather large collection, some system resource collectors were founded on existing library collections (Cade, 1994). This pattern was also used in Pennsylvania and Michigan (Courtright, 1994). In other systems, there simply was not a large collection to build on, and so one had to be established. As Robert Bullen put it, "Some systems bought books by the ton. They needed to build up a regional collection for the system."

Carol Morrison reminisced about the difficulty. "We needed 100,000 volumes at the system. There were 40,000 at the Reddick Library. Later we separated from Reddick and only took 10,000 volumes. As a result we were working frantically to just meet the minimum."

Sometimes it seemed that there was an emphasis on miscellaneous services. Systems "got things" for members (Tyer, 1994). Systems also "did things" for members. "We planned programs, we did exhibits" (Morrison, 1994). Storytelling was reported by several respondents, and Tyer reported that youth consultants did local programming.

One of the most significant development activities during this period was the formation of new libraries where none existed and the expansion of existing library service areas (O'Brien, Stoffel, 1994). Walter Curley, the first director of the Suffolk Library System in New York, reported establishing 15 to 16 new public libraries during his 6 years as director of the system.

> Systems were to help public libraries develop, but to do it in a way that provided continuing support. Previous efforts to help public libraries hadn't provided the continuing support. That's how systems were different. (Morrison, 1994)

B. Economies of Scale

In addition to library development, systems were needed to do things beyond the scope of a single library—things that a single library could not do on its own. Jim Scheppke also spoke of "obtaining more economies of scale in public library operations" as an initial reason for establishing systems. Clarence Walters described systems as

. . . a central wholesaler of library services. Systems became a "middle-man" because
there was a belief that they could provide services more cost effectively and efficiently on
a larger scale. During this period there was much interest in adopting the automated
methods used in business. Centralized ordering and processing was major initiative in a
number of library systems. The feeling was that repetitive tasks could be done at a lesser
unit cost on a larger scale. The Wayne-Oakland Library Federation was known for its use of
conveyor belts and other assembly-line techniques for centralized cataloging and processing.

Other tasks that were suitable for centralization included printing and duplication. In some areas, the system undertook building or service studies for libraries (Walters, Stoffel, 1994). A bookmobile was another economy of a scale project, seen as an effort to serve the unserved further afield from existing libraries (O'Brien, 1994). All of these were services that individual libraries alone could not afford.

After World War II some public libraries developed audio visual collections. Because of the high cost of these materials, especially 16-mm films, many libraries found it almost impossible to offer audio visual services to residents of their area. As a result, film cooperatives were organized in the late 1940s and early 1950s. As systems were formed in the 1960s, it was natural for systems to include audio visual collections among their services. These were reported by Roberta Cade as existing in New York. Lamont reported film and audio visual services provided by systems in Illinois. Scheppke reported a 16-mm film collection in the West Texas Library System.

Then as now "everybody's favorite service" was van delivery service—the most concrete embodiment of economies of scale. Robert Bullen said that he hired a driver, bought a van, and set up a delivery route as almost his first task as a new system employee in 1967. "Delivery was very important in the early days. Simply moving things around the big area of the system was a very important service" (McDonald, 1994).

C. Resource Sharing

Resource sharing was a major reason for system formation. Some state libraries had created teletype networks for interlibrary loan, but as Holly Carroll put it, "These were blind requests. You didn't know who had what." As systems took over interlibrary loan work, union catalogs were created. Walter Curley described the building of a union catalog as "laborious." The Suffolk Library System also constructed a union list of serials. As Curley put it, "There were no competitors then to provide these services and so it was worth the effort." Clarence Walters described the union catalog at the Wayne-Oakland Library Federation. "It was motorized to expedite the searcher's efforts." Interlibrary loan was almost universally a first system service. In some cases, interlibrary loan was based on the collection of a large member library. Robert Bullen remembers such an instance in which the library was paid 50 cents for each book loaned from the collection to the other system members. Jim Ubel reported that tools were available to help with interlibrary loan. He cited the microfilm catalogs of Southern Illinois University at Carbondale, the University of Illinois, and the Illinois State Library.

For more direct sharing, universal access or reciprocal borrowing programs were established. "We wanted to break down the boundaries of circulation with universal access" (Curley, 1994). McElroy reported that in New York, users of one library could have library cards not only at all other member libraries in that system, but from all the libraries in all other systems. In Illinois, regulations required that each system have a reciprocal borrowing program by the end of the first 5 years of service (Trezza, 1994).

Simply working together on a variety of fronts, the power of cooperation was discovered. A simple scheme such as routing copies of professional magazines among members made a library as a system member more powerful than it had been as a nonsystem member (McDonald, 1994).

D. Catalyst

Systems also served as a catalyst or tester of new ideas. One system promoted the library use of paperbacks by buying 10 copies of various paperback titles and encouraging system members to display them on tower racks in their libraries. In 1968, this was a revolutionary idea (Stoffel, 1994). Bridget Lamont also mentioned the catalyst role. She said that systems could encourage their members to join in larger and more innovate cooperative ventures. The catalyst role sometimes resulted in demonstrations of services to show how a new idea would work.

E. System Workers

Who came and who was recruited to work in library systems in the early days? Most came with a public library background. Experience was an especially important qualification for the system administrator because there had to be equality between the system administrator and the heads of the member libraries. Walter Curley emphasized the need for experience and noted that in New York there was an effort to get a senior person in each area. He said that it was important to have someone with a reputation, someone who could speak with authority. Other qualifications included problem-solving skills, communication skills, and having a vision for this new approach to library services (Bishoff, 1994). Robert Rohlf observed that people who were comfortable dealing with multipolitical levels seemed to be attracted to system work. He contrasted this to those who would prefer to operate libraries. He also observed that many system staff came from state libraries. Of course, a MLS was required for top level staff. Occasionally, sometimes recent and inexperienced MLS graduates were recruited to work with the systems, primarily because of low salaries and the remoteness of some jobs (McClarren, Klinck, 1994). Generalists were needed for the most part. The one specialist that proved the rule was the children's consultant. Cade noted that there was a children's consultant in every system in New York and she counted that as very significant.

F. Other Considerations

As systems were set up, the role of the state vis-a-vis the new systems was critical. "The role of the state library is basic. The state library provides the money and ensures the accountability. In Illinois we placed as few restrictions as possible on systems. All we required was that they establish a headquarters library, buy a certain number of books every year, and after 5 years have a reciprocal borrowing program" (Trezza, 1994). Roberta Cade echoed the leeway given to systems as they developed in New York. Requirements there included a certain number of degreed librarians, a director with 8 years experience, and the establishment of a union catalog.

Some activities that formerly had been undertaken by the state library agency were passed on to systems. Continuing education, consulting, and training were particular examples of this trend. "The state library wanted to be out of the business of supporting public libraries directly" (Morrison, 1994).

Systems during this period were funded either with state money or with federal (LSA or LSCA) money. It is interesting to note that the system concept was apparently saleable in a number of state legislatures. McDonald attributes this to the powerful idea of extending beyond the walls of existing libraries to library systems. In some states, system funding was seen as a way to get money into local libraries. But once the money was allocated, system membership was often used as a way to shore up struggling libraries. In Illinois, system membership was necessary in order to receive state grants.

Systems during this period were public library entities. Al Trezza said that his view was always that systems eventually would be multitype but that the process started with public libraries because it was deemed to be more saleable to the legislature. Not one single system in Illinois had the word public in its name even though all 18 systems were public library systems when they were established.

Not all those within the library community view the advent of a system approach as beneficial. Jim Scheppke expressed his views on what he sees as the failures of library systems:

> I must say that I believe systems overall have done more harm than good in improving public library services. In the broader historical context, I think systems were a reaction to the failure in most states, to move public libraries toward "larger units of service." This

was the rallying cry of public library leaders before about the middle of the century, but by the 1950s and 1960s it became apparent that the predominant pattern of mostly small, mostly municipal public libraries was not going to change despite decades of effort. The response to this was to redefine the concept of "larger units of service" to encompass federations of independent small and medium-sized libraries. This was a noble experiment, but in my view it was an unsuccessful one. On the whole, public libraries have not been significantly strengthened; economics of scale have not been realized; too many public libraries are still not managed by qualified staff; and, as a result, many public libraries will not be able to compete with other emerging information providers in the 21st century. In hindsight, systems were a band-aid solution to a problem that has only grown more serious in the past several decades and may prove fatal in the decades to come. The real solution is still the same as it was 50 years ago—large, strong, well-managed consolidated library systems serving entire metropolitan areas, and in rural areas, large, strong well-managed consolidated regional libraries serving multicounty areas.

G. Significance of the Period

Scheppke's comments not withstanding, most observers believe the system movement expedited the establishment of new public libraries and the expansion of service in others. It also provided a framework for cooperation on a number of fronts. As one respondent put it, "We could have done a lot of those things without the system. But we would not have done them if it hadn't been somebody's job to organize cooperation."

Systems offered a range of supportive services to existing libraries as well as services that were only possible with the economies of scale. Resource sharing was enhanced by cooperative relationships, union catalogs and van delivery service. In their catalyst role, systems demonstrated and encouraged new modes of library service. Adaptions from the business community were notable here.

On the other hand, some respondents worried that too much was done for member libraries:

> Perhaps we did too much. We went out on the bookmobiles, we took books to libraries. We cataloged. We solved problems. We weeded. We listened. We consulted. We basically continued each library as an island. We didn't foster enough communication among the libraries. We perpetuated the idea that librarians did not need degrees or training. We made it easy for "anybody to do it" and perhaps we made some of our present day problems. (Klinck, 1994)

"We had a youth consultant to do local programming. In the long run this didn't help local service. We were too much of a provider. We seemed to have assumed the role of 'Papa handing out the weekly allowance'" (Tyer, 1994).

A new type of library work was born with the advent of systems. Being new, it seemed to attract librarians with the zeal and enthusiasm characteristic of all pioneers. The excitement of setting up systems still was obvious in the interviews with those who had been there. "There were remarkable, key people involved in systems then who could see a future that would change forever libraries as we had known them" (Morrison, 1994).

V. System Snapshot—Circa 1994

Jumping ahead 30 years the author asked several questions designed to give an overview or snapshot of systems today. In analyzing the services that were mentioned by the interviewees, a total of 42 services were identified. Since the question was phrased in terms of "most important system service," this list should not be construed as complete or exhaustive. As with prior system emphasis, today's services can be grouped into four categories: library development, economies of scale, resource sharing, and catalysts.

A. Library Development

When systems began, library development meant improvement of library service. While that definition still holds, the activities in the development category have changed. In the beginning, the activities included forming new libraries where none existed, working with many smaller libraries to create larger units of service, or improving the service. There was a special emphasis on helping rural libraries. In today's system, the major vehicle for development is continuing education and training. Nine respondents listed it as a "very important reason" for systems to exist today. Barratt Wilkins put it at the top of his list. O'Brien said, "CE is big. It assists librarians and trains them to use technology to serve their users. It keeps librarians informed so they can be information brokers." McDonald described continuing education as a "critical system service." Training made Bridget Lamont's top three reasons for systems to exist. Curley said, "Systems have the responsibility for continuous training. It's not good enough for somebody from the state to come out every 3 months." Nancy Bolt elaborated on the rationale of systems (as opposed to state libraries), taking responsibility for training. "We need people on the spot in the area to plan continuing education programming and meet training needs. Those are the same people who do the hand-holding with staff and boards. It is important to offer these services as locally as possible."

Another way to improve member libraries is through consulting. Sometimes this is general consulting. Sometimes it is a more specialized consultant role such as advising on the selection and purchase of new technology.

Jim Ubel talked about library development in the sense of establishing new libraries and building larger units of library service. He said it was "almost as important as resource sharing." Joe McElroy also expressed the special need for systems in rural areas. "Without systems in rural areas, the libraries would revert back to isolation. They would return to rural institutions bound within their four walls."

B. Economies of Scale

A whole range of cooperative ventures can fit under the rubric of economies of scale. This then provides the rationale for organized cooperation. As Al Trezza pointed out, "Unorganized cooperation never works. The system can make a better case to state funding authorities and others for monies that benefit the entire group." Joe McElroy said that state money is what made the difference in having automation or not among libraries that he has worked with. Other reasons for libraries to work together are not only to get the monetary resources, but also to get the human resources to undertake complex projects such as automation or other technology initiatives. Lou Wetherbee said, "It's the aggregation of resources that the system provides to do things libraries can't do alone." In a monetary sense, this can be easily seen with automation projects, which provide circulation and other services for member libraries. Linda Crowe pointed out that many smaller libraries could not afford an automated system of their own, but as part of a cooperative, sophisticated automation is possible. Almost everyone linked automation to resource sharing.

Automation projects are not always in the form of an integrated automation system which automates circulation and certain other functions. CD-ROM technology has allowed many library systems to build databases of member holdings even when members are either not automated or automated via disparate systems. Holly Carroll reported this as a useful resource sharing tool at the NOLA Regional Library System. A similar project has been developed at the North Suburban Library System.

Walter Curley observed that centralized processing was fading as an effective and cost-efficient system service. Joe McElroy credits this change to the rise of vendors who could provide similar services for less money. He recalled a system processing center where processing costs were 50% of the cost of the book. Service was switched to a local vendor at 89 cents per book and bills were processed faster.

Delivery continues to be a vital service but it has taken on a new dimension. Delivery still means a van and a driver, but sometimes it is not a system van and a system employee. Instead, it is a contract with a commercial firm. Another van delivery change can be seen in the North Suburban Library System where a "just in time" service was developed to accommodate a big influx of new members when the system converted from a public library system to a multitype system. Instead of the "just in case" schedule of a regular delivery route, drivers stop at libraries indicating materials to be collected. The system installed a computer with a voice card. Members call and, using a preassigned number, request a stop for the next business day. Similarly, items that come to the system for these libraries will be delivered to them on the next business day. Called Next Day Delivery, the new delivery scheduling mechanism has been in operation for about 2 years and had proven very popular with system members.

C. Resource Sharing

Resource sharing in library systems today is seen as the most important reason for systems to exist. This is a big change from systems' beginnings in the 1960s and 1970s when library development issues were the primary reason for system formation. Bishoff says resource sharing is key. Bolt, Carroll, Lamont, Morrison, O'Brien, Ubel, and Weibel all listed it as a most important reason for systems to exist. Although many hastened to define resource sharing in its widest sense, Mike O'Brien pointed out that different systems sought different paths to helping members share resources. Curry said, "The products and services that facilitate resource sharing have changed, but the philosophy is still the same. Systems create an environment and an opportunity for cooperative projects." She described her system's use of Ariel computer stations as a new tool for accomplishing the old resource sharing goal. Another new product envisioned by Holly Carroll is the development of a regional database of local information.

Linking libraries together in a variety of ways facilitates resource sharing. Courtright called it connectivity. McDonald said it was communication and labeled it a critical system service. It means not only facilitating the physical sharing of materials but also linking libraries together electronically, passing along information from the system and encouraging communication and cooperation between system members.

Crowe described the systems of today as telecommunication centers. The best example of a system as a telecommunication center is seen in the Southeast Florida Library Information Network (SEFLIN), which has mounted a Free-Net on behalf of member libraries (Curry, 1994). Other interviewees reported organizing Internet access for their members (Courtright, Calabrese, 1994).

Resource sharing also means sharing human resources. Calabrese said that the system's mission was to "spur networking" and to help libraries connect to the outside world. Carroll added emphasis to the need for professional networking opportunities. She said school librarians especially needed to get together because they were so isolated in their ordinary work environment.

Some products and services developed in systems early days continue to be useful such as union lists of serials (Ubel, 1994), facilitating document delivery (O'Brien, 1994), organizing universal access and reciprocal borrowing programs (McElroy, 1994), and collection development projects (Ubel, 1994). McDonald pointed out that linking the haves and have nots among member libraries was still important. She said, "The system's role is to bridge the gap between the technological haves and have nots. Unfortunately, the gap is widening."

D. Catalyst

Sara Laughlin said the single most important reason for systems to exist today is to act as a change agent. She went on to say that this is not a change agent dedicated entirely to technology, but rather a change agent who would spend at least 50% of the time working with people. She said she spends many hours working with school boards, library boards, and directors pushing them to make changes. She pointed out that options are limited for many of these entities. "They need the network to be a buffer, to take risks, to be a coattail to ride on, to be a source of expertise and help." Alice Calabrese also put this goal at the top of her list. She called it "supporting membership innovation," and said the system role was "to stir the pot, and promote creativity." But she went back to put the emphasis on support and not on the innovation itself.

Travis Tyer called it being a "catalytic agent." He said that systems were hard to define and that each system took its definition from its membership. He said that system staff have to be visionary and bring participants together and help them do things they cannot do alone. He pointed out that systems are necessarily less political than a state agency might be. He said systems have more freedom to work with their members and to implement a course of action tailored to their needs. Jan Ison called it being a catalyst for innovation. Joe McElroy said it was keeping abreast of new developments. Bob Rohlf described systems as the glue and the leadership for member libraries.

E. System Workers

Systems still need good leaders—leaders that Liz Bishoff characterized as "holistic people who bring vision and can focus on the big picture." Cade described these leaders as "aware of the world and what's happening in the community and in librarianship generally." Laughlin also described a system leader as a change agent, someone who "sells change and explains constantly and adapts it and makes it work." Liz Bishoff said that the leader should be a risk taker and pushing the edge but should also have management skills and be able to make rapid decisions. She also said that the leader should be responsive to system members. Sara Laughlin said, "More and more I see systems as market-segment driven. It's not one size fits all anymore. A system must do different things for different members. The challenge is to keep up."

There is a new emphasis on technological skills for system staff. Some staff members need to be technological experts (Curry, Stoffel, Trezza, Tyer, 1994), but everybody on the system staff should be open to technology, not intimidated by it (Curry, McDonald, Wetherbee, 1994).

Cade alluded to the changes in business practices in the several years since systems have been established. Old management styles were hierarchal and top down whereas new management styles are flatter, process driven, and bottom up. System staff must work at being consensus builders. Facilitation and coordination are the tools of consensus builders. Elizabeth Curry said that it is especially critical for people who work at the system to be good facilitators, especially in critical circumstances. Most members believe that a group solution is paramount.

Laughlin said the staff simply had to like people. Ison said she needed staff members who could be liason people. Tyer called it team building skill. O'Brien reiterated the importance of getting to consensus. He said, "Members will complain if they are not happy."

Negotiating and lobbying are specialized refinements of these skills. Alice Calabrese said that in her job she negotiated and coordinated group contracts for members and that she found it important to be a lobbyist, to keep abreast of legislative developments, and to be aware of how legislation would affect all types of libraries and to pass on that information. Carroll echoed the importance of negotiating contracts and group discounts. She said that NOLA had saved members $800,000 in the last year by working with over 55 vendors to negotiate discounts.

In 1964 there was general agreement that all top system staff should have a MLS degree. In 1994 the agreement has evolved. Elizabeth Curry said that a higher level of technological skill was required, and she envisioned a system staff that would be half librarians and half nonlibrarians but with high-level technological skill and experience. Cade said that the MLS members on the staff must be experienced. Ubel said that system consultants should have a salary range comparable to a second or third career move in order to ensure that they come to the position with experience. Linda Crowe described the ideal system worker today as "a self-starter and independent. Somebody who makes the job his/her own. It's a job for a creative person," she said.

With regard to what system staff do not do, it was obvious that it is no longer common for system staff to act in place of local library workers on a daily basis. On the other hand, consulting still seems to be an important system service in rural systems.

Lou Wetherbee summed up what it takes to be an effective system worker today.

When the goals aren't clear you need a thick skin, you need to be entrepreneurial, and you need to be a risk taker. State funding is not stable. You have to have workers who are not the typical library professional who expects a monthly check and standard duties. But librarians who move to system work seldom go back. They find systems more free-wheeling and find their leadership skills of more use. System work can be very exciting.

VI. How Systems Are Different Today from Systems in Their Formative Years

A. Technology

Clarence Walters said that systems reflect changes that have taken place in libraries during this period, especially with regard to technology. He went on to say that the technological changes were somewhat more intense in systems than in libraries. Automation is of greater importance today than it was when systems were young. Similarly, other technology initiatives such as establishment of Internet nodes, Free-Nets, and even system CD-ROM databases show that technologically based activities are much greater in systems today than they were in the beginning.

B. New Solutions to Old Problems

With regard to other services, many respondents said that the goals have remained the same, only the activities are different. Kathleen Weibel agreed that the goals were similar but said that systems were now redefining how services are provided. Roberta Cade called to mind the observation in the 1960s of a writer in the *Harvard Business Review* regarding railroads. He noted that the problem with the railroads was that they thought they were in the business of operating trains. What they did not realize, he opined, is that they were really in the transportation business. Perhaps some observers have thought systems were in the backup reference and interlibrary loan business. But now systems are finding new ways to support libraries in their reference and interlibrary loan endeavors. Nancy Bolt said that two systems in Colorado are almost entirely out of operating backup interlibrary loan service. Member libraries have equipment, have completed retrospective conversion projects, and have joined a database. As a result there is no need for the system to be involved directly in the interlibrary loan process. She named this trend the "changing flavor of systems" with the new flavor being self-sufficiency for member librarians. Joe McElroy said that continuing education initiatives have shown members how to do interlibrary loan and they have discovered that it is easier for them and faster for the patron if requests are handled at the local library rather than at the system. As a result, the system statistics for interlibrary loan are down. Apparently, the traditional backup reference service is also changing. McElroy reported on decreasing reference statistics as well. On the other hand, Linda Crowe reported a new reference backup service featuring an 800 number for system members to obtain quick reference answers.

Another new way systems are fulfilling the old goals is with the development of tools such as system-wide CD-ROM catalogs. Mike O'Brien said that library automation projects and other automation tools were enabling members to do for themselves what system staff used to do for them. He said, "Now we are more teachers than doers." Jan Ison said, "We are asking our members to do a lot more and to make decisions. We used to make decisions and do things for them." Mike O'Brien said more and more systems are moving toward the facilitator role and forsaking the provider role. "This is a major change in just the last several years," he said.

C. Staff Changes

Speaking of system staff, Bob Rohlf said that in their formative years system staff were more pioneers and innovators, whereas now they are more facilitators and coordinators. Stoffel said staff were probably more sophisticated now, reflecting the higher sophistication of staff at member libraries. Nancy Bolt noted that more libraries were directed by persons with MLS degrees. System workers today must be very productive. Sara Laughlin estimated that the average system worker today works 25% harder without a commensurate increase in salary.

D. Increased Complexity

Harry Courtright characterized systems as being more complicated now. He said, "In the beginning it was simpler. The system offered services that everybody used. Now there is a range of services for members to choose from and each service has its own finance plan." Alice Calabrese said it was important for systems to look at themselves in a new way, an that it was not necessary to build a staff, as had existed in systems past. Rather she spoke of using technology, outsourcing, and bringing in consultants to accomplish the services that systems provide their members. Klinck said that system staff work with system members differently now. "In the old days systems sent staff out to member libraries. Now system staff has less need to visit. We help in a whole new way."

E. Multitype Membership and Partnerships

Several other trends are observable in systems now and seem to have import for the future.

Systems in Illinois, Kansas, and Colorado became multitype in the 1970s and 1980s. Florida systems began as multitype entities. The multitype trend seems to be gathering momentum.

Jan Ison reported that the Lincoln Trail Library System is now working with other information providers; in her case the Cooperative Extension Service. She said the trend now is to link at every level. "If we don't we won't exist in the future," she said. Elizabeth Curry also spoke about linking with other organizations. She said that SEFLIN had partnered with a local newspaper and others to mount the SEFLIN Free-Net.

Nancy Bolt sees a trend among systems in Colorado to operate over system boundaries. She said funding does not go as far as it used to and so there is an incentive to look at other systems and share services. Some systems are developing a cooperative database, others are contracting for cataloging, and still others are working on intersecting courier service.

F. No Collections

McDonald observed the trend in library acquisitions to move away from a book budget and toward an access budget. The same trend has affected systems. For the most part, systems no longer build or support a central system collections or pool collections. Instead they concentrate on helping members access each other's collections as well as materials beyond the system boundaries.

G. Concerns

Some respondents reported that the evolution of system services caused some concern. Harry Courtright worried that systems in Michigan have lost their constituency in the state legislature, jeopardizing state funding for systems in the process. Jim Ubel observed that systems in Illinois were more independent in their formative years than they are today. Elizabeth Curry said that systems had less need to justify their existence but more need to justify their viability. McDonald said there was more of a trend in Ohio to fund systems locally. She felt this was good because system members had more ownership if they were paying for the service. Joe McElroy noted a trend regarding state funding in California. He said more money went to direct subsidies to local libraries such as interlibrary loan reimbursement at $2.48 per item rather than on general funding for systems. Lou Wetherbee sees systems becoming more entrepreneurial. She said in Texas systems had been encouraged to privatize and to seek 501-(C)(3) status. Speaking of money, Liz Bishoff noted that there seemed to have been more money in systems for new ventures in the beginning years than there is today.

H. Conclusions

In general, the pace of change is quickening for library systems as it is for every other aspect of life today. Systems are still in their catalyst role, working with members in new cooperative ventures. Member libraries are less isolated.

Many services that were performed by the system in the 1960s are now performed by members. Presumably this is an indication of the increasing strength and vitality of libraries, and more libraries are system members. In the early days of systems, it was a public library movement. Now multitype systems are more common. More cooperation on a wider scale is the result.

I. Another Point of View

Scheppke has another point of view:

> I don't think systems have changed much since I ran one 15 years ago. They are still mostly dependent on state and federal dollars for their existence. They have not, for the most part, been successful in achieving significant economies of scale for their member libraries. They have not proven to be very entrepreneurial in looking for new ways to be of service to their members. Most systems today are not the dynamic, customer-driven, self-sufficient organizations that they were intended to be. This isn't entirely the fault of the systems. The member libraries that are supposed to benefit from the systems, have not held them accountable for higher performance. But the underlying and insurmountable problem is the original, mistaken premise that federation can achieve the same results as consolidation. Two or three decades of experience have proven otherwise.

VII. External Factors Affecting Library Systems Today

A. Customer Service Revolution

Sara Laughlin named the customer service revolution as one of the most important external factors acting on systems today. Customer service is only the positive way of asserting that systems must be accountable. That accountability reflects the prevailing trend to distrust government generally. Scheppke called it evaluation. He said, "I would like to think that we would begin to see some hard-nosed evaluation of the effectiveness of systems. What little has been done to date has been a whitewash, in my opinion."

B. Political Trends

Another way that the larger trend of distrust of government is played out is in tax caps which were noted by Bullen and Calabrese as a potential negative factor affecting systems.

Linda Crowe elaborated on the political trends. She said, "Government is totally in chaos. Counties are going out of business. Restructuring of government is taking place as a result. In California, a constitutional convention is planned. Libraries are caught up in this. There is a task force looking at financing and governance of public libraries. Systems may be eliminated or may become multitype as a part of this process." Bob Rohlf sees the political pressures as pressures to change, especially for systems to consolidate or combine. Jim Ubel said that politics in Illinois have been increasingly a factor in system funding.

C. Funding Trends

Nancy Bolt said that state funding for systems in Colorado ranged from 50 to 85% of their total budgets. She said that some Colorado systems are entrepreneurial and have made money in cataloging or in continuing education or other activities. This has been essential because state funding has not kept up with inflation. Alice Calabrese predicted that systems will turn more and more to fees for additional funding. At Southeast Florida Library Information Network, Elizabeth Curry said that the system operated primarily on dues from members. "That makes us accountable," she said. But state funding is needed for research and development. The uncertainty of these funds is troublesome. Joe McElroy echoed the sentiments that local funding builds accountability. He said, "Cooperation is better if members pay something. It makes our services more appropriate."

This squeeze on the budget has meant that some systems, like some governments and some businesses, have contracted out what used to be inhouse services. Joe McElroy noted that delivery had been contracted out by the Alliance Library System in Pekin, Illinois. He said that at his own Heritage Trail Library System he could see a future in which consulting help for member libraries would be provided from an outside source.

D. Technology

The biggest external factor affecting systems today is new technology. It was named as a top priority by nearly half of the persons interviewed. Nancy Bolt said, "It will affect everything but especially reference service and interlibrary loan. It is changing the kind of services systems provide. In the future it will be the system's job to bring libraries into the national information infrastructure—kicking and screaming if necessary. Systems must be advocates for the national information infrastructure and new technology."

Alice Calabrese said, "We need technology more today than ever before, but in a different way. Now technology means you can't do it alone. The Internet links you to the world and you need training to be able to use the

Internet." She said that technology was changing the way that systems get information and keep members apprised. Holly Carroll echoed some of these sentiments. She predicted that system services regarding interlibrary loan and reference service as we know them would be meaningless in 5 to 10 years whereas technology training issues have become so big that they represent 50 to 70% of the system's work. She said that NOLA now had an Internet trainer on staff who provided a great deal of one-to-one training.

Lou Wetherbee said that the paradigm has not emerged for libraries in a technological environment. "As a servant of libraries, a possible system role would be to take the initiative and help libraries make choices about technology." Liz Bishoff pointed out the myriad of policy issues embedded in the electronic information environment and suggested that a possible system role would be to help member libraries come to grip with these issues.

E. Competition

In the mix of the societal issues and new technology comes a new trend that is already having a big impact on systems. It is competition. Harry Courtright described it in detail. He said that Wayne-Oakland Library Federation (WOLF) processed 250,000 books for member libraries in 1992 at a cost of $1.25 per volume. Now the same service is provided to members by a commercial firm at less than $.50 per volume. Courtright predicated that reference services could be taken over by for-profit vendors. Jan Ison said, "What used to be traditional library work is now done by others in the commercial sector." Bridget Lamont suggested that libraries might make use of for-profit training facilities rather than use the training provided by the system. Clarence Walters suggested that competitors might be an aid to libraries and systems. Travis Tyer called for constant attention to identifying competitors. He used the analogy of a public library looking at a bookstore to determine what the bookstore is not doing and doing. On the other hand, McDonald said, "As end users can access everything and as libraries can access everything, what will systems do?"

In the end, Robert Bullen worried that conservatism would hold back libraries and library systems. Kathleen Weibel noted that the expectation and vision of system leaders were the most important external factors determining systems for tomorrow.

F. Are Systems a Middleman Service?

Respondents were particularly asked to respond to the prevailing trend to cut out the middleman, eliminate the bureaucrat, and decentralize everything. The respondents, for the most part, acknowledged that this could be a valid criticism of systems. Several spoke of accountability. Holly Carroll said systems must continually justify the services members need and defend them to funding authorities. Elizabeth Curry said that systems should look at accountability and cost benefit analysis and strategic planning in order to be viable.

Several respondents did feel that systems could improve their accountability. Jim Sheppke said, "Enlightened systems should be working actively to 'doom' themselves. Unfortunately, most system leadership will likely be highly resistant to any efforts to change the status quo." Bod McClarren said that systems are duplicating services that local libraries are offering. Joe McElroy said that more and more system work will be contracted out. "I don't know why every system needs to operate its own reference service, for example," he said.

Several respondents encouraged system leaders to seize opportunities. Linda Crowe said if systems have valuable services to offer they will exist, but if they do not seize opportunities, systems will go away. Klinck said systems will be out if they do not see the bigger picture. Courtright pointed out that only provider systems were now in danger of being charged with this trend. He characterized the new Library Network as being in the position of serving as a broker for services that formerly were provided by the system. Kathleen Weibel said that systems are serving as brokers or flashpoints for new ideas and information. "The nature of the cutting edge has changed and systems have a different perspective from member libraries."

Many systems have spun off their middleman tasks. Sara Laughlin reported that the big networking staff was gone from her system. Mike O'Brien said that the Suburban Library System had already cut out the middleman. "Cataloging and processing was middleman work. "We don't do that anymore. We flattened the organizational structure."

For those systems which feel that the middleman charge sticks, Bob McClarren suggests a counter attack. "Apply political pressure," he said. Bob Rohlf said that a small politician could make a big issue out of the middleman bureaucrat issue. "My advice is to consolidate where you can because a large membership will keep this from happening." Several respondents recommended a public relations effort to ensure that system services were known and appreciated. Jan Ison said that the perceived benefit that the state legislature sees in systems is essential. Alice Calabrese said that systems need to be more pro-active. "We need to market and sell the system."

A number of respondents disputed the label of "middleman." Al Trezza said, "Systems aren't middleman. Systems are *it*. Systems help libraries afford things. The state is too far away from the local library to do what systems do." Nancy Bolt said that member libraries are always suspicious of the state agency but that systems, not having that stigma, were much more effective in working with local libraries. Barratt Wilkins also said that systems were not middlemen and not bureaucratic and were just not set up that way. Carol Morrison also questioned whether the middleman charge related to systems. "We coordinate and facilitate and this is different."

McDonald said that systems should embrace the decentralized trend, that it did not mean systems' doom, and that system leaders should not get hung up on structure. She pointed out that there is always a need for professional judgment and quality control and therefore there is always a role for systems. She characterized this as facilitating the human network and being a catalyst for forming partnerships. Jan Ison echoed this optimism, "There are so many new things and there will always be work to do."

Elizabeth Curry had a slightly different view. She said,

> In our member libraries' organizational chart, we are not "middlemen." We're off to the side. We're their cooperation department. We're their research and development department. We are an extension of the library staff. If we are perceived as middlemen then we haven't given up our old services. For example, linking systems used to be a big deal. Today, because of the Internet, this is commonplace. Systems don't want to be a buyer of services off the shelf. Rather, systems should be organizations that facilitate cooperation.

VIII. Future System Funding

A. Background

Typically, systems as defined in this chapter operate on state or federal funding with some fees for service from members. Florida, Ohio, and some California systems are notable exceptions because these systems are largely supported by either dues or fees paid by members.

B. State Funding

Funding patterns are changing. In New York, additional state funds are being channeled into public libraries directly rather than into systems serving public libraries (Cade, 1994). In Michigan, Public Law 89 which establishes public library systems is being changed to allow systems to serve a multitype library clientele. Funding is expected to change as a result (Courtright, 1994). In Indiana where Area Library Services Authorities (ALSA) are being merged with the Indiana organization that brokers OCLC service (INCOLSA), Sara Laughlin reports that the new organizations expect to receive the $2.4 million now going to the ALSAs and INCOLSA. She said that additional monies are not expected this biennium. Formerly, ALSAs received most of their funding from the state. In California, systems receive state money for services provided to members such as interlibrary loan, reference, delivery, and continuing education (McElroy, 1994). But even these payments may cease in light of the state's planned constitutional convention. In Illinois, state funding for systems was cut by one-third in 1992, but was largely restored the next year. No additional changes are foreseen in the next several years (Calabrese and Ison), but additions to the level of funding are predicted as programmatic additions rather than as generic additions (Lamont, 1994). Short-term (e.g., 2 year) projects are seen as more saleable to the state legislature (Calabrese, 1994). Al Trezza echoed these sentiments. He said, "State funding is a sound idea (for Illinois library systems). I see the formula for system funding being adjusted but not changed, and there have to be good reasons for more money. A more viable approach to increased system funding is a grant program (for special projects) from the Illinois State Library.

In Florida where systems were more recently established, state funding is new (1993–1994) and local funding is the mainstay. The concept is to allow natural multitype coalitions of libraries to form as nonprofit corporations and to apply for start-up funding from the Florida State Library. Typically these monies are federal Library Services and Construction Act (LSCA) grants for 2 years. The usual amount is $25,000 the first year and $75,000 the second year. In describing the process, Florida State Librarian Barratt Wilkins stressed the importance of devising a local plan during this 2-year period because the local libraries would be asked to fund the cooperative after the initial period. He said that in the two oldest cooperatives (circa 1979), the Tampa Bay Library Consortium and Southeast Florida Library Information Network (SEFLIN), members pay as much as $35,000 per year. SEFLIN also has an associate member category that allows smaller members to pay reduced membership dues. Not all of Florida's cooperatives (as they are called) are as expensive. The Central Florida Library Consortium has memberships in the $300–$400 per year range. The maximum amount of the new state funding for Florida's cooperatives is $200,000 and it must be matched 10% by local monies. A cooperative must provide the Florida State Library with a plan of service. The state library reserves the right to withdraw state funding if the plan is unacceptable.

C. Changing Funding

Almost every person interviewed for this chapter agreed that funding for systems was changing. Several attributed the changes to the prevailing financial climate. Lou Wetherbee characterized the trend as "no government and privatize everything." Liz Bishoff said, "Systems will no longer be funded just because they're 'good.' System funding will be scrutinized much more closely and the funders will want to know what they're getting for their investment." Alice Calabrese said, "There's a great need for accountability. The tax payer revolt fuels this. It's frustrating if you're administering a system, but you must prove your case."

Predictably, interviewees recommended a variety of remedies or approaches to the changing nature of system funding. Liz Bishoff recommended that system leaders embrace and pursue multiple sources of funding. Travis Tyer said, "I'd like to see more sources of money for systems, sources that aren't political." Lou Wetherbee suggested that systems should be joining with other community groups and pursuing such activities as establishing Free-Nets. Elizabeth Curry, at the Southeast Florida Library Information Network, has established a Free-Net-like service. She said, "Systems should be creative and should look toward partnerships with related organizations." She suggested that systems seek out nonlibrary organizations. She said that in Broward County, the *Sun Sentinel* was SEFLIN's first partner for its Free-Net. Other partners, participants, and volunteers represent 155 community groups and organizations. She said, "The Free-Net has captured the community's imagination" and "SEFLIN established the Free-Net at members' behest. We do what they want." At the Lincoln Trail Library System in Champaign, Illinois, a productive partnership has been established with the Cooperative Extension Service with exchanges of databases and training as a result (Ison, 1994).

D. Local Funding

One approach to improved system funding is increased reliance on local or member funding. Dues and fees are the usual mechanisms for this. Marty McDonald reported that local money is the primary support (51%) of Ohio's systems. She predicted that this figure would increase in the future and noted that dues represented a big commitment to accountability. Another approach to member funding is shared costs. The most common example of this is funding for an automated system used by participating member libraries. Since such a service is vital to the operation of member libraries, members give full attention to the project. One respondent said that the most successful systems almost always operate a successful automation program. Joe McElroy said, "Cooperation is better if members pay something. It makes use more appropriate."

Local funding is being considered in Indiana. Sara Laughlin said that schools and public libraries have been getting increases and that the new Indiana systems would be looking to them for increased support. Les Stoffel predicted a gradual increase in member library financing—either fees for services or membership fees. He recalled that Betty McKinley, the former director of the DuPage Library System in suburban Chicago, was a proponent of member library fees for service. Jim Ubel said that he saw more and more of a trend for system members to share costs. He cited the shared automation system as an example. "Cost sharing makes things happen," he said. He described state funding vs member funding as the difference between dining at a buffet or a la carte.

E. Entrepreneurial Activities

Interviewees were particularly asked about the probability or viability of systems as entrepreneurs. Several respondents quickly answered negatively. Walter Curley said, "No. Entrepreneurial activities are not desirable or possible for systems." Bob McClarren said, "Systems would be ill advised to set up entrepreneurial activities. libraries have never been in the entrepreneurial arena; systems have no experience here, either. Mike O'Brien said. "If entrepreneurial means money making, I'm not sure that's appropriate." Carol Morrison said, "I hope systems aren't going to assume a substantial entrepreneurial role. I feel the same about systems as I do about public libraries. We're a public good."

Jan Ison said that she was not sure that she could see an entrepreneurial role for systems, but she noted that systems could be customers for each other. Ison has experience here. The Lincoln Trail Library System which she directs has sold printing services to other systems. In Michigan, Harry Courtright, director of The Library Network, also reported that printing services had been sold outside of the system membership. Bridget Lamont worried that the use of state money in setting up entrepreneurial activities might jeopardize state funding for systems. She suggested that systems might share services. Holly Carroll said, "The regionals (systems) work together in Ohio. There's a lot of collaboration especially regarding continuing education." Bishoff called this "bartering services." Perhaps the philosophical problem with entrepreneurial services is the notion of making a profit on tax payers' money. Or, more to the point, perhaps the problem is risking (and losing) taxpayers' money. To avoid this conundrum, Jim Ubel said he preferred to think of such services as cost recovery rather than entrepreneurial.

In general, respondents had little experience and not great enthusiasm for the idea of systems as entrepreneurial entities. Jim Scheppke said, "Sure there are entrepreneurial opportunities for systems. But I am not encouraged that systems will seize those opportunities. Most have not done so in the past. Most will remain more or less 'on the dole' as they have since they began." Kathleen Weibel concurred that entrepreneurial services were hard to do. Alice Calabrese alluded to a "business spirit" that would be necessary in system leadership for entrepreneurial activities to succeed. As a former director of Northern Illinois Learning Resources Cooperative (NILROC), Calabrese negotiated 5-year contracts for certain services on behalf of NILROC members. The contracts saved members up to 20% on these services, but members paid NILROC a small surcharge for negotiating and handling. Calabrese said that her experience had given her a different perspective on what a cooperative organization might do for its members and make a little profit in the process. Bob Rohlf named this system role, "buyer/broker of services." Holly Carroll described an extensive discount program that she has organized for NOLA, but it does not result in any revenue to the system. Several systems in Illinois operate insurance consortia—offering everything from employee assistance plans and health insurance to directors and officers insurance. In some cases the plans are open to other libraries and systems outside of the organizing system. In all cases, a small surcharge is paid by participating libraries and systems.

There seemed to be some concern about who the target market might be for entrepreneurial services. If the target market is the general public, this represents not only a new role for many systems but also a whole new market. Systems in many states have targeted their services toward their members exclusively. Roberta Cade said that systems in New York would not dare to compete with local library services in whatever entrepreneurial services they might offer in the future. Patricia Klinck said that library service to the public should be free, but that she could envision systems mounting entrepreneurial or fee-based services in affluent areas. The Peninsula Library System and the South Bay Cooperative Library System are already operating several entrepreneurial services for the general public including a coffee shop, a video rental center, and a business reference service in the name of a member library (Crowe, 1994).

If the target market is member libraries, some respondents had difficulty with this concept. Nancy Bolt said, "Members have already been paid for; members are free." Bridget Lamont shared that opinion because state money was involved but suggested that systems market their services outside of the state. Joe McElroy said that he had thought of fees for value-added services to members. The example he used was van delivery. "Member library X gets scheduled daily van delivery but decides it wants additional delivery—perhaps on Saturday. This value-added service (more than basic service) would be available for a fee." But McElroy said that he did not feel that a fee-based service, especially related to a service as basic as van delivery, would be approved by the state library. As Mike O'Brien noted, "If the state pays, they have a right to set the tone."

Mike O'Brien and Les Stoffel suggested that a proper risk-taking entrepreneurial activity for a system might be to experiment with new technology or untested library products at the system level and with system monies. If the experiment failed, it saved money because only one test for all member libraries had been mounted. If the experiment was successful, then the new service or technology was deemed safe for all members to use. Marty McDonald sees a possible future role for systems in the continuing education and training area. Sara Laughlin said that the one way a system's entrepreneurial initiative could be successful was if it added value and was something really wanted. Clarence Walters said that systems should look at their competition in devising entrepreneurial enterprises and learn from them. He said that systems must assume this role. He also pointed to training and brokering of services as possible areas for systems to explore. Barratt Wilkins sees Internet access and related services as a possible money maker for systems. Holly Carroll described library systems in Ohio as "lean and mean and getting more so." She said she saw marketing initiatives as a necessary fist step toward entrepreneurial activities and that systems really did not have a choice. "We must go for outside funding and make money," she said.

The interview question concerning entrepreneurial roles did not define the word "entrepreneurial." From the answers, it was obvious that each respondent had a different concept in mind. Some envisioned systems setting up for-profit businesses to serve either the general public or other systems or libraries outside of their membership. Others envisioned fees for services to members. A third variation involved members paying for a service that they wanted. Shared automation systems are the best example of this activity. Cooperative activities with other systems and other entities ranging from The Cooperative Extension Service to the Broward County *Sun Sentinel* are another approach. Even though strong reservations were expressed about entrepreneurial activities generally, successful examples of each type of activity exist. It would seem that entrepreneurial activities, however they are defined, are a growth area for systems.

F. The Future of Library Service and Construction Act Funding and Other Grants

The LSCA, now 38 years old, is the only federal grant program to be passed by Congress solely dedicated to libraries. The case has been made earlier in this chapter that LSCA and LSA (the earlier act) were one of the major reasons that systems exist today. The act expired in 1994 and a 1-year extension has already been approved. The American Library Association created a task force to propose a substantially revised act. A basic outline for that has been drawn and approved by the Council of the American Library Association. In general terms the new proposal has two titles. One is concerned with technology. The other is aimed at serving the unserved and the underserved. There is a per capita amount to public libraries which serve children living in poverty. The new proposal, like its successor, would be administered by state library agencies. Changes to such a major pillar of system creation and funding would necessarily have an impact on systems. In some states, LSCA funding is regularly channeled to systems and has become the basis for ongoing operations. Holly Carroll has followed the development of the new LSCA proposal carefully. She noted that the way it was structured might lead to more competition for LSCA funds and that systems might realize less support than is currently the case. Elizabeth Curry expressed the hope that the new bill would increase funding for the multitype projects. In the current LSCA, the best funded title, Title I, is only available to public library applicants. In the new bill, both titles would be available to multitype applicants.

Of course, other grant programs are open and available to systems. Lou Wetherbee said, "Federal money is available to build the information super highway. If systems can define a role here, they are logical recipients of these grants. But it is very competitive." Elizabeth Curry defined the problem. "It's tough to find out about and to write these grants. Often the information is received at the last minute and the granting source is unfamiliar."

Finally, some systems are seeking funding from the private sector. Sara Laughlin said it was necessary to look toward external funding. "Maybe Ameritech," she mused. Barratt Wilkins also mentioned private sector funding for system projects as a possibility. At the North Suburban Library System in suburban Chicago, a foundation is being established as a vehicle to receive private sector funding for system projects. The foundation will also serve as an umbrella foundation (modeled after community foundations) for funds established by member libraries. In this way the foundation will be a member service, aiding members with their own fund-raising projects and freeing them from the time-consuming and tedious work associated with setting up and operating a foundation and a funding agent for system projects.

IX. System Snapshot—Circa 1999

A. General Considerations

Respondents were asked to forecast how systems would function in 10 years. Alice Calabrese, the first person interviewed, said that predictions for 3 years out were more realistic. In looking at the responses, and in consideration of the volatile funding and technology environment, it is obvious that decade-long predictions are not very realistic. It is suggested that these observations will probably come to pass in approximately 5 years.

B. Physical Aspects

There was a general agreement that systems would still exist in the foreseeable future, although Jim Scheppke expressed concern:

> This is not a pretty sight. Unfortunately, if I had to bet, I would bet that systems are still hanging on 10 years from now, despite a widespread consensus in the library community that they do not earn their keep. Public library directors will have much bigger problems

than 'what to do about systems.' State libraries, unfortunately, may not be able to work up the gumption to pull the plug. Systems may join the ranks of other government bureaucracies (the Rural Electrification Administration comes to mind), whose time has come and gone, but who sadly live on.

Almost one-third of the respondents predicted that there would be fewer systems than there are today. This is a trend that is already happening in a variety of ways in California (Bishoff, Crowe), Indiana (Laughlin), Michigan (Courtright), and Illinois (Ubel). In some cases it is a de facto merger. The South Bay Cooperative Library System is managed by Linda Crowe, the director of the neighboring Peninsula Library System, and in Michigan, 13 members of the Huron Valley Library System joined The Library Network. Two other members joined another neighboring cooperative (Courtright). Clarence Walters views this change in system numbers positively. "This is a natural development. It shows examination and evaluation of system structure." Joe McElroy used a dental metaphor for systems. "We're the dentist and our job is to get rid of tooth decay. Some services and some dentists will go away because of better dental hygiene today."

As a result of mergers, systems will be larger; that is, serving geographically greater areas (Courtright, McDonald). Sara Laughlin envisioned systems across state boundaries. Travis Tyer said that systems might be larger but would serve fewer members as a result of mergers and creation of larger units of services among public libraries and mergers of school districts. Speaking from experience, Jim Ubel said that larger systems bring with them a new set of problems, including van delivery, communication costs, and other equity issues.

Several interviewees predicted that the system headquarters building would cease to be important in itself. Linda Crowe described it as "the demise of the system headquarters building as a place." She said she saw systems in the future as much more decentralized. Bridget Lamont also did not envision big system buildings in the future, but rather suites of offices. Sara Laughlin described future systems generally as "a lot less physical." Marty McDonald said, "Focus on the service, not the structure." Holly Carroll said that she imagined that future systems would still be geographically based, that is, serving a geographically contiguous area. "It facilitates training and getting together," she said. But in light of the preceding comments, the question arises: In the future, when electronic connections are pervasive, need a system be geographically based? Lou Wetherbee predicted that the future front door of the system would not be a physical door, but rather the system's Internet home page or gopher. While no respondent described a "virtual system," it is an image that comes to mind in light of the comments.

C. System Funding and Membership

Today the majority of libraries who are members of systems pay little or no dues and are encouraged to be system members by their state library agency.

Typically the state agency is the primary controller of funds going to systems, but system governance is at least nominally at the local level. This arrangement leads to confusion for the system administrator. Who is the system staff to please? The state agency, where most of the money comes from, or the member libraries who control the governance or at least the level of satisfaction with system performance? The author's observation is that system administration is typically more responsive to the source of funding than it is to the source of governance. Governance can be convinced in order to get the money.

One respondent predicted that systems would metamorphisize into branches of the state library with system employees becoming state employees, but this was only one comment and one that flies in the face of the relatively well-established trend toward decentralization and smaller government.

Several interviewees said that future system funding would be different but no one was willing to say specifically how it would be different. Nancy Bolt said there were "rumblings" and predicted that system funding would be decentralized. Certainly the variety of sources outlined in the preceding chapter show decentralization to be a trend.

Generally speaking, state funding for systems is flat at best. In some states there are new programmatic grants available to systems for start-up costs for a new program or for fixing an old problem. At a time when state money is hard to come by, focused and short-term funding is typically easier to sell in the state legislature than a general increase to system funding.

At the same time, categorical aid, usually sought by either school or public libraries, is up for legislative consideration. Unfortunately for systems, a person no less than New York Assemblyman Edward G. Sullivan, who is known as a friend to libraries, has said that he can sell categorical aid easier because it is sexier (Cade). As a result, state funding for systems is pitted against state funding for local libraries. Unless systems have a constituency of highly motivated and satisfied members, there is no constituency to make the case for funding systems over local libraries.

Liz Bishoff said, "Systems have to be market driven. They have to know who their customer is." It would seem that even though the majority of system funding might come from the state, the customers or the consumers of the services are the member libraries.

The composition of member libraries in systems in changing. Back in the 1960s when systems were new, all were public library entities. In 1974, Illinois was the first state to establish multitype systems. Since then, Colorado, Kansas, and Florida have created multitype systems. Several other states have affiliate membership available to types of library members. Michigan is planning a conversion of its public library system to multitype. The conversion to multitype gives new meaning to Bishoff's admonition to "know the customer."

Alice Calabrese sees much more emphasis on system service to school libraries. "They will be primary users in the way that the public library has been a primary user in the past 10 years." If there were a multiplicity of needs before when systems only served public libraries, that number must now be multiplied by four if systems now serve public, academic, school, and special libraries.

Systems began with a heavy emphasis on public library development. That put the focus on the beginning, smaller, poorer, often rural public library. Given a larger multitype membership overlaid with the electronic environment, those libraries that do not come up to a certain standard might seem irrelevant. This is not a new battle. Systems have long struggled with the conundrum, "Shall we be inclusive and take in every self-designated library and concentrate on bringing the least library up to the average level of the others?" or "Shall we be a cooperative of libraries of a certain standard and work on lifting all members to a higher standard?" Les Stoffel sees higher standards for system membership in the future along with a higher standard of service at the local level.

At least two interviewees saw the general public as users of system services in the future. Elizabeth Curry said that electronic access to Free-Nets and the Internet would position systems to serve end-users, "but via member libraries." Marty McDonald also saw end users in systems' future because of electronic access. Liz Bishoff said that if a library or a system had information on the Internet and people from wherever, maybe not taxpayers, could get in, they would expect service.

In any case, systems will continue to be different from each other. Cade said, "A lot depends on who you're serving." And Weibel said, "The cutting edge in Shawnee (Library System) is different from the cutting edge in North Suburban (Library System). She went on to say, "It's wrong to think that the cutting edge comes from things outside, such as doing something first with technology. The cutting edge comes from reflection and from moving forward from where you are."

D. System Workers

"People who need orderly chaos should be in networking now." That is how Marty McDonald described the ideal system worker now and in the future. Several respondents saw smaller permanent staffs at the system headquarters. "I see a smaller core staff and lots of contracts," Kathleen Weibel said. She went on, "Some systems will have specialists on the staff but others will have contracts with specialists." Joe McElroy described it as, "more machinery and fewer people." Linda Crowe said she had just saved $65,000 by contracting out the operation of the system's integrated automated system. She described it as "re-engineering" and "a new way to provide services."

So who is left working at the system? Walter Curley thinks systems will require more experienced and qualified leadership as they get larger. Lamont and Laughlin speculated that system staff would be more specialized. Don Wright said that he hoped systems would recruit "good dreamers" and "crack-erjack people at the top." Nancy Bolt observed that the last of the first generation of system leadership would be retiring in the next several years. She wondered where the new leaders would come from. Bob Bullen suggested that the new leaders might be directors of member libraries—persons who would know the system and had thought about the possibilities. Travis Tyer said that risk takers were needed to find the money and to meet the challenges of tomorrow.

E. System Services

Kathleen Weibel said, "There will be less of the traditional backup system services. Wherever you are, the system will help you move to the next stage, but then it will quit it." Sara Laughlin said, "Services will be more targeted. There will be smaller markets and perhaps more eccentric services." Holly Carroll said that new services would be more focused, especially technology focused. Clarence Walters said that systems needed to look at what they were doing and examine each service and make some decision about which services would disappear so that other services could be assumed. "But systems are not very good at dropping things," he said.

Automation and technology are a recurring theme of many predictions for the future of system services. Liz Bishoff sees systems as "automation hubs." Joe McElroy said, "We should concentrate on automation and technol-ogy and bring the library community along." He said that automation at the Heritage Trail Library System used to mean the automated circulation system used by a number of the member public libraries. An automation committee with a multitype membership has been formed to look at all areas of library automation and technology. Nancy Bolt spoke of a technological revolution, now in process, that is changing libraries and systems in ways we do not know and cannot predict. Travis Tyer said that systems should be heavily technology directed. Clarence Walters sees a role for systems as "guiding libraries in the new world by means of training and continuing education." Kathleen Weibel said that she hopes systems will be more of a player in resolving the information policy issues that arrive with library involvement with the Internet and other electronic communication vehicles.

Marty McDonald made the point that technology was only a tool. Jan Ison said that 20% of the information highway was reserved for the public domain. "If we (systems) could manage that 20%, that's a role," she said. Lou Wetherbee said that libraries and systems should be looking at local information. "Libraries should switch from being retrievers to providers and publishers of local information," she said. She noted that ASCII text files were easily mounted on the Internet. She said that all the local information mounted need not originate with the library or the system. She used the example of the Seattle Public Library which mounted a database of information on Puget Sound. It is a menu choice on Seattle's home page but it is a database provided by another organization.

Elizabeth Curry said that training and continuing education were becoming a major system role. "It could be 50% of what we do," she said. Marty McDonald described continuing education as systems "most lasting role." Several other interviewees listed it as an important service now and in the future, especially because of the new technology in libraries.

If technology projects and continuing education programs are the major focus of system services in the future, what about the traditional services that systems have provided? Resource sharing still seems to rank highly in importance according to many of those interviewed. Mike O'Brien said that resource sharing was good because of long established automation and delivery programs. He predicted more emphasis on document delivery. Alice Calabrese pointed to the need for systems to facilitate access internationally. Jan Ison said that patron initiated interlibrary loan in the Lincoln Trail Library System which she directs has given a new dimension to resource sharing.

On the other hand, Lou Wetherbee describes retrospective conversion and all kinds of catalogs as yesterday's services. She used the example of a patron who was writing a paper on school choice. "The patron went to the OPAC and found several citations. But when the patron got to the shelf, none of the materials was available. Catalogs are guides to information that might not be there," Wetherbee said. She encouraged enrichment of catalogs and the use of on-line resources. "The future is electronic and graphical," she said.

Delivery of materials and information was still seen as a viable system service by at least two respondents, although both were quick to point out that delivery can be accomplished in a variety of ways, including van, fax, and electronically. The traditional system role is to operate a van delivery service. The new system delivery role is seen in setting up electronic delivery mechanisms, including bulletin boards, Free-Nets, and fax servers.

Consulting has been a traditional role for systems. At one extreme it can simply mean system personnel serving as a sounding board for a staff member in a member library. At the other extreme, it can mean a study of a service, an analysis of personnel policies, or expertise in certain areas such as technology or children's services. Consulting has been a major service for systems in the past. It was still mentioned by some of those interviewed, but it was not described by anyone as a major system service. One person, a system director, wondered if the system's automation consultant should continue to serve as the primary automation advisor to the system's largest public library. "What's the difference between continuing education, consulting, and doing all of the public library's work for them?" he asked.

Negotiating discounts has been a long-time system service. Discounts have been appreciated by members but have seldom been a particular focus of system resources. Discounts have now become "collective buying" and when access to higher priced technology is involved, discounts become "negotiating licensing agreements." This role is seen as a growth area for systems. Bob Rohlf spoke of brokering contracts and Patricia Klinck said, "The information broker role will grow." Jim Ubel said that equalization of telecommunication costs was an issue for him. As systems broker expensive services such as Internet access, they may become involved in complex billing procedures. Thus what had been a relatively minor and simple system service becomes major and complex.

Leadership activities which include keeping members informed about developments and issues have been a staple among system services. Such activities are a continuing expectation of system leadership. Bob McClarren added to the list of leadership initiatives a system might undertake. These included: (1) testing new products and services; (2) taking responsibility (beyond offering continuing education courses) for human resource development in the professional environment; (3) providing system staff who could serve as the research and development arms of a member library needing such assistance; (4) taking a leadership role in area planning on behalf of member libraries; and (5) helping member libraries to merchandise themselves.

Several traditional system services were notable by their absence. Audio visual services and collections were mentioned by one interviewee in the past tense. Interlibrary loan was only mentioned in the context of patron initiated interlibrary loan or electronic interlibrary loan. Reference service was mentioned by one respondent as being phased out and by another as an example of a service that one system could provide for another system or systems.

In summary, there was general agreement that system resources should be focused on a few services needed and desired by members, rather than scattered among many services. The majority of those interviewed said that automation and technology initiatives and continuing education will be the principal focus for system services in the future.

F. System Behavior

How systems will behave in the future has been touched on earlier in this chapter. In the section on System Funding, the dichotomy between system funding and governance was outlined. System governance is being reexamined in many areas, especially as systems merge, realign, or contract out for their administrative decision making. The trend seems to be toward governance that reflects the wishes of the most powerful system members. The larger trends toward process decision making and accountability will also have an effect.

Systems in the future will be service oriented (Bishoff), focused (Carroll), and market driven (Bishoff). New ideas will come from outside of the library world (Calabrese), and systems will seek partnerships with a variety of organizations and entities, some in the for-profit sector (Calabrese, Curry, Ison, Weibel).

The trend toward partnership will also extend to other systems. Nancy Bolt envisioned systems working together to decide which services will be centralized and which will be decentralized. Mike O'Brien described it, "Some systems will provide services and some will buy services."

X. Conclusions

Systems were created in the 1960s in response to societal trends for regionalism, assistance to rural areas, and a broader federal role in all types of activities. A lot has happened in the intervening years. The trends now are exactly opposite: decentralization, local control, no faith in government, accountability at all levels, and no new taxes. New technology is changing the way Americans get their information and go about their everyday lives. It is also changing the nature of library service.

As a servant of libraries, systems are changing too. First of all, they are no longer just public library systems. They are multitype systems serving academic, public, special, and school libraries.

Systems were created to help with public library development. All that remains is the first part of that original purpose. "Systems were created to help." The challenge today is similar but the landscape, the clientele, and the methodology are vastly different.

Finally, systems, quo vadis, or where are you going? From the information gathered in this chapter it is clear that systems have the oppotunity to lead libraries into the information age. The characteristics of systems of the future are:

1. larger in geographical terms
2. fewer in number
3. funded from a variety of sources, some entrepreneurial
4. staffed by a range of professionals including MLSs but also including information professionals

   5. smaller—having a smaller regular staff and providing some services
      via contracts with other services providers
   6. consumer focused—this is focused on the expressed wishes of members
   7. technology based—organizing a myriad of higher technology proj-
      ects for the benefit of members
   8. always changing their services
   9. more focused and fewer services
  10. out of the traditional backup interlibrary loan, reference, and basic
      consulting services
  11. smaller—having fewer members because of higher technological
      standards for system membership
  12. into Internet access and providing leadership in organizing access to
      local information via some Free-Net-like model
  13. more emphasis on continuing education and training
  14. working with a wide variety of partners, including other systems and
      other public and private organizations

XI. Suggestions for Further Study

Further study into the current status of systems and their future development
is suggested, particularly (1) a comprehensive and unbiased review of systems
in the United States, (2) a report from consumers of system services regarding
their opinions and suggestions for future system development, and (3) comprehensive evaluation of systems especially aimed at answering the questions
raised in this chapter by Jim Scheppke. Specifically, an analysis of libraries
in states having and not having systems and a comparison might show what
difference systems have made.

Acknowledgments

The author acknowledges the staff of the North Suburban Library System for their help and
encouragement as this chapter was written. Mary Wheeler is especially commended for her
unflagging assistance with every aspect of this project. NSLS Information Service staff were
tireless in their efforts to search and procure obscure references. The author also thanks the
staff of the Suburban Library System's Reference Service for their services and Donald J. Sager,
the author's husband, for his counsel and assistance throughout the project. Finally, special
thanks are due to the persons interviewed for this paper. Without their experience, thoughtfulness,
and inspiration, this chapter could not have been written.

Appendix A

Questions Asked of Interviewees

   1. Library consortia or systems began developing in the United States
in the 1960s. In Illinois one reason for system development was the need for

public library development. In your opinion, what were other reasons for systems to develop?

2. How would you characterize the work of systems in the early days (their services to members, tasks assigned to system staff members, etc.)?

3. What is the single most important reason for systems to exist today?

4. How would you characterize the work of systems today (services to members, tasks assigned to staff members, etc.)?

5. How would you characterize the differences between systems today and systems in their formative years?

6. What do you see as the most important external factor acting on systems today that will change them in the future?

7. The trends to "...cut out the middleman," "...eliminate the bureaucrat," and "...decentralize everything" would seem to spell doom for systems. Do you agree or disagree, and why?

8. How do you see funding for systems changing? Is there a substantial entrepreneurial role that could be cultivated?

9. Imagine systems 10 years from now. How will they be different from the systems today?

10. What systems (perhaps including one close to your heart) would you say are on the cutting edge of system development and why?

Appendix B

Names of Persons Interviewed—September 6 to October 24, 1994

Lizbeth Bishoff, Vice President, Member Services, Online Computer Library Center, Inc., 6565 Frantz Road, Dublin, Ohio 43017-3395

Nancy Bolt, Dep. State Librarian and Assistant Commissioner, Colorado State Library, Colorado Department of Education, 201 E. Colfax, Denver, Colorado 80208

Robert Bullen, 414 Wing Lane, St. Charles, Illinois 60174

Roberta G. Cade, 33 Berkshire Boulevard, Albany, New York 12203

Alice Calabrese, System Director, Chicago Library System, 400 South State Street, Chicago Illinois 60605

Holly Carroll, Director, NOLA Regional Library System, 4445 Mahoning Ave. NW, Warren, Ohio 44483-1932

Harry Courtright, Director, The Library Network, 33030 Van Born Road, Wayne, Michigan 48184-2453

Linda Crowe, Director, Peninsula Library System, South Bay Cooperative Library System, 25 Tower Road, San Mateo, California 94402-4000

Walter Curley, Parnassus Imprints, 270 Communication Way, Suite 4A, Hyannis, Massachusetts 02601

Elizabeth Curry, Executive Director, SEFLIN, 100 S. Andrews Avenue, Ft. Lauderdale, Florida 33301

Jan Ison, System Director, Lincoln Trail Library System, 1704 W. Interstate Drive, Champaign, Illinois 61821

Patricia Klinck, State Librarian, Vermont Department of Libraries, 109 State Street, Pavillion Office Building, Montpelier, Vermont 05609

Bridget Lamont, Director, Illinois State Library, 300 S. Second Street, Springfield, Illinois 62701-1796

Sara Laughlin, Coordinator, Stone Hills Library Network, 112 N. Walnut, Suite 500, Bloomington, Indiana 47409

Robert McClarren, 1560 Oakwood Place, Deerfield, Illinois 60015

Martha J. McDonald, Executive Director, Creater Cincinnati Library Consortium, 333 Vine Street, Suite 605, Cincinnati, Ohio 45220

Joe McElroy, System Director, Heritage Trail Library system, 405 Earl Road, Shorewood, Illinois 60436

Carol Morrison, Information Network Consultant, DuPage Library System 127 S. First Street, P.O. Box 268, Geneva, Illinois 60134

James M. O'Brien, System Director, Suburban Library System, 125 Tower Drive, Burr Ridge, Illinois 60521

Robert Rohlf, 4531 Penn Avenue, Minneapolis, Minnesota 55409

Jim Scheppke, State Librarian, Oregon State Library, State Library Building, 250 Winter St. Ne, Salem, Oregon 97310

Les Stoffel, 1352 Turvey Road, Downers Grove, Illinois 60515

Dr. Alphonse F. Trezza, 2205 Napoleon Bonaparte Drive, Tallahassee, Florida 32308

Travis E. Tyer, Alliance Library System, 515 York Street, Quincy, Illinois 62301

Jim Ubel, System Director, Shawnee Library System, Greenbriar Road, Cartersville, Illinois 62918

Clarence Walters, Program Director for State and Public Libraries, Online Computer Library Center, 6565 Frantz Road, Dublin, Ohio 43017-3395

Kathleen Weibel, Director of Staff Development, Chicago Public Library, Harold Washington Center, 400 S. State Street, Chicago, Illinois 60605

Louella V. Wetherbee, Library Consultant, 3958 S. Better Drive, Dallas, Texas 75229-6207

Barratt Wilkins, Director, State Library of Florida, Division of Library and Information Services, R.A. Gray Building, Tallahassee, Florida 32399-0250

Donald Wright, 1715 Chancellor Street, Evanston, Illinois 60201

Reference Citations

Bishoff, Lizbeth. Interview with author. Wheeling, IL, September 27, 1994.
Bolt, Nancy. Interview with author. Wheeling, IL, October 19, 1994.

Bullen, Robert. Interview with author. Wheeling, IL, September 27, 1994.
Cade, Roberta G. Interview with author. Wheeling, IL, October 24, 1994.
Calabrese, Alice. Interview with author. Wheeling, IL, September 6, 1994.
Carroll, Holly. Interview with author. Wheeling, IL, September 26, 1994.
Courtright, Harry. Interview with author. Wheeling, IL, October 10, 1994.
Crowe, Linda. Interview with author. Wheeling, IL, September 27, 1994.
Curley, Walter. Interview with author. Wheeling, IL, September 27, 1994.
Curry, Elizabeth. Interview with author. Wheeling, IL, October 17, 1994.
Ison, Jan. Interview with author. Wheeling, IL, September 15, 1994.
Klinck, Patricia. Interview with author. Wheeling, IL, September 27, 1994.
Lamont, Bridget. Interview with author. Wheeling, IL, September 20, 1994.
Laughlin, Sara. Interview with author. Wheeling, IL, September 28, 1994.
McClarren, Robert. Interview with author. Wheeling, IL, September 23, 1994.
McDonald, Martha J. Interview with author. Wheeling, IL, October 18, 1994.
McElroy, Joe. Interview with author. Wheeling, IL, September 15, 1994.
Morrison, Carol. Interview with author. Wheeling, IL, September 19, 1994.
O'Brien, James. Interview with author. Wheeling, IL, September 15, 1994.
Rohlf, Robert. Interview with author. Wheeling, IL, September 27, 1994.
Scheppke, Jim. Written response to author's questions dated September 27, 1994.
Stoffel, Les. Interview with author. Wheeling, IL, September 28, 1994.
Trezza, Alphonse F. Interview with author. Wheeling, IL, October 19, 1994.
Tyer, Travis E. Interview with author. Wheeling, IL, September 21, 1994.
Ubel, Jim. Interview with author. Wheeling, IL, September 15, 1994.
Walters, Clarence. Interview with author. Wheeling, IL, September 19, 1994.
Weibel, Kathleen. Interview with author. Wheeling, IL, September 21, 1994.
Wetherbee, Louella. Interview with author. Wheeling, IL, October 19, 1994.
Wilkins, Barratt. Interview with author. Wheeling, IL, October 14, 1994
Wright, Donald. Interview with author. Wheeling, IL, September 26, 1994.

Bibliography

American Library Association (1956). *Minimum Standards for Public Library Systems.* Prepared by the Standards Committee and Subcommittees of the Public Library Association.
Casey, G. M. (1978). *The Public Library In The Network Mode: A Preliminary Investigation.* Illinois Regional Library Council.
Gregory, R. W., and Stoffel, L. L. (1971). *Public Libraries in Cooperative Systems, Administrative Patterns for Service.* American Library Association.
Hamilton, B. A., and Ernst, W. B., Jr., eds. (1977). *Multitype Library Cooperation.* R. R. Bowker Company.
Huwe, T. K. (1993). Information specialists and the cooperative workplace: Challenges and opportunities. In *Advances in Librarianship* (I. Godden, ed.), Vol. **17.** Academic Press, San Diego.
Joeckel, C. B. (1935). *The Government of the American Public Library,* pp. 351–355. University of Chicago Press, Chicago.
Joeckel, C. B. (1948). *A National Plan for Public Library Service,* p. 155. Prepared for the Committee on Postwar Planning of the American Library Association.
Leigh, R. D. (1950). *The Public Library in the United States,* p. 227. The General Report of the Public Library Inquiry, Columbia University Press, New York.
Realities of the public library system concept in Wisconsin (1968). In *Proceedings of the Twelfth Institute on Public Library Management, Division for Library Services.* Department of Public Instruction.

Regional Library Study FY '93 (1993). State of Vermont, Department of Libraries, Executive Summary, unpaged.

Regional Policies in the United States (1980) Organization for Economic Co-operation and Development, Paris, Part A, IV. Regional Policy, 24.

Shaughnessy, T. W. (1975). *An Overview of the Development of Larger Units of Service and the Central Library Concept.* ERIC Reports. ERIC Document Reproduction Service: Arlington, VA.

Trezza, A. F., ed. (1987). *Not Alone, but Together.* A Conference on Multitype Library Cooperation, Florida State University.

Woodsworth, A. (1991). Governance of library networks: Structures and issues. In *Advances in Librarianship* (I. Godden, ed.), Vol. 15. Academic Press, San Diego.

The Future of Technical Services: An Administrative Perspective

Nancy H. Allen
University of Denver
Denver, Colorado, 80208

James F. Williams II
University of Colorado at Boulder
Boulder, Colorado, 80309

I. Institutional Perspective

Any discussion of technical services must take into account the institutional context within which today's libraries operate. That context, whether for private or public institutions, academic, or public libraries, is one heavily influenced by government activity and public policy issues. These issues have been identified for higher education organizations by the Association of Governing Boards of Universities and Colleges (AGB) in a report containing recommendations based on five major societal factors: (1) the growth of domestic and international economic pressures, (2) the continued influence of demographic change, (3) racial and cultural tensions, (4) the exponential pace of scientific advances, and (5) a deepening national crisis of values and ethics and the negative impact of that crisis on our ability to create a sense of community. A similarly broad view of context indicators would include the organizational development trends observed by Benveniste (1994) that are relevant to all kinds of institutions: worldwide competition for new ideas; education of the work force; feminization of organizational culture; new technologies, particularly in communication and information; institutionalization of rapid change; and new understanding of organizations. With factors such as these influencing our perspectives on the educational environment, 10 public policy issues for higher education in 1994 were identified and discussed by the AGB:

1. Tight budgets due to competition for public funds.
2. Public agency oversight of institutions and demands for greater accountability regarding finances, administration, and academic affairs.

ADVANCES IN LIBRARIANSHIP, VOL. 19

3. Increasing demands for more productivity and access at reasonable costs.
4. Student-aid reforms: new student-aid legislation regarding direct loans, national service, etc.
5. Slow growth in funds to support university-based research, and more emphasis on research that supports economic development.
6. Institutions will be asked to do more in addressing societal problems.
7. All institutions will be affected by health care reform.
8. Intercollegiate athletics will be under scrutiny, with a focus on cost containment and gender equity.
9. Colleges and universities will be asked to do more to advance public school reform.
10. Elimination of mandatory retirement in 1994 will affect the finances and faculty demographics of many institutions.

Clearly, this list applies to other types of organizations outside of higher education, and thus the list becomes illustrative of the kinds of public policy issues facing all of society's institutions and agencies. A cursory review of these issues and trends by library administrators will reveal the strong and lasting influence that each one will have on the future of scholarly communication and library operations in general throughout the remainder of the 1990s.

Within the context of these public policy, higher education, and societal issues and trends there is a very strong expectation by higher education administrators that their library directors/deans will continue to function as skillful and effective managers while continuing to grow as effective leaders. Managers will be expected to manage complexity, to create an ongoing agenda for planning and budgeting, to organize and staff in order to achieve that agenda, to execute that agenda through a process of controls and problem solving, and to maintain an environment of predictability, order, and key results. Leaders will be expected to lead change, establish direction for the management agenda, align people in order to develop the most effective possible human network for achieving the management agenda, motivate and inspire personnel once they have been properly aligned, and accomplish this while producing dramatic and useful change. In order to assume these leadership responsibilities, today's library deans/directors will have an increasing personal responsibility to strengthen their ability to deal effectively with interpersonal relationships, think and behave in terms of systems, approach decision making from the standpoint of trade-offs and leveraged resources, think and act with flexibility, and maintain balance by coping with disequilibrium caused by a volatile information environment.

II. The Present and Future Academic Library

Today's academic library functions in an environment where the mission of the college or university is not only to teach, but also to create a culture (driven by technology) where the academic community is continuously learning and skilled in the process of lifelong learning. To a considerable extent, public libraries are also furthering these instructional and lifelong learning missions, taking a central role in helping to reeducate today's knowledge workers. To accomplish these missions, digital technologies coupled with telecommunications, have already been accepted as new and integrating media for teaching and learning, and for scholarly discovery and communication. Through these new media, in the long run, institutions will deemphasize physical collections. This deemphasis will ultimately be accompanied by the expectation that codified information and knowledge will become society's primary wealth-producing assets.

Today's library is dealing with the innumerable changes brought about by the new media and the way those media have changed the way information is organized, retrieved, and disseminated. Academic and research libraries have among their missions the role of functioning as a bridge to the past and future of the scholarly record. Information technology has already had many profound effects on the process of academic communication and on the ways libraries support their historic missions of acquiring, preserving, and making recorded knowledge available. Information technology will also generate more change, introducing themes of the future which include new organizational structures, new visions for the future of scholarly communication, and thus new roles for librarians as educators, publishers, preservers, and organizers. For a snapshot of current discussions in the library and information science profession on the library of the future, see Drabenstott (1994).

These transitions herald an exciting future for technical operations in libraries. Libraries in their transitional roles will continue to be essential in the process of delivering information when and where it is needed to support the creation of knowledge and culture, at an affordable price. Technical services operations have been responsible for access systems and for cost-effective methods of connecting library users with the materials they seek. In today's volatile information environment, library administrators are demanding new automation skill sets for staff, while the diverse technological environment within our institutions requires even more coordination or connections among administrative functions. It is an environment where multiple data streams from publishers, bibliographic utilities, library automation vendors, and a host of other external telecommuted sources require much greater effort to track and integrate. Even greater operational efficiencies of scale are needed. Fiscal constraints already threaten our ability to maintain access to both physical and virtual resources. The market-driven library systems vendor community does not have sufficient ongoing research and development capital to deliver systems at the rate and on the scale of change in libraries, and library directors are continuing to operate under heightened expectations by institutional administrators and users for faster, better and affordable information systems and infrastructure. Technical services operations will continue to be at the core of the integrated solutions which must be brought to bear on this environment of pressure, change, and opportunity.

III. Technical Services Today

Since the early 1990s, a number of textbooks, guides, and investigations into technical services have been prepared. These volumes (and the journal literature cited in their bibliographies) present a remarkably common identity for technical services today, although most of them are written from a predominantly academic library perspective (Godden, 1991; Racine, 1991; Leonhardt, 1992; Intner and Fang, 1991; Gorman, 1990; Evans and Heft, 1994). Christensen (1989) provides a bibliography of the literature of the 1980s on the state of technical services. A review of these works yields a description of the library organizational patterns which have been practiced in a vast majority of libraries for the past quarter century.

The part of the library called technical services currently has a hierarchical organization chart and continues to use a hierarchical management structure (although the role of committees and task forces in library management overall continues to evolve). Found in this organization chart are departments responsible for placing orders for both monographic and serial material, for tracking orders, receiving materials ordered, and for reconciling receipts with invoices. Other departments are responsible for finding bibliographic information describing these material, for editing bibliographic information, for creating bibliographic information where none could be found, and for maintaining bibliographic information which already resides in the catalog. Yet other units are charged with checking in serial items and for maintaining information about the physical condition and location of each serial item. Other staff groups are responsible for the physical labeling, marking, care, and protection of the materials, including all aspects of the relationship with the companies doing binding and repair. Other staff groups are responsible for all dealings with a very large publisher—the U.S. government—and those staff generally take care of all or most of the previously described work for materials generated by that publisher.

The widespread mission of the staff undertaking these functions is: Get library material onto the shelves as quickly as possible so that library users can see them. Get high quality information about the library collections into the catalog as quickly as possible so that library users can find information. Keep the material in good shape so future library users will be able to use it.

There are perhaps four or five commonly found organization charts for these operations, and no single method of organization is right or wrong. Measures of efficiency and quality show that any number of reporting lines work as long as redundancy is kept to a minimum and the physical movement of material and staff is rational. Communication among and between work units with related or dependent workflow must be effective. The use of computer-based systems to transfer information about library material to the various staff units handling either the material or information about the material is certainly one of the most dominant factors in determining the organization of work and staff.

For example, one library might organize staff according to the location of OCLC workstations, workstations accessing the local system, and workstations dedicated to access to an order vendor's information. Another library might have funded and installed a network so that all systems can be accessed from any staff workstation. One library, not having enough money to put a networked workstation in front of every staff member, might schedule staff into shared workstations, which has an impact on the organization of work units. The extent of funding for microcomputers and terminals, for networking, for the support of telecommunication systems, and for technical staff capable of linking vendor systems to local systems will also determine, at least to some significant extent, the organizational choices selected. The availability of workspace and the size of the library are obviously other factors.

A. What Has Caused Change So Far?

Since the 1960s, with the exception of our current goals of speed in materials processing and bibliographic control, the mission of technical services may not have changed so much as the methods. Timeliness as part of the mission has changed—in the 1960s and 1970s, enormous backlogs were so common in large- and medium-sized libraries that the idea of fast cataloging or processing was not always on the list of goals, and it took a very long time to identify and acquire new materials prior to the widespread use of approval vendors, blanket orders, or other "gathering plans" (Lockman, 1990). In the early 1960s, the approval plan system was developed, and statewide cooperatives began to emerge. From one of the state cooperatives, the one in Ohio, a national bibliographic database emerged, supported by the MARC standard for bibliographic descriptions. This made the on-line copying of someone else's cataloging possible, a fundamental change which triggered many others, including the development of local on-line catalogs which flourished after 1975. These changes in libraries were triggered by the search for less expensive ways to operate, supported by changes in the computer and telecommunications industries. In addition, the availability of cataloging in publication (CIP) data offered the opportunity to shift labor costs from the library to the publishing industry. However, tinkering practices developed, related to both CIP and member copy, and large staff investments emerged along with copy cataloging.

IV. Technical Services in the Future: What Will Cause Change?

The search for savings and changes in the computer and telecommunications industries are still among the triggers for change in technical services. Added to these two factors are advances in software for information access and changes in the publishing industry.

A. Change Agent: The Search for Savings

Whether libraries are located in the public or private sector, fixed or shrinking resource bases will be the rule for the 1990s. Further, the library director has to face impossible dilemmas in decision making for budget planning. The trend line on journal prices is steeper some years than others, but it continues to rise. The trend line on monographic prices continues to rise. The number of libraries receiving funding to cover the full cost of materials inflation is small. The struggle to reserve funds for the purchase of monographs continues to result in round after round of serial cancellations.

But perhaps the most dramatic change in the collections formula became apparent only in the early 1990s: the rising percentage of the materials budget dedicated to leasing or acquiring machine-readable information (at this time, primarily journal index files or services, but increasingly data sets, or multimedia). Although large research libraries may now be reporting that digital information represents about 1% of the material processed (Gozzi, 1994), it certainly represents more than 1% of the cost. Data are not readily available on the percentage of materials budget dollars spent on CD leases; on journal indexes available on a free or subsidized basis to users through FirstSearch, Dialog, etc.; or on site licenses for PAC-affiliated databases, but from all accounts and informal surveys, there is no doubt that it is an ever-increasing percentage. A significant part of the trend from ownership to access, by 2000 this sector of cost may well exceed the journal inflation rate as the dominant factor causing libraries to acquire fewer printed resources.

It is now the case that U.S. libraries are moving beyond the initial aspects of technology exploration where grant or other external funding enabled leading edge pilot projects to explore new uses of microcomputers. Libraries are operationalizing the support structures needed to access on-line files and services. Permanent funds, both in the materials budget and operating budgets, are required.

With journal prices continuing to erode the number of books acquired, and with the relatively new cost of digital resources competing with all other components of the fixed material budget, a number of effects follow:

1 Library directors need to reallocate or to find more funds for the equipment and systems required for the use of digital resources.
2. As equipment, supplies, and telecommunication costs rise to support digital resources, S&E budgets begin to drain staff budgets. Funds generated from vacant positions are a major support for equipment investment.
3. With a declining staff size, more labor-effective processing methods are sought.

These effects take a while to show up in statistics since most survey data do not reflect the number of positions held vacant on a temporary basis. Nonetheless, hiring freezes, staff reorganizations, and other methods of moving dollars from staff to equipment continue as common practice because library directors generally attempt to prevent collection dollars from being spent on equipment. Since the decline of spending on staff, matched by a corresponding increase in spending on automated systems in the member libraries of the Association of Research Libraries (ARL), is now documented through analysis of ARL annual statistics (Dillon, 1993), the trend of spending more on automated systems at the expense of staff is here to stay.

After time, and with continued constraint on library budgets, another effect has already begun: collection development budgets are used increasingly for the hardware and software needed to provide access to digital information resources. The lines are fuzzy already. For years, many libraries have supported OCLC costs with collection budgets. Information acquisition as well as information access will be supported by the same fixed (or if one is lucky, inflation-adjusted) allocation. And of course, the economics of collections are creating an independent effect of declining resources available for purchase of material, as indicated by studies of buying power and budgets in research libraries (Association of American Universities Research Libraries Project, 1994, p. 40).

Given these circumstances and projections, what can be done to make technical services even more labor effective? Through the use of automated systems, many efficiencies have already occurred, although it has been shown time and time again that libraries add value rather than reducing cost through the application of technology. Peggy Johnson, discussing her survey results, says that although libraries badly want to reduce costs through automation, few libraries see any savings. Instead, libraries report new or improved patron services, speed of processing operations, or improvement in the library's image (Johnson, 1991, pp. 120–121). Internally, then, effective use of automated systems does indeed improve speed and efficiency.

Several other options for improved efficiency have been proposed, and although library directors will not necessarily elect these options, when budgetary restrictions force them into action, these efficiencies will eventually be pursued.

1. Contracting with External Agencies for Service

If the information professional's primary job is to identify, filter, organize, and synthesize information on behalf of library users, then it may be necessary in some environments to outsource some library operations in order to stay within budget and concentrate the management piece of the job on those aspects that have the greatest impact on service. A survey done in 1994 (Bush, Sassé, and Smith, 1994) established the growing choice of vendor services in acquisitions, cataloging, and collection development.

Outsourcing basically means that competitive bidding is used to reduce the cost of operating certain functions. It should be seriously considered when operational expenses are growing faster than budgets; when demand for quantity and quality of services outstrips the ability to provide the services; when the skills to evaluate, implement, and manage certain operations do not exist; and when the time and energy devoted to managing certain operations interfere with the ability to focus on the mission of the organization. Cost-cutting or generation of revenue might not be the only reason for considering outsourcing operations, but when outsourcing works, the key resulting benefits include:

1. the ability to define the cost of operations
2. the library can rely on fixed or predictable costs over time, and
3. external operations can be curtailed more easily and naturally than can internal operations.

If a contract to outsource is developed, it should concentrate on responsibility, costs, and performance standards. At a minimum, it should address vendor selection and negotiation, materials processing, maintenance of local files and databases, adherence to national standards, level of detail in creation of local files and records, external information access levels and sources, retrieval and delivery specs, additional fees and charges, user satisfaction measures, subject or staff expertise, service types and levels, reporting level and frequency, error tolerance, terms for equipment (ownership, replacement, maintenance), space utilization and costs, and the locus of responsibility for overhead.

The manager of outsourced operations must understand that the degree of fiscal flexibility differs for in-house full-service operations and for out-sourced operations. For in-house operations, the fiscal flexibility is low and overhead is high. For outsourced operations, fiscal flexibility is high and overhead is generally low.

If a decision is made to outsource a particular operation or function, the analysis of whether to do so should include the short- and long-term fiscal implications, transition plans, personnel impact, cultural impact, security, loss of control, and the performance record of the provider (Woodsworth and Williams, 1993, p. 21). The Stanford University Libraries (SUL, 1995) report on the SUL project to reengineer technical services workflow will certainly serve as a model for such analysis. The report recommends outsourcing whenever that is possible, identifies risks such as those concerning quality control, and suggests major changes in centers of responsibility for processing in order to eliminate duplicative work loads and to increase efficiency.

a. Cataloging. Is the contract the path to "faster, cheaper, better?"   Not at all a new phenomenon, the change in cataloging operations will be in degree. OCLC could, for example, become the nation's cataloging contractor. With two new services (TECHPRO and PromptCat), OCLC moves from retrospective conversion contracts to current cataloging programs. Through TECHPRO, libraries are able to contract for cataloging of special formats of materials, special languages, etc. Through PromptCat, libraries contract to receive automated delivery of copy cataloging for items ordered from participating vendors. PromptCat allows libraries to address their needs through various options, including immediate or delayed setting of holdings, record selection, record delivery, tailored reports, and the inclusion of vendor-supplied information. Further, the link between library approval vendors and PromptCat is an interesting one, with a number of possible effects. For years, libraries have been able to send off copies or originals of card cataloging in order to have it replaced with machine-readable cataloging along with hold-ings information for the local and national catalogs. Libraries have, for some time, been able to acquire cataloging along with approval books, although as with other workflows for copy cataloging, there has been mixed success in handling this in a manner which does not involve redundancy and/or local tinkering with records which does not result in additional access functionality.

The connection between cataloging and acquisition vendors is not a new connection; what *is* new is the relationship with OCLC.

OCLC is not the only option for contract cataloging. Regional OCLC providers such as AMIGOS provide a range of cataloging services. In any cooperative, one might find cataloging services, such as those in DALNET, where Wayne State University performs contract cataloging for area hospital libraries that are members of the Detroit Area Library Network. Further, large research libraries may perform specialized cataloging. Even at the holdings level, resource sharing groups may be collectively funding the creation of local data records to enhance access to holdings and location information on journals needed through interlibrary loan.

Contract cataloging is not the only option for reducing costs. From an administrative perspective, a number of analyses must be completed before making a decision on contacting. Lowering the unit cost of any technical services operation can perhaps be done by using lower level and less expensive staff. This trend toward deprofessionalizing technical services has been underway for years (Gorman, 1987). There is a limit to this solution, and that limit is caused by the extensive use of systems. In most support staff job classification schemes used by public, academic, or government libraries, the use of complex information systems, the need for extensive training, or the need to understand rules, interpretations, policies, and standards (such as AACR2, etc.) leads to an increase in the classification level and pay grade. It is apparent that the trend toward lower level staff in technical services has reversed and that although most technical services operations are performed by preprofessional, support, or clerical staff, those staff are not entry level staff, and the use of student or part-time staff is effective only in limited areas. Still, in some libraries, further reorganization to maximize the use of less costly staff can be undertaken.

Many libraries are still permitting redundant workflow, with numerous searches in various files for the same item at different stages in the process from order to labeling. A systematic effort to find the greatest effciency for the most reasonable quality level can also lead to considerable staff savings.

The balance between quality and quantity must be determined by each library, of course, but in looking at the greatest cause of expense in in-house copy cataloging operations, perhaps most pernicious is the search for perfection. It seems that the debate over quality versus quantity in cataloging continues to rage (LeBlanc, 1994), with proponents of minimal level cataloging arguing for some basic access rather than none for backlogs or stored collections, and with cataloging purists insisting on thorough review of all copied cataloging regardless of source. A great deal of time and effort is being spent by many libraries changing cataloging or adding local information in ways that do not actually help users find library material (Rush, 1994).

According to this study, in their effort to seek local perfection, libraries are actually deleting useful access points, creating incorrect information by meddling with punctuation, subtitles, or places of publication. Although most library directors are not at this time taking the advice of Mr. Rush (to totally eliminate copy cataloging in the individual library), any increase in the use of OCLC's services may lead in that direction. OCLC and the Library of Congress, with a relatively small community of major research libraries acting in partnership, could quite reasonably supply a growing percentage of all cataloging, along with provision of holdings data.

This trend would be synchronous with the existing pattern where fewer libraries are doing cataloging in OCLC and more in local/regional systems. Why does a library director support cataloging in the local or consortial system instead of in OCLC? Because of the cost of OCLC telecommunication and searching. Using the local system as a cataloging source and reflecting holdings only in that local/regional system saves money. Using a non-OCLC cataloging source for L.C. records also saves money. This same cost-conscious library director will compare the overall cost of local staff to the overall cost of entirely contracting out the process, and will decide on the basis of savings. If the staffing plan is very efficient, pay rates are low, and use of automated systems are maximized, local cataloging may still be less expensive than the contract.

What will be the effect of increasing the use of external contracts for technical services on overhead, equipment, and supplies budgets? In theory, the fewer computers and telecommunication lines supported locally, the lower the cost. Library directors may be focusing on staff savings as a way to pay for contracts, but they may have other categories of savings to anticipate as well.

What other impacts might be anticipated from an increase in libraries' reliance on external contracts in the area of copy or original cataloging? A significant impact not often discussed is in the area of maintenance of holdings and location information. If it follows that journal price inflation, fixed or reduced library collection budgets, and improved interlibrary lending technologies will increase reliance on interlibrary loan and other document delivery options, then accurate information about holdings will be of increasing importance. At this time, the OCLC pricing structures do not provide any incentive to libraries to keep holdings information current; instead there are disincentives. The current OCLC pricing structure rewards the contribution of original cataloging, not holdings information. This, among other cost factors, has led to a decline in the reliability of OCLC holdings information, especially in the area of journal summary or volume holdings data. In order to access accurate holdings data for interlibrary lending, libraries must search local systems or must belong to consortia with union catalog arrangements that are maintained throughout the consortium via OCLC. The lack of a cost-effective national infrastructure for ready access to holdings information is a primary cause of the relatively poor fill rates on interlibrary lending requests, especially for libraries that have endured journal cancellations projects over recent years. Still, technical service units struggle to keep local catalog holdings information current and accurate for local users. The need to invest in these laborious efforts will remain, whether or not cataloging is done in house or externally, or via a contract. It is most likely that the importance of finding mechanisms for record exchange, uploading, overlaying, and depositing to OCLC and to regional cooperative catalogs will increase with the need for resource sharing.

    b. Resource Sharing Contracts.   Contract cataloging has been the target of a fire storm of opinion (Hirschon, 1994), but we might anticipate other areas of technical services where contracts or resource sharing agreements could emerge as savings sources. These would have a direct effect on local technical services staffing requirements.

As the technology supporting document delivery from remote locations improves in reliability, quality, and cost, regional cooperatives will certainly begin to look at alternatives to binding and retention of materials duplicated in the region. It is now feasible to contract with neighboring libraries for binding and retention of paper material so that each participant shares in the bindery contract and only one location is planned for back runs of selected serials. This resource sharing contract concept has (for the most part) failed in regard to initial selection, but has yet to be tried on any scale for retention once the peak use period of the journal has passed. Bindery contract administration, bindery processing, and space savings would result. University of California libraries using the two regional depositories have edged toward storage "contracts" for bound journal volumes. Although UC libraries do not collaborate to decide which libraries should retain journal runs locally, the regional depositories will not retain duplicates. With the regional storage sites in place, and with enough pressure on local library space, the next step would be cooperative retention planning on a large scale.

As changes occur in the U.S. government depository program because of federal shifts to electronic distribution (compact disk products) or to centralized federal databases accessed via telecommunication, libraries are highly likely to challenge the need to permanently retain all depository material when a number of libraries in the same region have supported overlapping depository profiles or when there is more than one regional depository collection. Again, high quality and lower cost document access technologies will continue to make it more feasible to craft contracts or agreements for retention and access. These would be less expensive than duplicative depository processing and retention, and multiple commitments to storage space.

   c. Acquisitions Contracts. Libraries have probably gone as far as is practical to go with acquisitions contracts. Approval plans, blanket orders, foreign material gathering plans, and publication notification services are in widespread use today. Perhaps the most forward-looking project related to acquisitions contracts has been the one launched by the Association of American Universities (AAU) and the Association of Research Libraries to improve access to and delivery of international research sources. This project focuses on the development of a collaborative program of participating institutions sharing responsibility for collecting foreign imprint publications and sharing those collections through network-based access mechanisms. The initial AAU/ARL acquisitions projects concentrate on Latin American resources, scientific and technical publications from Japan, and materials that originate in Germany (*ARL Newsletter*, p. 3).

   The next logical development to these kinds of contracts will connect the cataloging contract with the acquisitions process and could, in fact, even avoid the acquisition process. There has already been one published assertion that approval plans, bibliographer's workstations, and mechanical selection systems can replace or reorganize most traditional collection development activities (Sassé and Smith, 1992).

   For some time, prepublication cataloging has been available through approval vendors. Now through OCLC PromptCat, a library may order through an approval vendor, and when the material comes in through the approval plan, the vendor will already have sent notification to OCLC to add a cataloging record and holdings to the purchasing library's OCLC file. Taking this one step further, it should be possible for a library to browse through the cataloging for new approval books, and whenever it is interested in something it has *not* selected (for reasons of price, or peripheral interest, or for some other perfectly good reason) it can add a record to its catalog anyway which points to the interlibrary loan address. This seems like an odd idea—listing items *not* selected in the on-line catalog—but it is already being done by every library loading the Center for Research Libraries tapes. But if this practice were adopted on a grander scale through approval systems, how would technical services units maintain these records? How could locations be held current? What systems would be designed to maintain ''access'' or ''pointer'' records as compared to records for owned materials? Depending on answers to these questions, new roles for technical services units might well emerge.

   d. Contracts for Preservation. Bindery contracts are today's version of outsourced preservation services. But tomorrow's preservation functions are even more likely to require outsourcing. Preservation and/or regeneration of digital content, access to previous generations of digital viewing equipment, and methods of dealing with previous generations of digital storage media are not currently in the repertoire of most library preservation units. Most time and effort are spent on saving acid paper documents, or nitrate films, etc. Unless more cost-effective methods of both paper and electronic preservation are found, some obvious negative effects will result. Both theoretical and practical angles on these thorny problems are outlined by Graham (1993). After describing technical solutions to identification and preservation of true electronic copy such as encryption (transforming a document with complex computer-generated algorithms to be unlocked with secret keys or with combinations of public and private keys), hashing, and time-stamping, Graham asserts, with some humor, that this is indeed a role for librarians and libraries. "Some librarians may draw back from the apparent complexity of the technologies that support electronic information. But these technologies should present no difficulty to minds that can easily deal with corporate authorship and with the acquisition of monographic continuations" (Graham, 1993, p. 35). Perhaps this is to be a new unit within the preservation department, but it could clearly be contracted out as well, with the library maintaining its historical responsibility for intellectual preservation and overcoming barriers related to information format.

B. Change Agent: The Pressure on Library Space

"So, when is it all going to be electronic?" chorus the nation's Provosts and Presidents, the Boards, and the Trustees.

The federal investment in explorations of the virtual library is making it difficult to get commitments for expansion of library space. University administrators will leap on any reasonable indication that more research material will be digitized and accessible over the Internet since those indicators would seem, on the surface of the argument, to support reductions in the size of the projected space deficit for local paper collections. The Library of Congress has announced a digitization project (Library of Congress, 1994) to convert a million images to digital format. Although that sounds like a lot, it turns out to be a shared effort with selected research libraries, and the project will first attend to the digitization of special collections, following on the model of the American Memory Project. What else is likely to happen in regard to the conversion from existing paper publications to digital storage formats? Without an enormous investment, not much. Research libraries are not able to find funding to keep up with current purchases, the Commission on Preservation and Access is unable to find enough funding to get a running start on cooperative digital preservation projects, and the million images at the Library of Congress would turn into only 4000 book-length volumes if the project's focus were not on special collections. To help library directors combat the persuasive set of fallacies which are making it harder and harder to argue for new library space, the Association of Research Libraries published a SPEC kit entitled *2001: A Space Reality in 1994* (Kaufman and Mitchell, 1994).

An unpublished e-mail survey conducted in 1991 by Cathy Tweedy in support of a space planning effort at Colorado State University revealed that a majority of the ARL libraries have either finished construction of additional library space in the past 5 years or intend to begin building projects in the next 5 years. It appears that the prospect of a cost-effective space solution based on digital publishing or on conversion to digital forms is not regarded by most ARL libraries as a near end solution.

> The 120 research libraries that are members of ARL now report holdings approaching 400,000,000 volumes and over 300,000,000 microform units. . . . There is little real likelihood that all of the material—even taking into account duplication between collections—will ever be converted into some electronically accessible form. Nor should such ideas and efforts be encouraged considering the nature, value, and use of that material. (Stevens, 1993)

However, there is the real possibility, and likelihood, that all libraries needing additional space will not get funding. If new buildings are not funded, the options include remote storage, replacement with microformats (including digitization), conversion of conventional to compact shelving, large-scale weeding, or even more dependence on document delivery. Most likely, all of these methods will be used in combinations to be determined by local funding and other circumstances. What will the impact be on technical services? Remote storage requires an investment of labor in records maintenance since location information changes. Similarly, microformat conversion requires creation and maintenance of indexing and location systems on a different level than those for separate monographic or serial cataloging. Large-scale weeding is not widely practiced in research libraries for a number of reasons related to those libraries' collection missions, but weeding of duplicates and superseded editions is commonly done on a limited scale. Weeding and withdrawal projects on a larger scale can indeed generate badly needed space, but are costly in technical services and deselection staff time. Not even counting the professional collection management time required to weed stacks, a casual cost estimate is highly likely to determine that it would be less expensive to purchase a range of stacks than it is to weed, withdraw, and dispose of the equivalent number of volumes. Because more and more libraries must consider more aggressive withdrawal planning, some interesting and complex formulas have been presented which project future demand while calculating costs of various solutions to space limits (Lee, 1993). Again, the technical services' effort is in holdings, location, and bibliographic informa-tion maintenance, a work load destined to increase.

It could also be the case that the pressure on library space and the lack of funding for large new buildings or for additions to existing buildings will finally force real interlibrary collection acquisitions cooperation. If some improvements in the cost of commercial document delivery and/or the cost and speed of interlibrary loan were also to happen, substantial cooperation might result. In this case, still fewer dollars would be spent locally, and more dollars would be spent on access systems. Most likely, serial collections would be the first area for purposeful cooperative collection reductions. In the technical services units of cooperating libraries, the serial acquisition and cataloging units would initially see an increased work load in record adjust-ments and order management due to cancellation projects. Cataloging units might create pointers from one local catalog to the record in the cooperative or union catalog. But eventually, the serial ordering, check in, bindery/conser-vation management, and serial records units would have less to do. Of course, any free person hours created by this scenario would need to be transferred to the document access unit, whether that is located in the order unit, the interlibrary loan unit, the circulation unit, or a new unit to be found in the future library's organization chart.

C. Change Agent: Less Paper, More Digital?

Among the trends predicted in the OCLC symposium by Arnold Hirshon (1994, p. 16) in his advocacy of contracting cataloging are "print publications will decrease substantially in importance" and "electronic communications will become more and more prevalent and eventually will be the major form of scholarly communication." Note that he did not assert that paper publications will decline substantially in number.

Most information professionals will agree that more and more is going to be available in digital forms over the Internet (or the emerging NII). Digital image technologies are making it possible for libraries to create trans-mission copies for resource sharing, but that availability will not necessarily be the factor creating change in libraries. Instead, it may be a combination of greater availability, greater access, and better software which will finally make a change for libraries. After all, as client-centered organizations, libraries are likely to continue to try to acquire what their users want and need, not simply what is available. Will readers *want* to abandon print publications in favor of digital ones?

1. Will There Be Less Paper to Process?

The AAU study on the question of electronic publishing (Association of American Universities Research Libraries Project, 1994) is perhaps one of the more authoritative predictions of the future. In this study, the AAU Research Library Project team envisions a 20-year transition period from paper to digital publishing, with a rapid increase in digital communication taking place immediately, with copyright and intellectual property law acting to restrain the pace of change, and with the publishers acting as a market-sensitive, generally conservative force taking steps and stages to complete the transition. Even in the year 2015, the AAU report predicts that 50% of recorded knowledge will be disseminated in the way it is being disseminated now, using the "classic" model of paper publishing.

Libraries are certainly buying less material with the same budgets. This loss of buying power is most severe for monographs because of the commit-ment to serial subscriptions and the well-known serial cost inflation trends (Perrault, 1994).

A related question central to a vast number of legal and marketplace questions in trade and academic publishing is: in that transition, how long will libraries have to choose between digital and paper copies of the same documents? Will digital publishing turn out to be a lot like paperback publish-ing, except for the enormous investment required in equipment and software by consumers and libraries?

Several big questions for technical services units remain unresolved today, and there is not much evidence for projection of trend lines. Nonetheless, looking at similar questions, one might make some predictions.

2. How Will Digital Publications Be Accessed?

Two conflicting practices for electronic journals are developing. The MIT library developed a thoughtful and intricate system of acquiring, describing, listing and indexing, posting, maintaining, and archiving a number of elec-tronic journals (Geller, 1992). This model accepts the premise that digital publications should be fitted into the existing workflow and that the intellec-tual content of these should be treated in the same ways content is treated when it has a physical rather than digital form. Other libraries have created similar procedures and policies (Sassé and Winkler, 1993) and often for selected titles in demand by user groups. However, a greater number of libraries are not acquiring, cataloging, listing or indexing, or archiving elec-tronic journals at all, although the users of those libraries regularly read the publications. Instead they are creating gopher or web page pointers to the indexes and files of the electronic publications. This phenomenon is illustrated by the many pointers to the electronic journal project created by the CIC (Big Ten libraries) and housed at the University of Illinois, Chicago.

It is apparent that a new form of copy cataloging is possible; instead of creating a copy of cataloging to add to the local system, a pointer is created in the local system connecting with the original cataloging copy which is posted in a public, network-accessible file somewhere else.

Once this capability exists from within any on-line catalog, bibliographic utilities, individual libraries, or consortia can provide sets of pointers rather than cataloging so that bibliographic information can reside in one electronically available location rather than thousands of them. The concept behind client-server network architecture should be possible for on-line catalogs, with local systems storing indexes to cataloging locations rather than cataloging. If this happens from within catalogs instead of through gopher indexes as is now the case, the traditional function of a catalog will need to be reconsidered once again since, for instance, the University of Colorado catalog could list not only Center for Research Libraries holdings side by side with University of Colorado holdings, but could also list selected sets and publications from Canada, Germany, France, or Rhode Island. But wait, cataloging capability cannot race ahead of user wants and needs! A rational approach from a user perspective will assert that locally owned and available library resources should be searchable separately, either by search limit capability or through menu structures reflecting separation of data sets for owned versus accessible resources. This same approach will not be needed for digital publications since they are equally accessible when housed in the library's own computer, or in a foreign country, as long as they are in ftp sites.

It is certain that changes in the underlying concepts of bibliographic and content analysis will be needed for digital information sources, but what about the Provostial hope that it will all eventually become electronic. What will happen to technical services when there is less paper flowing through it units?

D. Change Agent: User Demands for Access

1. Elimination of Backlogs

After all paper collections housed in backlogs are treated on a project processing basis by staff previously dedicated to current cataloging, there will be a local assessment of priorities. A study of 12 Canadian OPAC's (Cherry, Williamson, Jones-Simmons, and Gu, 1994) demonstrates that few research libraries represent their collections fully in the library catalog. This is not due entirely to the lack of funding for retrospective cataloging. Much library material was never added to the catalog as a result of policy. Examples abound: video collections, government publications, ephemera, special collections and archives, microfiche sets, etc. In the interest of fuller access to all collections, many libraries are likely to address these historical deficiencies in catalog content, and retrospective cataloging will certainly continue. Indeed, additional arenas for retrospective cataloging are likely to surface, such as projects to provide access to (at least selective) federal documents which are now accessible only through the paper index *Monthly Catalog to Government Publications.* Retrospective, project, or backlog catch-up work will continue to be a substantial work load or candidate for outsourcing contracts. There must be an end to this source of work, where the value to users will not meet the test of cost.

2. Chapter Level Information

It is possible that cataloging units will undertake descriptions at a more detailed level. Monographic material, proceedings, and research literature could be analyzed at the chapter or section level. "Two modes of enhancing cataloging are to provide access to works, not packages; and to imbue the subject index with information on attributes of topics so users can explore the subject representation more fully via the catalog" (Younger, 1993, p. 80). Since, like journal indexing, this has never been performed by libraries but rather by commercial information providers as an added value over the "free" basic descriptive information provided by libraries, it is not at all clear how this level of cataloging will be delivered. Younger's discussion of enhanced cataloging implies that the incorporation of enhanced cataloging to any great extent into existing cataloging domains would require expert systems, computer-assisted indexing systems, or other software support not currently commercially available. In reporting on a project at the California State University system libraries to assess the feasibility and desirability of enhancing cataloging for monographs in content information, Weintraub and Shimoguchi (1993, p. 168) observe that "[AACR2] provides for the inclusion of chapter-level information through content or summary notes . . . but traditionally, catalogers have not taken advantage of this option. This is due in part to restrictions in time, staffing, funds, storage, and technology that have existed in cataloging operations and tools until recently." The authors urge a new approach to this idea, asserting that enhancement of content information for monographs is not only feasible, but desirable and consistent with most projections of patron demand and the need for informed decisions in the process of resource sharing.

A different type of enhanced cataloging would be required if the type of publishing envisioned by the Columbia Project (*University Support for Electronic Publishing*, 1994) ever materializes. A group of librarians, scholars, and publishers met at Columbia University in September 1994 to engage in tactical discussions on the best way to influence the development of scholarly publishing patterns which would support the widest possible free flow of information to the world's scholarly community. One of the major tactics recommended at this meeting was the concept of encouraging faculty to publish only in ways that facilitate the free flow of information both locally and well beyond the campus. One publishing method which would meet these goals involves the development of preprint systems and preprint servers on campuses around the globe. Each academic discipline would maintain preprint systems which would gather and disseminate preprinted works in all media. If this proposal were to become common practice, it would portend a new form of enhanced record cataloging. The entire preprint system, including databases, indexing, and access systems, and distribution/access systems could become the responsibility of technical services units.

Some enhanced cataloging programs are available now. These fall into at least two categories. One category is represented by commercial services providing internal document indexing access to paper documents of a monographic or reference nature, for a fee. Presently, the Blackwell TOC service is available on subscription, and the service through FirstSearch called ProceedingsFirst is on-line to thousands of libraries. Such programs and services are not coming out of libraries, but are instead part of the expanding number of commercial information services and products. They echo the journal indexing business to a great extent. If current trends are to continue, technical services units will not undertake this sort of cataloging or indexing as a rule, and commercial information providers will continue to stake this territory out as something for which to charge. In part, this is because library directors will be (by necessity) more interested in the staff savings possible through a reduced need for cataloging paper than in the additional access possible by enhanced cataloging in-house.

The other category is represented by many projects under way to provide access to the internal content or structure of digital text documents. Using standard mark-up indicators, access can be created to the entire document with searching capability extending substantially beyond the on-line catalog, MARC-based level of access. Probably among the most visible of these projects is the Center for Electronic Texts in the Humanities (Gaunt, 1994), but a number of projects exploring the capability of the virtual library are extending applications of text encoding standards.

3. HyperMARC

One scenario proposed by a number of authors addressing the future of MARC is that there is a need for entirely new assumptions on which to base cataloging standards; it has been suggested that all current cataloging theory rests on a mistake (Carpenter, 1992, p. 96): "the metaphor of a fixed-form display caused a whole branch of theory to form. It was a necessary mistake; fixed-form displays require a uniform heading to work easily." Carpenter proposes shifting focus from references to a fixed form of a name to creating links among various forms of the name. The idea of links moves into concepts more akin to hypermedia structures, and Michael Gorman, on this topic says, "that change would consist of replacing the unitary MARC record containing complex information and with few and weak links to other related unitary records. Its replacement (MARC III? HyperMARC?) would be a system based on multiple records for each physical object, set of physical objects, intellectually distinct part of a physical object, and work. Those records would contain simple data and would be linked in an articulated, complex and sophisticated manner." He goes on to say that "the elegance and flexibility of the system would reside in the various ways of linking these records to create a complex structure expressive of all the bibliographic relationships between works and objects" (Gorman, 1992, pp. 91–92). If this situation were ever to come true, the role of the cataloger would evolve from one where the emphasis is on description to one where the emphasis is on linkages which anticipate user needs as well as those which link works, objects, and forms of name. Pat Moltholt further expands this concept when she forecasts

> We will move from linear applications to hypermedia-based settings that provide tremendous freedom to follow thoughts and move through information or knowledge motivated by one's own view of the world or, indeed, to build worlds. Digression will be the norm and constraint unacceptable. . . . We need to spearhead research on the epistemology and application of inter-concept links so that users find consistency as they navigate in information or knowledge space and can reliably anticipate the results of their movement, or their leaping about. (Moltholt, 1993, p. 20)

These ideas help us draw some outlines of the new roles for those currently using cataloging codes and rules to make order for library users. "The truly radical approach would be to have catalogers performing such tasks as systems design and quality control, in addition to actually working with the public" (Wallbridge, 1991, p. 68). These concepts appear to be taking hold, as evidenced by the fact that at least one school of library and information science is now teaching mark-up language (SGML) as a system which must work together with existing standards such as MARC to support linkage-based finding systems on the World Wide Web.

E. Change Agent: Pressures on the Organization

The idea of catalogers serving as bibliographers, subject specialists, and working with the public is a good one which has been widely practiced for a very long time, and in most types of libraries. It hardly bears emphasis here. However, the underlying idea of a change in emphasis from processing to public services is questionable. Some staff shifts are likely, especially in the event of fixed budgets and a need for more staff devoted to accessing rather than acquiring collections. A great many writers (e.g., Williams, 1991, p. 32;

Martin, 1993; Intner, 1993) have commented on the increase in technical skills, the challenges of finding highly qualified staff to operate in the multisystem, multiformat environment of technical services, and of the trends toward fewer librarians and more technology-literate paraprofessionals. As libraries invest in microcomputers for staff use, multitasking enabled by integrated office software and Windows-like operating systems will create flexible staff workstations supporting fluid transitions among disparate job duties. But those who have argued that the most appropriate role for technical services professionals is in the arena of access system design, delivery, and maintenance are probably seeing the middle distant future most clearly. This role will require new teams of professionals and technicians from computing, information systems, telecommunications, and resource management specialties (Woodsworth et al., 1989). "The ability of librarians to be imaginative, to move outside of the library and into broader information roles, will be a measure of the future librarian. While it is likely that the profession will shrink and the credentials for membership broaden, the roles of designer and guide will be needed well into the future" (Moltholt, 1993).

Although current library organizations may have the systems office located inside the technical services division, as does the University of Michigan Library, most of the time, the systems office is a separate organization reporting to the director or a deputy director. With this reporting line, the systems office is centrally situated in order to support all library units' technology requirements. However, if a great deal of the responsibility of technical services relates not only to files and databases maintained or created by technical services, but is equally related to intersystem links, software development, and maintenance, the organizational connection between the systems office and technical services may shift. If it does not shift, then only the library owned and operated files will be maintained by technical services, and this is likely to be a declining part of the system responsibility, with an increasing part of the work lying in systems. The taxonomy for technical services (Intner, 1992) where technical services is at the center of a circle and "automation," or systems development and maintenance is a ring surrounding technical services is likely not to be the concept description for the future organization. Rather, technical services will be one user of the integrated system in which the library participates, and the management of all connections to that external system will be more predominant in the organizational hierarchy.

What of the changing relationship with public services, including reference, interlibrary loan units, and lending units? Although it may be true that the inner structures used to organize technical services divisions or departments have not changed greatly, there are new pressures at work forcing changes in how technical services fits into the library as a whole. Some sharp differences in perspectives between public and technical services librarians remain.

> their purposes are miles apart. Catalogers provide a product that is never judged too harshly, since it is only out of kindness and a sense of duty that libraries provide catalogs at all. It is a free service and, perhaps, not worth more than its price. Catalogers send their products (read: entries) out into the world, and, if users cannot decipher them, it shows how ignorant they are. If using the catalog requires several time-consuming searches, it isn't the cataloger's business. . . . The reference librarian . . ., on the other hand, is directly accountable to clients. (Intner, 1993)

Although this rather unkind portrayal of the cataloger may be exaggerated to make a point, the point can certainly reasonably be documented in many libraries across the land. Where will these dichotomies lead us in an era of access? The theme of focus on access while continuing to acquire ownership brings some blurring of lines, or convergence of missions which are explored in a series of papers edited by McCombs (1991).

Will these changes ever finally lead to the predominance of the matrix, nonhierarchical library organization chart? Automation seems to be the key predictor of the likelihood of that. Research on organizational change in the Association of Research Libraries shows that "libraries with a longer history of automation are more likely to see a decrease in the number of organizational levels and a flattening of the organizational structure" (Johnson, 1991, p. 61). This is combined with specialization, so that the number of units or departments in the library either stays unchanged or increases (Johnson, 1991, p. 62) with automation. So, one might project that eventually, the nature of the units will change, their number will increase, and their reporting structure will become flatter, with more interunit contact and exchange. When? Not very soon. Library organizations, according to Johnson's research, are very slow to change. After packing a stimulating discussion of indicators of the convergence of public and technical services with a series of organizational diagrams to demonstrate the options for organizational theories in place today, McCombs (1992) urges the "reassessment of the status quo," evolution, and a new emphasis on relationships among work units. She also points out that in order to change, librarians must develop tolerance for ambiguity, and concludes with a question about forging a new organizational structure: "Do we have the courage to attempt to define our own destiny and make one of those discontinuous leaps?"

F. Change Agent: Advances in Software

Since the 1970s, computer hardware costs declined for both mainframe and microcomputer systems, and new, more portable, and cost-effective storage systems have been available to libraries, once again primarily due to an emerging consumer market for office and home microcomputers. Although the compact disk is termed interim technology by a great many industry observers, it appears that as of this writing it is only now just moving into the consumer market as multimedia storage for the office and home computer consumer. It probably has a lively, colorful future which will have a number of effects on libraries.

The most dramatic effect is likely to be supporting the trend away from text-based information transfer toward image-based transfer. The video kids of today are learning to read with home multimedia and microcomputer software highlighting the ABCs and 123s. Although they are still comfortable with the bedtime story from a book, by the time many of them enter school, they are far more comfortable with pictures then text. The recent shift (supported by cheaper computer memory) toward graphical interfaces is consistent with the preferences not only of today's generation of video kids, but with the clear preference for intuitive, picture-symbol systems replacing, introducing, or supplementing command-driven and not necessarily mnemonic alphanumeric codes for word processing, spreadsheets, computer-aided graphic design, computer-aided management systems, and other business and home software.

Today, libraries are adding memory, upgrading from older microcomputers, and investing in systems to support graphical user interfaces. Contemporary integrated library systems either come compatible with the graphical operating systems or use linked user interfaces to provide this comfortable, intuitive front end. The concept of windowing, or linking between and among various information-seeking activities, is very attractive. People no longer want to stop doing one search to find something else. In fact, the completion of one search might involve using a completely different database or system to find the information required. Human curiosity can perhaps best be satisfied without forcing a completely linear, one step at a time logical progression. This represents a fundamental capability, and a trend which has some educators a bit worried. Will the next few generations of students be able to concentrate on the texts which have until now always been used to convey cultural, historical, scientific and other human knowledge? With film, hypertext, video, Windows, multimedia, and interactive teaching technologies, will they still be able to allow their minds to float above the text, with imaginations following from mere words on a page?

If libraries are to continue to fulfill their cultural role as the institutions which protect past knowledge for future generations, they may need to switch gears, being part of an endless process of translating text to image.

The existence of image-based teaching systems means that the acquisitions, cataloging, classification, and processing of image-based materials could require new skills for library staff, and will no doubt mean the library must invest in new systems to provide access to all varieties of imaging systems, and image products carrying information. Each picture or illustration in printed works, and each image in networked image libraries would need to be accessible—cataloged in some way. These and other developments will certainly mean that new software will have a significant impact since the workloads involved in image access would seem insupportable without help.

1. Natural Language Search Systems

At present, however, most libraries contain information predominantly in text or numeric form. New types of access systems are being developed by a merger of the fields of computer science and linguistics.

A few pilot projects are currently exploring the possible roles of natural language search engines. These search software systems create thesauri during the search process using principles of language systems such as frequency and word order to analyze word occurrence and create finding guides to content. Other linguistics-based systems, "probabilistic retrieval where documents are retrieved and ranked based on techniques that predict probability of relevance" (Norgren, Berger, Buckland, and Plaunt, 1993), have extraordinary potential to improve the quality of search results.

The availability of such systems to analyze the topics of full text documents eliminates the need for classification systems which rely on a cataloger to select from controlled vocabulary systems to assign topic terms to describe any item. Further, the full content can be indexed and accessible, depending on the internal structure of the digital document or item. Boolean searching, now an option or even built into the design assumptions of the current release of most integrated library systems for PAC searching, is primitive compared to "conditional search modifiers that can be invoked heuristically" (Belkin and Croft, 1987).

This sort of system, either linked to the conventional controlled vocabulary or keyword retrieval search engines in use now through searching of standard format descriptive records, portends an entirely new way of working in cataloging units. At Carnegie Mellon University, HELIOS, a natural language search system used to access the full text of a special collection, will be linked to their on-line catalog. However, in the future, if the trend line on computer capacity continues, natural language systems could actually replace current search engines in some cases, and could in other cases be an integrated part of the search engine designed for integrated library systems.

The Library of Congress/OCLC project for a national authorities database is moving ahead. Other such developments include the Library of Congress' use of the OCLC Site Search Z39.50 server software and the Newton search engine server software to load and immediately index cataloging copy received from other countries. But is there a better solution to be found in software design? It would be foolish to speculate on the timing of general commercial access to natural language systems, but once this happens, even with special, limited applications, questions about the functionality of authorities systems will arise that are even more profound or radical than the call for vocabulary and name control through HyperMARC.

2. Artificial Intelligence

Expert systems have five primary uses:

1. To make existing expertise more readily available, particularly in multiple locations.
2. To reach new levels of expertise by accelerating complex problem solving.
3. To free the expert to handle difficult cases while the system handles the more routine ones.
4. To preserve expertise that might be lost through retirement or resignation.
5. To enhance training through observation and analysis of the reasoning used by the system to reach its decisions (Ford, 1991, pp. 8–9).

For years, those who could follow the intricate and scientific explorations of computer-based information storage and retrieval research in journals, such as *Information Processing and Management: An International Journal,* have been tracking the development of artificial intelligence and expert system applications. But for just as many years, it has seemed to most library directors that these tentative efforts, on such a limited scale, have not meant very much.

So, with such attractive characteristics, when the potential staff savings of artificial intelligence or expert systems seems to be so great, and when the economic imperatives for libraries are clear, why have so few artificial intelligence applications been available? The answer seems to be that the cost, either to a library or to a vendor, of software development is simply too great for the limited market potential.

Artificial intelligence systems have been designed as prototypes, and time and again, the decision has been made not to put the system to a real test because the cost of upgrading from prototype is too great. Instead of designing systems to take full advantage of decision making without staff, artificial intelligence systems have been successfully developed which enhance the decision-making capacity, or the efficiency of staff. These helping or enhancing systems are likely to be those most rapidly emerging on the library software marketplace, as artificial intelligence shells are marketed which are easily learned and applied by library systems staff or other staff working on developments of artificial intelligence projects. Another area where intelligent systems might succeed is where the system might be flexibly applied as part of user interface systems (Denning and Smith, 1994). User interface systems may have somewhat greater market potential than systems designed to improve staff efficiency.

In a review of artificial intelligence applications in cataloging and acquisitions (Hawks, 1994), the conclusion is: do not give up yet! Despite the number of articles written about expert systems, development in the library world has been limited, with almost no operational system in widespread use. Bailey (1991) compares the development of expert systems to the development of home-grown automated systems and those marketed by vendors. "When did everyone start buying automated systems? The answer is, once a few entrepreneurial libraries and vendors developed viable ones."

3. Wide Area Information Networks

In the previous discussion of the choices for access to electronic journals, another development arena was mentioned. The shift from mainframe to mini-microcomputer networking based on client-server architecture has many ramifications for technical services which are already reflected in questions about what a catalog is or should be, and where the information seeker will look when trying to find a resource.

In theory, information collections could be scattered physically, yet an information seeker could rely on a single integrated listing of resources linked to finding aides, indexes, natural language search tools, or library catalogs, each of which could be the most appropriate search tool for the information resource. With more advanced applications of standards like the Z39.50, and with financial and data transactions standards, the information seeker should be able to forward her request to any selected resource, to any group of them, or to do a single search in all of them. How soon will this occur? Z39.50 compliant software is indeed coming right along. Most library catalog vendors have developed both client and server Z39.50-compliant software, but the functionality and variety of applications of the standard are still deficient. The true connectivity of scholar-level, comprehensive, sophisticated search qualities, with logic, limiting, filtering, saving, and reconfiguring search sets and searches is not yet possible among disparate systems and files.

An optimist would say that the trend, however, is clear. Interactivity between and among disparate systems and files will certainly take place at some time, although by the time it does take place, it may be based on entirely new and widely applied standards for bibliographic description and access, such as the concept of linkage rather than referral to a single form of name and such as natural language search systems rather than systems tuned to sets of controlled vocabularies.

It is not too soon to come to some conclusions about the purpose of a catalog and its place in a distributed, client-server information retrieval environment. Those environments exist now on many campuses and are represented in the structure (or nonstructure) of the Internet. What difference will it make to technical services units? The library will not be the only organization creating and maintaining information files and systems. Library staff are therefore likely to be expected not only to maintain files and systems funded through library funds, and related to library-located collections (both digital and traditional), but to create and maintain links between "library" catalogs and other catalogs.

To put this another way, library catalogs will no longer point to only what the library has, but may even devote more listings on its menus to what is not in the library: indexes to journals the library does not own, other library catalogs, full text files located on local computers and computers on other campuses, or commercial document delivery services like UnCover. From the user's perspective, the local library catalog which retrieves citations to documents is not the main thing on the list. Rather, the document itself is the main thing on the list.

V. Conclusion

A new order for the dissemination of information is certain, and the underlying stimulus for change in library operations is technology. Information technology has already enabled the creation of a vast choice of information sources, and the information industry offers a bewildering array of possible services. Changes in technology in the future will have a lasting impact over what is economically feasible for libraries. The economic, legal, social, and organizational frameworks which will emerge are still very obscure, but libraries in their transitional roles will continue to be central to the delivery of information when and where it is needed. Technical services operations, with shifting and changing materials, priorities, work loads, and system responsibilities, will therefore continue to be central to the integrated solutions which must be brought to bear on the new order for information dissemination.

References

Association of American Universities Research Libraries Project (1994). *Reports of the AAU Task Forces.* Association of Research Libraries, Washington, DC.

Association of Governing Boards of Universities and Colleges (1994). *Ten Public Policy Issues for Higher Education in 1994* (AGB Public Policy Series No. 94-1).

ARL Newsletter (1994). "AAU/ARL Demonstration Projects." **176**, 3.

Bailey, C. W. (1991). Intelligent library systems: Artificial intelligence technology and library automation systems. In *Advances in Library Automation and Networking.* JAI Press, Greenwich, CT.

Belkin, N. J., and Croft, W. B. (1987). Retrieval techniques. *Annual Review of Information Science and Technology* **22**, 109–145.

Benveniste, G. (1994). *The Twenty-first Century Organization: Analyzing Current Trends, Imagining the Future.* Jossey-Bass Publishers, San Francisco.

Bush, C., Sassé, M., and Smith, P. (1994). Toward a new world order: A survey of outsourcing capabilities of vendors for acquisitions, cataloging and collection development services. *Library Acquisitions: Practice and Theory* **18**, 397–416.

Carpenter, M. (1992). Does cataloging theory rest on a mistake? In *Origins, Content, and Future of AACR2 Revised* (R. P. Smiraglia, ed.). American Library Association, Chicago.

Cherry, J. M., Williamson, N. J., Jones-Simmons, C. R., and Gu, X. (1994). OPACS in twelve Canadian libraries: An evaluation of functional capabilities and interface features. *Information Technology and Libraries* **13**, 174–191.

Christensen, J. O. (1989). *Management of Technical Services in Libraries in the 1980s: A Selective Bibliography* (Public Administration Series: Bibliography #P 2759.). Vance Bibliographies, Monticello, IL.

Denning, R., and Smith, P. J. (1994). Interface design concepts in the development of ELSA, an intelligent electronic library search assistant. *Information Technology and Libraries* **13**, 133.

Dillon, M. (1993). *Measuring the Impact of Technology on Libraries.* A discussion paper, OCLC, Dublin, OH.

Drabenstott, K. M. (1994). *Analytical Review of the Library of the Future.* Council on Library Resources, Washington, DC.

Evans, G. E., and Heft, S. M. (1994). *Introduction to Technical Services*, 6th Ed. Libraries Unlimited, Inc. Englewood, CO.

Ford, N. (1991). *Expert Systems and Artificial Intelligence: An Information Manager's Guide.* Library Association, London.

Gaunt, M. I. (1994). Center for Electronic Texts in the Humanities. *Information Technology and Libraries* **13**, 7.

Geller, M. (1992). *Handling Electronic Journals in the Academic Library: The MIT Experience.* Paper presented at the Third National LITA Conference, Denver, Colorado, September 13–16.

Godden, I. P., ed. (1991), *Library Technical Services; Operations and Management*, 2nd Ed. Academic Press, San Diego.

Gorman, M. (1987). The organization of academic libraries in the light of automation. In *Advances in Library Automation and Networking*, Vol. 1, p. 152.

Gorman, M., comp. (1990). *Technical Services Today and Tomorrow.* Libraries Unlimited, Inc., Englewood, CO.

Gorman, M, (1992). After AACR2R: The future of the Anglo-American cataloguing rules. In *Origins, Content, and Future of AACR2 Revised* (R. P. Smiraglia, ed.). American Library Association, Chicago.

Gozzi, C. I. (1994). Technical processing, today and tomorrow: A scenario for one large research library. In *The Future is Now: The Changing Face of Technical Services.* Proceedings of the OCLC Symposium ALA Midwinter Conference, February 4, OCLC, Dublin, Ohio.

Graham, P. S. (1993). Intellectual preservation in the electronic environment. In *After the Electronic Revolution, Will You Be the First to Go? Proceedings of the 1992 Association for Library Collections and Technical Services President's Program* (A. Hirshon, ed.). American Library Association, Chicago.

Hawks, C. P. (1994). Expert systems in technical services and collection management. *Information Technology and Libraries* **13**, 203–212.

Hirschon, A. (1994). The lobster quadrille: The future of technical services in a re-engineering world. In *The Future is Now: The Changing Face of Technical Services. Proceedings of the OCLC Symposium ALA Midwinter Conference, February 4, 1994.* OCLC, Dublin, Ohio.

Intner, S. S. (1992). Education for technical services: Challenges for the twenty-first century. In *Technical Services in Libraries: Systems and Applications* (T. W. Leonhardt, ed.). JAI Press, Inc., Greenwich, CT.

Intner, S. S. (1993). *Interfaces: Relationships between Library Technical and Public Services.* Libraries Unlimited, Inc., Englewood, CO.

Intner, S. S., and Fang, J. R. (1991). *Technical Services in the Medium-Sized Library: An Investigation of Current Practices.* Library Professional Publications, Hamden, CT.

Johnson, P. (1991). *Automation and Organizational Change in Libraries.* G. K. Hall & Co., Boston.

Kaufman, P. T., and Mitchell, A. H., comps. (1994). *2001: A Space Reality: Strategies for Obtaining Funding for New Library Space* (SPEC Kit 200). Association of Research Libraries, Washington, DC.

LeBlanc, J. D. (1994). Cataloging in the 1990s: Managing the Crisis (Mentality). *LRTS* **37,** 423–433.

Lee, H. (1993). The library space problem, future demand, and collection control. *LRTS* **37,** 147–165.

Leonhardt, T. W., ed. (1992). *Technical Services in Libraries: Systems and Applications* (Foundations in Library and Information Science, Vol. 25). JAI Press, Inc., Greenwich, CT.

Library of Congress (1994). *Digital Library Summary* (Briefing material prepared for the fall 1994 meeting of the Association of Research Libraries meeting.)

Lockman, E. J. (1990). A perspective on library book gathering plans. In *Technical Services Today and Tomorrow* (M. Gorman, comp.). Libraries Unlimited, Inc., Englewood, CO.

McCombs, G. M., ed. (1991). *Access Services: The Convergence of Reference and Technical Services.* The Haworth Press, Binghamton, NY.

McCombs, G. M. (1992). Technical services in the 1990s: A process of convergent evolution. *LRTS* **36,** 135–147.

Martin, S. K. (1993). Achieving the vision: Rethinking librarianship. In *Libraries as User-Centered Organizations: Imperatives for Organizational Change.* The Haworth Press, New York.

Moltholt, P. (1993). Libraries as bridges; librarians as builders. In *Libraries and the Future: Essays on the Library in the Twenty-First Century* (F. W. Lancaster, ed.). The Haworth Press, New York.

Norgren, B. A., Berger, M. G., Buckland, M., and Plaunt, C. (1993). The online catalog: From technical services to access service. In *Advances in Librarianship* (I. P. Godden, ed.), Vol. 17. Academic Press, San Diego.

Perrault, A. (1994). The shrinking national collection: A study of the effects of the diversion of funds from monographs to serials on the monographic collections of research libraries. *Library Acquisitions: Practice and Theory* **18,** 3–22.

Racine, D., ed. (1991). *Managing Technical Services in the 90's.* The Haworth Press, New York.

Rush, J. E. (1994). A case for eliminating cataloging in the individual library. In *The Future Is Now: The Changing Face of Technical Services. Proceedings of the OCLC Symposium ALA Midwinter Conference, February 4, 1994.* OCLC, Dublin, Ohio.

Sassé, M., and Winkler, J. (1993). Electronic journals: A formidable challenge for libraries. In *Advances in Librarianship* (I. P. Godden, ed.), Vol. 17. Academic Press, San Diego.

Sassé, M., and Smith P. (1992). Automated acquisitions: The future of collection development. *Library Acquisition: Practice and Theory* **16,** 135–143.

Stanford University Libraries (1995). *Redesigning the Acquisitions-to-Access Process.* Available: http://www-sul.stanford.edu:8000/sul-as-org/redesign/redesign.html.

Stevens, N. (1993). Research libraries: Past, present, and future. In *Advances in Librarianship* (I. P. Godden, ed.), Vol. 17. Academic Press, San Diego.

University Support for Electronic Publishing (1994). A draft document of the Columbia University working group, submitted to the AAU/ARL research libraries steering committee. Chapel Hill, North Carolina.

Wallbridge, S. (1991). New partnerships within the library. In *Managing Technical Services in the 90's* (D. Racine, ed.). The Haworth Press, New York.

Weintraub, T. S., and Shimoguchi, W. (1993). Catalog record contents enhancement. *Library Resources & Technical Services* **37,** 167–180.

Williams, D. (1991). Managing technical services in the 1990's: The ruminations of a library director. In *Managing Technical Services in the 90's* (D. Racine, ed.), The Haworth Press, New York.

Woodsworth, A., and Williams, J. F., II (1993). *Managing the Economics of Owning, Leasing and Contracting Out Information Services.* Ashgate Publishing Ltd., Aldershot, England.

Woodsworth, A., *et al.* (1989). The model research library: Planning for the future. *Journal of Academic Librarianship* **15,** 132–138.

Younger, J. A. (1993). Virtual support: Evolving technical services. In *Virtual Libraries: Visions and Realities* (L. M. Saunders, ed.). Meckler Publishing, Westport, CT.

Literary Text in an Electronic Age: Implications for Library Services

Marianne I. Gaunt
Rutgers University Libraries
Rutgers–The State University
New Brunswick, New Jersey 08903

I. Introduction

There is tremendous interest in the delivery of ASCII and image full-text data in all disciplines over computing networks. Having timely access to journal articles, news wire services, technical reports, and government information is becoming increasingly important to users. Numerous articles in the library literature address collection development implications of electronic data, access versus ownership, copyright and fair use in an electronic environment, cataloging remotely accessible data, preservation, and user education. One might wonder why in this current environment the electronic literary text is being singled out for a separate review. Could the service implications presented by these texts be so unique that they require distinct treatment from other full-text data? Certainly many of the issues addressed in this review will be applicable to more than just electronic literary texts. However, a close examination of what these texts are and how they are used should demonstrate that the move from print to electronic form is much more than just a change in production and delivery systems. For humanities scholars, many of whom still question the value and relevance of computing for literary study, the electronic literary text may change forever their definition of "text" and force a reconceptualization of literary study itself.

Even though the production of electronic texts for use in humanities research began in the mid-1950s, it has only been in the 1990s that the academic library community has begun focusing its attention on providing access to these materials as part of its ongoing service program. This is due in some measure to the availability of high quality data, the production of which is linked to the maturity of humanities computing and its centrality to research and instruction in the field. As a result, only a small body of library literature addresses the specific needs of humanists in an electronic

ADVANCES IN LIBRARIANSHIP, VOL. 19

environment. Much of what is currently happening is being reported at professional meetings and discussed on electronic bulletin boards.

Electronic texts need to be viewed within the context of how literary scholars and students work so that the issues of access, documentation, service, and preservation can be fully addressed. A significant challenge for librarians will come from working closely with electronic primary source materials and the opportunity to assist more directly in their creation. A brief history of how electronic literary texts developed and are being used is important for assessing their current and future impact on library services.

II. History

Until 1990 or so the development of electronic literary texts could probably be defined as a cottage industry. Since 1949 when Father Roberto Busa began the *Index Thomisticus*, which signaled the advent of computing in the humanities, most electronic texts have developed as by-products of individual research projects. Busa's goal was to trace Aquinas' concept of divine immanence, which he determined could be linked to the occurrence of certain words in his texts (Raben, 1991). By creating a word list or concordance, he could trace these occurrences. However, before the concordance could be created, an electronic edition of Aquinas' works was necessary. Hockey (1994b) estimates that this by-product process accounts for 95% of all the existing ASCII texts in the hands of individual creators or projects. The remaining 5% are packaged products used with specific software and published by a wide variety of sources. Cataloging the existing major electronic text projects in the humanities at the Center for Text and Technology at Georgetown University, Neuman (1991) lists six broad creator groups for electronic texts. Commercial vendors and publishers comprise only 11% of the 339 developers represented in his catalog. Other developers include individual scholars, academic centers, libraries and museums, and research and development agencies.

During the early stages of humanities computing, from the 1950s through the 1970s (Burton 1981a,b), most of the major work in electronic text creation was done at research centers in European universities where public money was provided for the study of language and its relation to cultural heritage. For a variety of reasons, the textual databases that were created at these centers were usually only available to the researchers working on them. A few very large and significant projects, whose electronic data are now generally available, were in the first stages of development. Work began in the 1950s on a new national French dictionary and, as a result, a corpus of French literature was compiled as the *Trésor de la Langue Française*. Search access to texts from this database and other French texts is currently provided by the University of Chicago as the *American Research on the Treasury of the French Language (ARTFL)*. Another dictionary project, the *Dictionary of Old English*, compiled at the University of Toronto, resulted in a complete corpus of Old English. While not a dictionary project, the *Thesaurus Linguae Graecae (TLG)*, based at the University of California at Irvine, was one of the first attempts to create a complete corpus focused on a particular literature. Its data are now available on CD-ROM. During the same period, electronic texts were also accumulating in the hands of individual scholars, scattered throughout the world, who were creating texts for their own research projects.

By the late seventies, humanities computing had matured sufficiently that there was a growing recognition of the need for access to electronic texts already created. One of the most tedious and time-consuming aspects of literary and linguistic computing was then, and to some extent still remains, the creation of the electronic version from which to begin the research project. Even now the availability of commercially produced electronic literary editions is limited. In an effort to preserve electronic texts that had been compiled by scholars who had moved on to other areas of research and to facilitate humanities computing by the sharing of electronic texts, the Oxford Text Archive (OTA) was established at Oxford University, United Kingdom, in 1976. The preservation of existing texts and the sharing of texts among researchers were laudable premises for the OTA. However, the problems confronting the OTA are illustrative of the state of electronic literary texts almost to the present.

In an assessment of the OTA sponsored by the British Library, Proud (1989) reports that many of the texts arrived at the OTA without sufficient documentation about the edition on which the electronic text was based. Frequently absent was information about the markup or encoding scheme or the basis on which certain electronic editorial or encoding decisions were made. Was the electronic edition a faithful transcription of the original text; was there internal consistency in the markup scheme; were certain features normalized, etc.? Normalization refers to a process whereby specific features of the text are changed to a consistent form, such as modernizing the irregular spelling in older texts. These are basic questions any scholar wishing to reuse the text would want to know. Since these texts were prepared for specific research projects, their compilers were intimately familiar with them and did not find it necessary to have written or electronic documentation of these features. However, without this kind of documentation it was also impossible for anyone else to check on the quality of the work. With or without this documentation the OTA accepted these texts for deposit, provided a print catalog of their holdings, and subsequently made the catalog available on the Internet. In judging the quality of OTA's texts, most scholars said they relied on the scholarly reputation of the compiler in deciding whether or not to reuse a text.

What the experience of the OTA and the first attempt at sharing the texts did was to highlight the necessity for standards to encode data.

III. Standards

Encoding or markup refers to all the information included in an electronic text other than the substance or content of the text itself. This typically may include formatting information, textual apparatus (references to all the variant forms of the text, which appear in critical editions), notes, and analytic and interpretive information. Until recently, most compilers, even those associated with major text projects, such as the *TLG* and *ARTFL*, had to develop their own encoding schemes or markup language, which were frequently dependent on the software program that was used to analyze the text. While certain projects, like *Project Gutenberg* at the Benedictine University of Illinois (Hart, 1990; Basch, 1991), believe that the best and most system independent way to share textual data is in ASCII format with no markup, for most serious literary and linguistic research it is necessary to identify more features of a text than just the words and punctuation. According to Sperberg-McQueen (1991, p. 35), "markup reflects a theory of the text," and without markup, "no electronic tools working with such texts are likely to know anything interesting about it." Potter (1988) asserts that traditional literary scholars will need to do some changing of their definitions of the "text" if they are ever to accept computer text handling.

Over the years, different encoding schemes have been developed to describe a variety of textual features, but it is not possible to combine these schemes in one text or through an entire database of numerous texts to denote different textual features. Hockey (1994b) notes that many of the early encoding schemes tended to either describe typographic features of the text rather than the structure of the text or used the same encoding scheme to describe both the typographic and structural features. For example, italic script may be used to denote titles or chapter headings but also foreign words or emphasized words. How can a retrieval system distinguish among the usages of italic script in a single text? In addition, for scholars to share electronic texts so that each could work on the data for their own research purposes what was needed was a markup system that was independent of the software program that would analyze it, that would describe the structure of the text, and allow for the exchangeability of texts without the need for conversion programs.

In 1988, the Association for Computers and the Humanities, the Association for Computational Linguistics, and the Association for Literary and Linguistic Computing embarked upon a project to develop such a scheme, called the text encoding initiative (TEI). It was to be based on the standard generalized markup language (SGML). SGML was originally intended for use in the publishing field (van Herwijnen, 1994) and became an international standard in 1986. Sperberg-McQueen (1991) describes SGML as a metalanguage that is descriptive rather than prescriptive. It provides a means to encode the components or structure of a text. The markup used in the text is totally independent of any software program that is used with the text. As a result, any text marked up in an implementation of SGML can be expanded or added to by someone else, operated on by a variety of software programs, and printed out in a variety of formats.

One of the important features of SGML is that it can also provide links to materials that are not in ASCII text format, for instance, images and sound, which are normally stored in separate files from the text. An SGML tag can be used to mark the image and indicate its format and file name. Within the humanities community, the multimedia Perseus Project in 1987 was one of the first projects to use SGML for its Greek texts. Publishers and data suppliers, such as Oxford University Press, Mead Data Central, and Random House, have moved or are preparing to move their data to SGML (Hockey, 1993b).

The TEI is an implementation of SGML that provides guidelines for humanities applications (Sperberg-McQueen and Burnard, 1994). Various working committees within the TEI were set up to provide guidance both on the features of the text to encode and how to encode them. SGML introduced the concept of document types. Every SGML document is regarded as being of a specific type, and that type is defined by the document's constituent parts in a structure. Every SGML document, including the TEI, has a document type definition (DTD) which defines the tag sets permissible in that text and their relationships to each other. The TEI DTD is modular in that the user selects from an optional set of tags which characterize a particular type of text, such as prose, drama, spoken texts, manuscripts, or dictionaries. A software program, called a parser, can be used to run against the DTD to validate the tags in that text, which provides for internal consistency in an electronic text. Different documents of the same type can be processed in a similar way. Documents may have incompatable DTDs yet still be SGML conformant.

Another important feature of a TEI document is the document header, which is loosely anlogous to the cataloging in publication (CIP) in a printed work. The header is believed to be the first systematic attempt to provide in-file documentation of an electronic text (Hockey, 1993b). Figure 1 is an example of a very simple TEI header. It has all the elements described next except the profile description, which is not applicable to this particular text.

The header's four major components include the file description, encoding description, profile description, and revision description. The file description contains the typical catalog elements of title, statement of responsibility,

```
<teiHeader>
<fileDesc)
        <titleStmt>
                <title>Ben Jonson's "Volpone": electronic edition</title>
                <respStmt>
                        <resp>originally deposited by </resp><name>Hugh Craig, Dept.
                        of English, University of Newcastle, Australia</name>
                        <resp>initial SGML tagging </resp><name>Jeffrey Triggs at
                                Bellcore</name>
                </respStmt>
        </titleStmt>
        <editionStmt>
                <p>Public Domain TEI edition prepared at the Oxford Text
                Archive
        </editionStmt>
        <extent>
                Filesize uncompressed: 197 Kbytes.
        </extent>
        <publicationStmt>
                <distributor>Oxford Text Archive</distributor>
                <address>Oxford University Computing Services, 13 Banbury
                        Road, Oxford OX2 6NN; archive@ox.ac.uk</address>
                <idno>2032</idno>
                <availability><p>Freely available for non-commercial use
                provided that this header is included in its entirety with any
                copy distributed.</availability>
                <date>9 June 1993</date>
        </publicationStmt>
        <notesStmt><note>This is a prototype header</note></notesStmt>
        <sourceDesc><p>1607 Quarto edition. Scolar Press facsimilie edition.
        </sourceDesc
</fileDesc>
<encodingDesc>
        <editiorialDecl><p>All speeches, speakers and stage directions are
        marked.</editorialDecl>
        <refsDecl>
                <p>Acts (div1) bear n attributes in the form A1.</p>
                <p>Scenes (div2) bear n attributes in the form S1.1.
        </refsDecl>
</encodingDesc>
<revisionDesc>
        <change><date>Jan 94</date>
                <respStmt><name>JAT</name><resp>Final corrections and
                parsing</resp></respStmt>
        </change>
</revisionDesc>
</teiHeader>
```

Fig. 1 TEI Header from Oxford Text Archive text, modified at Center for Electronic Texts in the Humanities.

publication or distribution information, and bibliographic description of the source text on which the electronic edition is based. The encoding description documents the relationship between the encoded text and its sources. It documents editorial principles and practices made before or during the encoding, such as how ambiguities were resolved or how text was normalized. The profile description can include elements describing the circumstances or situation in which the text was produced. This is especially helpful for spoken language corpora. Frequently, such characteristics as the ages of the speakers, their geographic location, and the time span of the study are relevant for spoken language data. This type of information, as well as any other relevant situational information, can be recorded here. The revision description provides a log to document the history of any changes made to the text.

IV. Uses and Users

Computers and the Humanities (*CHum*), the premier journal in the field of humanities computing, was founded in 1966. It began as a newsletter and later expanded to a journal. *CHum*'s appearance was indicative of the increasing level of interest and activity within hunanities disciplines for using computing technology for research applications. Raben (1991), *CHum*'s founding editor, provides an overview of its first 25 years, relating the progress made in humanities computing since then. Burton (1981a,b) chronicles the very early years of humanities computing. The progress made in humanities computing applications is directly related to several factors: the availability of an electronic edition of the text(s), the development of an encoding scheme to represent the text in electronic form, the availability of software to perform the required functions, and the availability of disk storage to access data other than sequentially. The variety of applications in which humanists have used computing is apparent from the research reported in the literature over the years.

Concordance production was the earliest application and still remains common because it employs the most basic computing functionality. Concordances are word lists where each word (key word) is accompanied by references indicating the location of the occurrences of that word in the text. *Micro-OCP* and *TACT* are two of the more robust and flexible software programs for concordance production.

Stylometry, or the measurement of style, which is used to compare texts or to establish authorship, is another application. Frequently the words studied in stylometrics are common words (Mosteller and Wallace, 1964; Kenny, 1978; Burrows, 1987). Retrieval systems which operate on common words are not like the traditional bibliographic retrieval programs librarians use for database searching. Full-text searching software frequently searches on content words only, leaving out the common "stopwords" which are thought to interfere, such as "and" or "while." Indexing every word and distinguishing between homographic forms are, however, important for literary computing. Burrows' (1987) work on the novels of Jane Austen analyzed the common words to show gender differences in the characters and to describe their style of speech.

Other applications include syntactic analysis, lexical analysis, morphological analysis, and computational linguistics. A simple but effective way to conduct syntactic analysis is to investigate tenses or clauses by searching for words or patterns found within specific syntactic units. Vocabulary studies use collocations and lexical analysis. Software programs that sort words by their endings are used in analyzing rhyme schemes or for the study of morphology. The field of computational linguistics has been one of the most active within humanities computing. Walker (Hockey and Walker, 1993) claims that a frame of reference in which a text is considered or an "ecology of language" is necessary to properly analyze texts by computer. This refers to the relationship between particular uses of language and the contexts in which they occur. For example, the language used in a personal letter is different from that in a scientific paper, a news article, or a novel. Biber (1989) has identified eight classes in his topology of texts as a prerequisite for comparative analysis. These include intimate and personal interaction, informational interaction, scientific exposition, imaginative narrative, general narrative exposition, situational reportage, and involved persusasion. Potter (1991) asserts that in an ideal world literary critics would have waited for more complete descriptions of languages from computational linguistics; however, they began their analyses as these descriptions were being developed.

Potter (1988) claims that literary critics have not taken literary computing seriously. She posits that mainstream literary scholars have rejected the notion of using scientific (technological) methods to derive any information about texts because they lack training in or appreciation of scientific methods and that the literary technocrats have become absorbed in programming and statistics and have forgotten that they were seeking information about literature. According to Potter, what literary computing offers to literary criticism is "evidence, precision of measurement, and universally accepted standards of validity." She cites two practical impediments to the advance of literary computing as a discipline: the lack of existing software packages to meet broad-based research goals, and the lack of a truly easy method for text entry.

On the latter point, many have cited the use of optical character recognition (OCR) to facilitate text entry, but it still has limitations (Hockey, 1994a; Mintz, 1993). Although moderately useful with modern texts, the shortcomings of OCR entry relate to footnotes and marginalia, nonstandard characters, words in italic, and material printed before the end of the last century where characters bleed together. More importantly, OCR presents only a typographic representation of the text. In many cases it is easier to include the markup at the time of data entry, which involves entering (keying) both the markup tags and the text in one process.

Olsen (1993) claims that computing methodologies have not received acceptance within the broader humanities community because their results have not explained more than we already know. He proposes that those who use computers to read literature have fallen out of touch with current literary criticism, namely post structuralism. He suggests that poststructuralist methodologies would offer a theoretical backbone heretofore missing in humanities computing. According to Wolff (1994), poststructuralist methodologies are concerned with interpreting texts within particular critical discourses that meet specific political agendas. He posits that what has characterized the goals for much of humanities computing research thus far is "the irrefutable meaning of a text." Those seeking this goal would be incorrect to assume that poststructuralist methodologies would be a better means to attain them since poststructuralists mistrust the "true and universal interpretation of the text." McCarty (1993) believes the value of the computer is to analyze the multidimensional space where texts reside to map out all the structures that produce meaning.

With the advent of the TEI and the use of SGML-based encoding, several SGML-aware programs have made it easier for developers to create a tagged text and to search and retrieve data. Among these programs are *Author/Editor* from Softquad in Toronto, *Omnimark* from Software Exoterica, also in Toronto, and *MarkIt* from Sema Group in Belgium. Electronic Book Technologies in Rhode Island has developed SGML browser, *Dynatext;* Open Text Corporation in Waterloo has developed *PAT*, an interactive retrieval system; and Softquad has developed *Explorer*. Several large university libraries are currently providing access to electronic texts on their network using *PAT*, namely Princeton University, the University of Virginia, and the University of Michigan.

V. Collection Development

A. Local

Libraries may provide access to electronic texts for their users without ever collecting the texts themselves. Some texts are available for free or low cost from a number of archives or research centers. Libraries may simply help users find the text they need from existing sources. This is acceptable to those users who have search software, are familiar with humanities computing applications, and understand the concepts of markup so they can work independently. This may not be particularly useful for novices, where additional service support will be required. A few sites (institutions, archives, and projects) are making their public domain texts available on the Internet for searching. This level of access may suffice for many users who find the texts they need. However, the number of texts currently available in this manner is still very limited. As a result, libraries have begun collecting texts themselves.

Two surveys undertaken by Price-Wilkin (1991a,b) regarding academic libraries' use and support of electronic text files demonstrate the growth of activity over a 2-year period. Only a quarter of the 27 libraries responding to his 1989 survey were actually collecting texts. In 1991, well over half of the 27 libraries responding had begun to develop local collections.

As with other materials, those responsible for formulating collection development policies for electronic literary texts need to identify their audience and know that audience's needs and skills. While scholars in most academic institutions are involved in literary research and instruction, the level of interest and expertise related to computing applications varies, sometimes leading to the decision not to acquire such materials. Shreeves (1992) suggests that the potential of computing to affect humanities scholarship cannot be ignored and that librarians must continue to build alliances with those faculty who are users and convert the nonbelievers through a process of demonstration, education, and experimentation. "If librarians have a role . . . it will be to act as facilitators providing scholars with the resources necessary to develop and test new theoretical models." Seaman (1994) reports that new faculty and students are recruited to computer-aided textual study through numerous nurturing activities. Demas (1989) suggests that as part of a library's research and development program, specific audiences be targeted and that their response and success with these formats be carefully studied.

In order to make a significant contribution to research and teaching, electronic texts must meet the highest standards of scholarship and editorial accuracy (Neuman, 1991). In a February 1995 posting to the *ETEXTCTR* listserv, Peter Shillingsburg, Mississippi State University, described scholarly principles for the development of electronic editions. He suggests that an electronic text that is not a new edition should be an accurate reproduction of a specific print edition, including font changes or basic formatting, and should identify the specific print edition that it represents. A newly edited representation of an existing work should identify its source text(s) and describe the editorial principles used in creating the electronic edition. Accuracy for both types of electronic texts requires adherence to these principles and careful proofreading. In addition to accuracy, collection development decisions may be made on other factors, including the richness of the text's markup or the editorial principles of the markup or the edition on which the text is based.

In an article on the importance of mainstreaming electronic formats, Demas (1989) discusses five practical strategies, which he believes will ensure an intellectually coherent collection. Mainstreaming refers to the processes by which all forms of information transfer are incorporated into existing policies and operations. While he does not offer specific criteria for each kind of electronic format, he acknowledges that collection development policy statements may need to be developed for specific formats and genres of electronic publication. For some types of materials, librarians may replace a print version with an electronic one. For example, the flexibility offered by a CD-ROM index or abstracting tool may cause a library to cancel the paper equivalent. Price-Wilkin (1991a) believes that electronic literary texts will not replace but duplicate print holdings. Meshing policies for electronic formats with those for print may depend on experimentation, the costs of electronic information, availability of products, software compatibility, hardware and maintenance, and staffing.

Selectors of electronic literary texts are confronted with two impediments to selecting materials: the lack of bibliographic tools to identify them, which will be discussed later, and the lack of reviewing media to evaluate existing products. The lack of reviewing media is complicated by the fact that there are no broadly defined standards of what constitutes a high quality electronic text. Rarely have there been multiple editions of the same texts from which to make comparisons. Shakespeare's works and the Bible are current exceptions. Reviews of large-scale products may be included in journals, such as *Computers and the Humanities*, or incorporated into journal articles discussing the status of electronic texts (Bolton, 1990; Shreeves, 1992). Frequently the best source of information concerning particular texts is on electronic bulletin boards, such as the *HUMANIST* Discussion Group, the Electronic Text Centers Discussion Group (*ETEXTCTR*), or the listservs of particular interest to the specific disciplines within the humanities.

Selection of electronic formats cannot be made without regard to the service implications they present. Unlike print materials that readers can use independently, electronic texts will require hardware, software, technical support, and user instruction. These factors must be taken into account as selection criteria are developed. For literary applications the choice of edition is critical. Since the electronic editions acquired are now most often based on a source text, the decision to acquire a particular edition will most likely be based on the merit of the printed text. However, the quality and authenticity of the electronic text must also be judged. Electronic versions of many printed works currently under copyright are not available. Individual scholars and even some publishers have chosen to produce electronic editions of works in the public domain to avoid copyright problems, which raises questions of editorial quality.

The choice of a particular electronic format of a literary text has implications for service delivery and support. Many libraries have started their collection of electronic literary texts with CD-ROMs. The packaged products combining texts and searching software with a user-friendly interface are usually easy to use. However, some CDs have very poorly designed user interfaces. Lack of clear documentation with some products is another potential problem, if the expectation is that workstations with data will be left for self-use by library patrons. The text in CD-ROMs cannot be unbundled from the software, thus limiting its application. Price-Wilkin (1991a) notes, however, that no single software program will provide for all possible types of applications. Providing local network access or remote access to CD-ROM texts may also be a problem. CD-ROMs are normally useful for instructional purposes, frequently include images, and may be useful reference sources for librarians and those outside the discipline.

Many texts are available in straight ASCII form without markup, but require a software program to make them useful. Providing texts in this way requires more staff support and user involvement. In addition, searching on datafiles that have no markup is somewhat limiting. Some vendors, such as Chadwyck-Healey, make data with markup available to be used with separate searching software. The level of research that can be achieved through this mode of access is dependent on the amount of tagging in the texts and the sophistication of the search software.

Collection development librarians need also to consider copyright and licensing agreements for electronic materials (Lowry, 1993). It is important to know in advance what restrictions will be placed on the use of the text, such as copying, printing, or downloading, and user population, among them. The cost of electronic texts may vary with the form of access. Single user access will be less expensive than multiple user access on a networked version. The publishers of most scholarly texts retain all rights of ownership but grant the licensee (the library) only those rights specified in the contract. The Coalition for Networked Information's project READI is developing guidelines for those negotiating contracts for networked information (Ubell and Tesoriero, 1994). Publishers and vendors have no models from which to draw practical information regarding pricing schemes and licensing agreements for the use of full-text information in a networked environment. Garrett (1991) discusses the Copyright Clearance Center's pilot projects to investigate how electronic full-text materials are being used. Lanham (1989) points out the intellectual property problems posed by interactive texts.

Demas (1989) notes that all the skills necessary to make these collection decisions are rarely found in one person or one part of the organization. Collection development librarians will need close collaboration with public services, technical services, and systems staff for some time to come as experience is gained in using these formats.

B. Cooperative

Cooperative collection development for electronic texts has occurred on a very limited scale. Because of copyright restrictions on electronic resources produced by commercial vendors, the typical interlibrary loan function commonplace for print sources is problematic. However, some libraries have formed consortia to purchase jointly several large-scale databases, such as those published by Chadwyck-Healey. The need for cooperative collection development for electronic texts in the public domain available freely from archives and other sources may not be necessary, as each library can have its own copies. Collaboration can exist, however, in the creation of new electronic texts to be put on the network for broad access. In order to avoid duplication in such conversion projects, bibliographic access for those texts already available and some form of register for new projects underway are necessary.

VI. Bibliographic Control

A. Identifying Sources

One of the more problematic aspects of developing the electronic text center will be identifying the electronic texts for acquisition. The difficulty in locating texts derives from the history of how many existing humanities text files were created and the relative immaturity of the publishing field in this area. Lowry's (1994) selective bibliography on electronic texts provides a reference list for information concerning electronic texts, which incorporates many of the sources one needs to search in order to identify materials. No equivalent to *Books in Print* exists for electronic data, and because only a small number of libraries have begun collecting and cataloging these texts, their appearance as cataloged records on the bibliographic utilities is still limited. There are, however, a number of sources for information concerning the availability of electronic texts, each with varying degrees of comprehensiveness.

Hoogcarspel (1994) and Neuman (1991) describe two ongoing humanities projects that are attempting to gather information about existing files; one on the individual text level and the other on the project level. In 1983 the Rutgers University Libraries, with funding from the Council on Library Resources, began an *Inventory of Machine-Readable Texts in the Humanities.*

The purpose of the *Inventory* was to identify electronic texts in all humanities disciplines that would be potentially useful for research and to publicize their existence by cataloging them on a national bibliographic network, RLIN. In addition to providing a bibliographic tool for the location of electronic texts, the inventory staff were some of the earliest users of the MARC format for machine-readable datafiles (MDF), now called computer files. The problems of using the MARC format to describe full-text humanities files are discussed later. The *Inventory* now describes more than 1600 individual records, many from the Oxford Text Archive, and continues under the auspices of the Center for Electronic Texts in the Humanities (Gaunt, 1994; Hockey 1993a).

The second project began in 1989 at the Center for Text and Technology at Georgetown University. The goal of the *Georgetown Catalogue of Projects in Electronic Text* is to gather information on the structure of projects that were producing electronic texts. Excluded from the catalog are lexicographical projects, computer-assisted instruction, relational databases, and tools for linguistic and literary analysis unless they contain full-text components. While the catalog itself does not identify individual texts, the projects it describes are potential sources for texts. The information in the catalog is made available for searching on the Internet (Neuman and Mangiafico, 1994).

Both the *Rutgers Inventory* and the *Georgetown Catalog* rely on personnel to monitor the published literature, especially journal articles, and electronic bulletin boards for information. Since both of these projects refer primarily to texts that reside elsewhere, there is no assurance that the texts reported on have been maintained or that the information concerning the project or text has not changed since it was last recorded. David Seaman at the University of Virginia Libraries announced in February 1995 on the *ETEXTCTR* discussion list that he was willing to maintain a database of information regarding TEI texts that are currently being created.

B. Cataloging

The rules for the bibliographic description of electronic texts appear in the *Anglo-American Cataloging Rules,* second edition, 1988 revision (AACR2), chapter 9 (ALA, 1988). The cataloging information describing a particular electronic text using AACR2 is transcribed into the MARC format record and is maintained in a local online catalog and normally also in a national bibliographic database. Most catalogers would probably agree that the MARC format is flexible and that there is a place in the record to record all the information desired, even if only in a note field. The information that humanities scholars believe is important to document an electronic text is included in the TEI guidelines under the "header" description. Since the header chapter in the TEI guidelines was developed by the Text Documentation Committee composed of humanities scholars, archivists, and librarians, it is not unusual to see that the header's contents have the characteristics of a catalog record with the addition of encoding and revision profiles. It was not, however, the intention of the TEI to have text compilers create catalog records but rather to have them supply all the information necessary to describe the text so that a catalog record could be created from it. As a result, one would assume that mapping from a TEI header to the MARC record would be very straightforward.

The required elements in the TEI header's file description map very well to MARC: statement of responsibility, title, bibliographic information concerning the source on which electronic edition was based, and a publication statement. Even the optional elements of edition, physical description, series, and notes have equivalent MARC fields. Using these search parameters in an on-line catalog would make the retrieval of a particular text similar to that of a printed book. However, the type of information contained in the profile and revision descriptions included in the header are analogous to information in social science data codebooks, and this level of detail is not normally recorded in a catalog record. The text of these descriptions could appear in a note field, but most likely would not be searchable through many on-line catalogs (Giordano, 1994; Hoogcarspel, 1994). This information could be reviewed only after records were retrieved by some other means.

Hoogcarspel (1993, 1994) reports that the *Rutgers Inventory* expands cataloging rules to provide access points for language, time period, genre, and subject headings for literary texts because users frequently look for electronic editions that way when beginning a research project. She notes that the primary thesaurus used for genre terms was developed for use by rare book and archive collections. While useful, it does not provide sufficiently descriptive terminology for the humanities computing environment.

Dunlop (1995) has suggested that a database of TEI headers available in print or on the Internet would be a valuable tool for humanities scholars. The TEI guidelines have taken this into account in their chapter on the independent header. The richness of the header data, which is in structured form, could be searched by a variety of software systems. Giordano (1994) notes that the value of such a database would be limited, however, by the lack of a controlled vocabulary. Most scholars, archives, and projects rarely have catalogers assisting in the creation of these headers, which results in a lack of authority control (controlled vocabulary) for uniform titles, personal and corporate names, subject, and place names.

VII. Service Implications

In order to provide local access to electronic texts, a number of research libraries have established electronic text centers within their organizations, most notably Columbia University (Lowry, 1990), Indiana University, Rutgers University, the University of Iowa, the University of Michigan (Price-Wilkin, 1991a; Warner and Barber, 1994), and the University of Virginia (Seaman, 1994). While each of these libraries has structured their center in a way that best meets their organizational needs, a number of issues are being addressed by all of them. First and foremost is determining a service mission.

A. Mission

There are numerous ways in which to provide services for these materials, but the amount of staffing, the available expertise, space, equipment, library and faculty interest, and budget are some factors that may affect the mission. Electronic literary texts comprise a significant portion of the full-text data at most existing centers but other humanities datafiles may be treated similarly. In determining the service mission, some questions to ask include: who are the clientele, what kinds of services will be offered, and who will be providing these services? Will there be a coordinator for the center and what are the coordinator's responsibilities? At what times and under what circumstances will service be offered? How will any staff training be accomplished, and will the center be incorporated in existing service space or a separate area?

B. Services

Services that the centers may provide include identifying and locating appropriate electronic texts and software, providing access to texts available on the Internet but not owned by the center, instructing users in how to operate searching software on their own texts or texts that the center provides, creating texts for the center or helping users create and tag their own texts, tagging and indexing texts that the center acquires, preparing headers for texts that users create, advising on software programs for text manipulation, assisting users with scanning (OCR) equipment, preparing documentation, and digitizing images.

C. Staffing

Providing access to full-text primary resources presents challenges that print resources or even some electronic bibliographic files do not. While a considerable amount of data is available in English, a significant body of literary text is in foreign languages, most notably Greek, French, Hebrew, Latin, and German, but in other languages as well. Broad language facility is most typically associated with catalogers and bibliographers, yet these librarians do not always share in public service responsibilities. New opportunities may exist for catalogers and bibliographers in providing service for electronic texts. Graduate students are also being used in several text centers because they bring additional language and subject skills for staffing support. In turn, they benefit from the experience gained in using computing applications which may be useful for their own research.

In addition to language facility, subject expertise is particularly useful when dealing with electronic literary texts. Typical data retrieval systems operational in most libraries for the on-line catalog or subject database operate on specific fields or key words. While this type of software can be useful for literary research, it is quite limited. Librarians need to be conversant with the kinds of research being done in language and literature studies so they can evaluate separate software programs and texts bundled with software (usually CD-ROMs) to determine their level of sophistication.

The need for technical expertise cannot be underestimated in dealing with electronic texts. While the plethora of workstations already in libraries for the on-line catalog, CD-ROMs, and other databases has already demonstrated the need for technical support, full-text data present the specific challenges already mentioned. Some text centers have sought the cooperation of their computing centers and shared staff resouces for setting up and maintaining equipment, networking, and maintaining texts residing on a local server.

D. Organizational Structure

Service for electronic texts can be successfully provided regardless of the organizational structure in which the service resides as long as responsibilities are clearly delineated and communication is effective. However, the experience of operating text centers in libraries suggests that there should be one person acting in a coordinator's role to oversee the operation. Among the responsibilities of the coordinator may be scheduling and training staff, monitoring the copyright and licensing agreements for access to the texts, preparing or assigning responsibility for preparing documentation, selecting equipment, overseeing network design, and coordinating or implementing publicity and outreach efforts. The selection of the electronic texts for the center is usually accomplished in cooperation with collection development librarians.

E. Access

Some electronic text centers have purchased ASCII data from publishers or through the OTA. They have determined that access to all or a substantial portion of their text holdings will be on the campus network with access provided through a common interface and search software (Price-Wilkin, 1991a; Seaman, 1994; Warner and Barber, 1994). This requires considerable planning and technical support. ASCII files need to be indexed before they can be run against a software program. The burden of deciding what to index falls to the librarian, who must predetermine how the texts will be used in order to index them to permit these queries. In addition, any tagging of the text to represent its structure, and thereby facilitate searching, will also need to be done. This is a labor-intensive process requiring specialized technical skills and involves an interpretation of the text itself. Training in using SGML and knowledge of the TEI guidelines are the technical prerequisites for this undertaking. Without tagging the text, users would be limited to simple string searching, which may only provide limited results. While staff and training are required, the benefits of this access mode are numerous. The database can grow as more texts are added over time; users can enrich texts by adding tags useful for their research; the specificity of searching is increased by the addition of tagged fields and elements; the text can be tagged for formatting on the screen; and as new SGML software is developed the texts can still be used. The amount of time required to instruct users is reduced as the number of specialized software programs decreases. Murphy (1994) evaluates some of the SGML editors that can assist both in tagging and validating tagged texts.

In addition to the texts themselves, a selection of searching software is necessary. SGML-aware software, such as Open Text's *PAT* software, is a common choice for networked database access (Seaman, 1994; Warner and Barber, 1994). EBT's *Dynatext* is another SGML-aware program, but as yet it has no networked version; Softquad's *Explorer* is another. General purpose programs such as *TACT* and *WordCruncher*, or specialized software such as *Micro-OCP*, *Storyspace*, *Kleio*, *Collate*, and *Guide* are examples of software being used for humanities applications. The most commonly used software for this purpose in existing electronic text centers is Open Text's *PAT* software.

Because the work of literary scholarship is an individual and private process, Price-Wilkin (1991a) notes that providing the faculty with remote access from home or office is desirable.

F. Training

Training is both a staff development as well as a user education issue. Providing access to primary resource material in an electronic form is a new service for most libraries. The concept of tagged texts, SGML, and the TEI are unfamiliar to many librarians, humanities faculty, and students alike. Librarians have rarely selected software with such specialized applications. The methods used to perform these services have yet to be incorporated into professional or academic degree programs. New librarians and recent graduate students are unlikely to address these topics in their curriculm. How then are librarians learning to cope with them?

Within the American Library Association (ALA) collection development discussion groups have provided the first impetus for dealing with electronic literary texts. The Center for Electronic Texts in the Humanities (Gaunt, 1994) conducts a 2-week seminar on the topic of tools and methodologies for humanities computing; the rare book school at the University of Virginia is offering similar workshops. ACRL's new electronic text centers discussion group and its electronic bulletin board, *ETEXTCTR*, provide support groups. Articles in the library and humanities computing literature provide current information. Programs at meetings of library associations offer opportunities for shared wisdom and practical experiences. Several professional organizations for the humanities disciplines have subcommittees on computing, which can be equally useful for librarians. As skills develop within each library they are shared among team members working with electronic texts.

User education has taken on several forms at libraries with electronic text centers. These include creating documention for various products, preparing brochures describing how to access services, and one-on-one instruction in the use of electronic data. Introductory classes are held for targeted groups when the library has materials of interest to them (Seaman, 1994).

VIII. Preservation

With a few notable exceptions, such as the TLG for Greek language and literature and the ARTFL database for French literature, most scholars have not had the luxury of a large database from which to select texts on which to work. They have had to create their own electronic texts in order to attempt a computer analysis. As Meserole (1990) notes, the body of information needed for literary research is not only the text itself but every scrap of information found in the corollary data that extends its literary boundaries. The work of literary scholarship requires considerable retrospective conversion of existing print resources in order to provide the basis necessary for research. The preservation of print collections through digitization may provide the foundation for the creation of large-scale database that will benefit humanities computing research. A report sponsored by the Research Libraries Group (Gould, 1988) and several articles elaborate on the present and future information needs of humanists (Farrell, 1991; Pankake, 1991; Wiberley, 1991; Wiberley and Jones, 1989). It is clear these scholars rely heavily on primary source material and want better access to it. The Getty Art History Information Program, the Coalition for Networked Information, and the American Council of Learned Societies have sponsored a national initiative (Getty AHIP, 1994) aimed at giving the arts and humanities a prominent role on the National Information Infrastructure. Their report outlines not only humanists' needs but the technical requirements to support them in an electronic environment. It also notes that "digitizing the centuries of existing humanities and arts information will be a long and expensive process that will only be worthwhile if it is built with an eye toward anticipated use and accompanied by software applications and tools that make possible a new dimension of learning and experience." The National Digital Library to be created by the Library of Congress (LC), in collaboration with other libraries, may benefit the humanities as LC's collections are digitized. However, for literary scholars, the intellectual content as well as the appearance of the text needs preservation in the electronic environment. Combined access to the image of the text with the ability to manipulate the data is critical. Hockey (1994a) warns that while digital imaging is important from an archival perspective, storing the image in a proprietary format linked to specific software will recreate all the problems that existed with text stored in a proprietary indexing program. It may be unusable for future applications. Lesk (1992) notes that preserving electronic information means moving information from old to new technologies as they become available, or as older technologies are no longer supported. Instead of preserving the medium, the information is preserved. In any case, the electronic record must be in a format that can migrate to new systems and be software independent. Taylor (1994) points out the archival role of libraries and the uncertainties associated with digital storage for the long term as compared to other more established formats.

Mohlhenrich (1993) describes a broad spectrum of research and development efforts in digital preservation using some humanities projects as examples. The focus is both on preserving print collections in digital form and on preserving the electronically stored data itself. As Garrett (1991) notes, in the electronic environment, text is easily and transparently modified, its authorship may be debated, and its modification difficult to trace. Electronic documents may be altered inadvertently or changed purposely. A mechanism for determining authentication of the electronic record is needed. Graham (1994) and Lynch (1994) discuss the many issues related to the integrity of digital information, whereas Haber and Stornetta (1991) relate one way to authenticate documents. Lynch (1993) gives a broad overview of the many issues related to networked information, including access, confidentiality, copyright, documentation, integrity, preservation, and standards.

IX. New Directions

Neuman (1991) notes increasing interest among publishers in electronic literary texts. Oxford University Press has developed its own electronic publishing division, and Chadwyck-Healey has begun two major electronic literary projects. Some publishers, unwilling to undertake their own projects, have signed contracts with developers to produce electronic editions of their standard critical editions. Publishers, for the most part, have focused their electronic developments primarily in the area of bibliographic databases and journal publication, not monographs. In a presentation discussing how the University of Chicago Press is gearing up for electronic publication, Owens (1993) says that it is easier for presses to work from author's manuscripts for journal articles than for monographs. In monograph production, much time is spent in reconciling the author's electronic file with the typesetting of the book. Each monograph is unique. For journal production the editorial and typesetting style and the coding are constant and known in advance. Decisions at the author and editor level are simplified. Many presses, especially smaller scale university presses, find it difficult and expensive to maintain current production operations while changing technology. Nonetheless, the University of Chicago Press is moving toward coding all their data using SGML, which will generate typesetting and form the basis for any future electronic delivery. Mintz (1993) reports on similar concerns of other publishers as they consider the legal, financial, and technological ramifications of moving to electronic publishing.

In some cases, university presses are collaborating with their respective libraries to experiment in electronic publication. *SCAN*, Scholarship from California on the Net, is one such example. A pilot project to facilitate broad scholarly access to the full-text of humanities journals and monographs on the Internet, SCAN is a collaboration of the University of California Press, the University Libraries at Berkeley, Irvine, and Los Angeles, and the division of library automation of the office of the president. The project is beginning with the journal *Nineteenth-Century Literature*.

Professional societies are looking for ways to assist their authors in the preparation of electronic editions (Neuman 1991). Projects, such as the Model Editions Partnership with David Chesnutt at the University of South Carolina as principal investigator, will give scholars preparing documentary editions a guidebook on how to structure their electronic text for both print and electronic publication.

Rubinsky (1993) suggests that we do not know how data will be used, viewed, and manipulated in the future. Many technological inventions of the past were used popularly in ways that were never envisioned. New and different applications were made of them. Electronic text may follow. Efforts expended in the present need to prepare us for all future applications. Hypertext (Landow and Delaney, 1991) and hypermedia have already changed our thinking about the sequential reading and analysis of text and demonstrated their power as pedagogical tools. Lanham (1989) suggests that technology will create a new rhetoric of the arts, as the arts create new relationships through digital equivalencies. Within the university the result will be a reexamination of the arts curriculum and the place of literary study in it. Both he and Rubinsky (1993) ask if we are in the book business or in the information business. Smith (1990) posits that the research library of the future will provide access to a consolidated electronic record of the world's scholarship achieved through a collaborative effort of research libraries to preserve the past in electronic format and by publishing electronically into the future. However, both Rubinsky (1993) and Smith (1990) note that we will drown in information unless easy access is provided by effective indexing or the future equivalent of the fast forward button on the video.

The particular needs of the humanist, who studies the text as object, may easily be lost in the quest to move from print to electronic distribution of text. The Center for Electronic Texts in the Humanities (CETH) (Gaunt, 1994), a collaboration of Princeton and Rutgers universities, was formed in 1991 to focus attention on the needs of the humanities scholars working with texts and computing. The activities of CETH include promoting the use of standards, providing educational programs, acting as a clearing house for information, and collaborating with other projects to support the development of tools and electronic texts.

X. Conclusion

The electronic literary text has the power to transform the concept of "text," the way that literary research is conducted, and the way humanities instruction is delivered. However, we are still in the very early stages of this development. In order for this transformation to take place, literary scholars will need large textual databases that contain both literature and other documents that surround their explorations. The development of a large body of electronic texts is a slow process that may be hastened by major preservation activities. The shift in primary source material from print to electronic in the humanities disciplines is a cultural change, which up to now has been hampered by a lack of standards and software. Libraries will be part of the development cycle of electronic texts as users are educated as to their potential and are assisted in developing their own texts, ensuring that standards are developed and used. As the availability of electronic texts increases, libraries must be prepared to acquire and provide access to them. As preservation projects emerge, we must ensure that the standards necessary to use these materials into the future are guaranteed.

References

American Library Association (ALA) (1988). *Anglo-American Cataloging Rules*, 2nd Ed. ALA, Chicago.

Basch, R. (1991). Books online: Visions, plans, and perspectives for electronic text. *Online* **15**, 13–23.

Biber, D. (1989). A typology of English texts. *Linguistics* **27**(2), 3–43.

Bolton, W. (1990). The bard in bits: Electronic editions of Shakespeare and programs to analyze them. *Computers and the Humanities* **24**, 275–287.

Burrows, J. (1987). *Computation into Criticism: A Study of Jane Austen's Novels and an Experiment in Method.* Oxford University Press, Oxford/New York.

Burton, D. (1981a). Concordance-making: Fifties. *Computers and the Humanities* **15**, 1–14.

Burton, D. (1981b). Concordance making: Early sixties. *Computers and the Humanities* **15**, 83–100.

Demas, S. (1989). Mainstreaming electronic formats. *Library Acquisitions: Practice & Theory* **13**, 227–232.

Dunlop, D. (1995). Practical considerations in the use of TEI headers in a large corpus. *Computers and the Humanities* (in press).

Farrell, D. (1991). The Humanities in the 1990's: A perspective for research libraries and librarians. *Library Hi Tech* **9**(1), 69–71.

Garrett, J. R. (1991). Text to screen revisited: Copyright in the electronic age. *Online* **15**(2), 22–24.

Gaunt, M. I. (1990). Machine-readable literary texts: Collection development issues. *Collection Management* **13**, 87–96.

Gaunt, M. I. (1994). Center for electronic texts in the humanities. *Information Technology and Libraries* **13**, 7–13.

Getty Art History Information Program (AHIP) (1994). *Humanities and Arts on the Information Highways, A Profile.* Final Report of a National Initiative sponsored by the Getty Art History Information Program, The American Council of Learned Societies, the Coalition of Networked Information. AHIP, Santa Monica, CA.

Giordano, R. (1994). The documenting of electronic texts using the text encoding initiative headers: An introduction. *Library Resources & Technical Services* **38**, 389–401.

Gould, C. C. (1988). *Information Needs in the Humanities: An Assessment.* The Research Libraries Group, Stanford, CA.

Graham, P. S. (1994). *Intellectual Preservation: Electronic Preservation of the Third Kind.* Commission on Preservation and Access, Washington, DC.

Haber, S., and Stornetta, W. S. (1991). How to time stamp a digital document. *Journal of Cryptology* **3**, 99–111.

Harloe, B., and Budd, J. M. (1994). Collection development and scholarly communication in the era of electronic access. *Journal of Academic Librarianship* **20**, 83–87.

Hart, M. S. (1990). Project Gutenberg: Access to electronic texts. *Database* **13**, 6–9.

Hockey, S. (1993a). Developing access to electronic texts in the humanities. *Computers in Libraries* **13**(2), 41–43.

Hockey, S. (1993b). Encoding standards; SGML and the text encoding initiative: What and why? In *Scholarly Publishing on the Electronic Networks, the New Generation: Visions and Opportunities in Not-for-Profit Publishing. Proceedings of the Second Symposium* (A. Okerson, ed.), pp. 59–64. Association of Research Libraries, Office of Scientific and Academic Publishing, Washington, DC.

Hockey, S. (1994a). Electronic texts in the humanities: A coming of age. In *Literary Texts in An Electronic Age: Scholarly implications and library services* (B. Sutton, ed.), pp. 21–34. Graduate School of Library and Information Science, University of Illinois, Urbana Champaign.

Hockey, S. (1994b). Evaluating electronic texts in the humanities. *Library Trends* **42**, 676–693.

Hockey, S., and Walker, D. (1993). Developing effective resources for research on texts: Collecting texts, tagging texts, cataloging texts, using texts and putting texts in context. *Literary and Linguistic Computing* **8**, 235–242.

Hoogcarspel, A. (1993). *Guidelines for Cataloging Monographic Electronic Texts at the Center for Electronic Texts in the Humanities* (CETH Technical Report, 1993). Center for Electronic Texts in the Humanities, New Brunswick, NJ.

Hoogcarspel, A. (1994). The Rutgers inventory of machine-readable texts in the humanities: Cataloging and access. *Information Technology and Libraries* **13**, 27–34.

Kenny, A. J. P. (1978). *The Aristotelian Ethics.* Clarendon Press, Oxford.

Lanham, R. A. (1989). The electronic word: Literary study and the digital revolution. *New Literary History* **20**, 265–290.

Landow, G. P., and Delaney, P., eds. (1991). *Hypermedia and Literary Studies.* MIT Press, Cambridge, MA.

Lesk, M. (1992). *Preservation of New Technology: A Report of the Technology Assessment Advisory Committee.* Commission on Preservation and Access, Washington, DC.

Lowry, A. (1990). Machine-readable texts in the academic library: The electronic text service at Columbia University. In *Computer Files and the Research Library* (C. C. Gould, ed.), pp. 5–23. Research Libraries Group, Mountain View, CA.

Lowry, A. (1993). Landlords and tenants: Who owns information, who pays for it, and how? *Serials Librarian* **23**, 61–71.

Lowry, A. (1994). Electronic texts in the humanities: A selected bibliography. *Information Technology and Libraries* **13**, 43–49.

Lynch, C. A. (1994). The integrity of digital information: Mechanics and definitional issues. *Journal of the American Society for Information Science* **45**, 737–744.

Lynch, C. A. (1993). *Accessibility and Integrity of Networked Information Collections* (U.S. Office of Technology Assessment Background Paper BP-TCT-109). Washington, DC.

McCarty, W. (1993). A potency of life: Scholarship in an electronic age. *Serials Librarian* **23**, 79–97.

Meserole, H. T. (1990). The nature(s) of literary research. *Collection Management* **13**, 65–73.

Mintz, A. (1993). Availability of electronic full-text sources: A look behind the scenes. *Database* **16**(5), 24–31.

Mohlhenrich, J., ed. (1993). *Preservation of Electronic Formats and Electronic Formats for Preservation.* Highsmith, Fort Atkinson, WI.

Mosteller, F., and Wallace, D. L. (1964). *Inference and Disputed Authorship: The Federalist Papers.* Addison-Wesley, Reading, MA.

Murphy, G. (1994). Software review: SGML editors. *CETH Newsletter* **2**(2), 6–8.

Neuman, M. (1991). The very pulse of the machine: Three trends toward improvement in electronic versions of humanities texts. *Computers and the Humanities* **25**, 363–375.

Neuman, M., and Mangiafico, P. (1994). Providing and accessing information via the Internet: the Georgetown catalogue of projects in electronic text. *The Reference Librarian* **41/42**, 319–332.

Olsen, M. (1993). Texts, signs and readers: Quantitative methods in socio-cultural history. In *Proceedings of the Sixth International Conference on Symbolic and Logical Computing*, pp. 5–32. Dakota State University, Madison, SD.

Owens, E. (1993). Electronic text and scholarly publishers: How and why? In *Scholarly Publishing on the Electronic Networks, the New Generation: Visions and Opportunities in Not-for-Profit Publishing. Proceedings of the Second Symposium* (A. Okerson, ed.), pp. 5–13. Association of Research Libraries, Office of Scientific and Academic Publishing, Washington, DC.

Pankake, M. (1991). Humanities research in the 90s: What scholars need; what librarians can do. *Library Hi Tech* **9**, 9–14.

Potter, R. (1988). Literary criticism and literary computing: The difficulties of a synthesis. *Computers and the Humanities* **22**, 91–97.

Potter, R. (1991). Statistical analysis of literature: A retrospective on *Computers and the Humanities*, 1966–1990. *Computers and the Humanities* **25**, 401–429.

Price-Wilkin, J. (1991a). Text files in libraries: Present foundations and future directions. *Library Hi Tech* **9**, 7–44.

Price-Wilkin, J. (1991b). Text files in RLG academic libraries: A survey of support and activities. *Journal of Academic Librarianship* **17**, 19–25.

Proud, J. K. (1989). *The Oxford Text Archive* (British Library Research and Development Report 5985). The British Library, London.

Raben, J. (1991). Humanities computing 25 years later. *Computers and the Humanities* **25**, 341–350.

Rubinsky, Y. (1993). Electronic texts the day after tomorrow. In *Scholarly Publishing on the Electronic Networks, the New Generation: Visions and Opportunities in Not-for-Profit Publishing. Proceedings of the Second Symposium* (A. Okerson, ed.), pp. 5–13. Association of Research Libraries, Office of Scientific and Academic Publishing, Washington, DC.

Seaman, D. M. (1994). A library and apparatus of every kind: The electronic text center at the University of Virginia. *Information Technology and Libraries* **13**, 15–19.

Shreeves, E. (1992). Between the visionaries and the Luddites: Collection development and electronic resources in the humanities. *Library Trends* **40**, 579–395.

Smith, E. (1990). *The Librarian, the Scholar, and the Future of the Research Library.* Greenwood, Westport, CT.

Sperberg-McQueen, C. M. (1991). Text in the electronic age: Textual study and text encoding, with examples from medieval texts. *Literary and Linguistic Computing* **6**, 34–36.

Sperberg-McQueen, C. M., and Burnard, L., eds. (1994). *TEI P3: Guidelines for Electronic Text Encoding and Interchange.* Association for Computers and the Humanities, Association for Computational Linquistics, Association for Literary and Linguistic Computing, Chicago/Oxford.

Taylor, M. E. (1994). Books, computers, and the Pushmi-Pullyu. *C&RL News* **55**(2), 84–86.

Ubell, R., and Tesoriero, M. (1994). *Negotiating Networked Information Contracts and Licenses* (DRAFT, November 15, 1994). Rights for Electronic Access to and Delivery of Information (READI), Coalition for Networked Information, Washington, DC.

van Herwijnen, E. (1994). *Practical SGML*, 2nd Ed. Kluwer Academic Publishers, Boston.

Warner, B. F., and Barber, D. (1994). Building the digital library: The University of Michigan's UMLib text project. *Information Technology and Libraries* **13**, 20–24.

Wiberley, S. E., Jr. (1991). Habits of humanists: Scholarly behavior and new information technologies. *Library Hi Tech* **9**(1), 17–22.

Wiberley, S. E., Jr., and Jones, W. G. (1989). Patterns of information seeking in the humanities. *College and Research Libraries* **50**, 638–45.

Wolff, M. (1994). Poststructuralism and the ARTFL Database: Some theoretical considerations. *Information Technology and Libraries* **13**, 35–42.

International Cooperation in Cataloging: Progress and Constraints

Jay H. Lambrecht
University Library
University of Illinois at Chicago
Chicago, Illinois 60680

I. Introduction

In an ideal world, each unique bibliographic entity would be cataloged only once. It would have attached to it a unique bibliographic record that could be shared electronically with every other library that acquired the work. The cataloger would know the language or languages in which the item was produced, would have in-depth knowledge of the subject matter, and would adhere strictly to an accepted world standard for description, subject analysis, and classification. This complete and perfect bibliographic record would be recorded in an electronic format that was shared by all the world's libraries. It would be distributed instantly to a single global bibliographic database, from which any other library could draw the record instantly for local use. The notes and subject terms could be translated automatically into a chosen language. The entire record would be transliterated automatically into a chosen script, if desired. Nirvana would be reached, and library administrators would be able to redirect immense resources, now wasted on duplicated efforts, to other vital library functions.

Building the ideal world of bibliographic cooperation is, of necessity, an international enterprise. It is not reasonable to expect that a single country, no matter how great its resources relative to other countries, could supply this service to the entire world. Libraries within each country are in the best position to acquire all the works published in that country. They are the most likely to have available the linguistic expertise that is essential to a perfect bibliographic record. They know local name use conventions, local geography, and the local sociopolitical context that may be necessary to provide adequate subject analysis. They know their national bibliographies and traditions, and how the catalog record might need to be enhanced to fulfill national needs when those vary from the world standard.

ADVANCES IN LIBRARIANSHIP, VOL. 19
217

The dream of international cooperative cataloging based on universal standards is closer now than it ever has been, but it remains beyond our grasp. The efforts of more than thirty years have resulted in conferences, committees, studies, publications, and a variety of shared standards. Unfortunately, they often do not free catalogers in one country from redoing much of the work that already has been done in another. If it is a good time to see how far we have come, it is equally important to note how much more work it will take to get to our destination.

II. Standards Designed to Achieve International Cooperation

The perfect world of international cataloging cooperation is not a new dream. Historically, the production and distribution of national bibliographies such as the *National Union Catalog* (United States), *British Museum General Catalogue of Printed Books* (United Kingdom), and similar sources have served some of the purposes of international cooperative cataloging. Bibliographic records in these sources, many of which were created in the country of a work's publication and by experts in local languages, name usages, and subjects, have served as aids to catalogers everywhere. The fact that they have been printed sources (until very recently) following national, not international, standards for description and the assigning of name and series access points, subject headings, and classification numbers has left them far short as sources of universally acceptable bibliographic data. Their utility has been compromised still further by the fact, as reported by the International Meeting of Cataloguing Experts (IMCE) held in Copenhagen in 1969, that "the requirements of the catalogue and of the national bibliography [are] different and that the usage of national bibliographies [is] therefore not a valid guide for cataloguing" (IMCE in *Libri*, 1970, p. 115).

Efforts whose exclusive aim was international cooperation in cataloging (as opposed to those that worked toward that purpose, although it was not their primary intent) date from the 1960s. Progress has been rapid on some fronts, and virtually nonexistent on others.

A. Standardization of Personal Name Access Points

Standards for the entry of personal names in catalogs were among the first to be addressed internationally. The most visible early effort was the International Conference on Cataloguing Principles (ICCP), which was held in Paris in 1961, and succeeded in bringing together experts from around the world and forging an agreement. It adopted as one of the sections of its famous

Statement of Principles (ICCP in Carpenter and Svenonius, 1985, pp. 179–185) (commonly known as the Paris Principles) a formula for determining the entry word for personal names in a catalog. The usage of the person's country of citizenship was to be the primary consideration; the conventions of the language that the author wrote in were to be considered only if citizenship was unknown.

From the principle of following the usage of an author's country grew the practical need to make an authoritative statement of national usages. That need was met with the publication of a provisional standard in 1963 (*National Usages for the Entry of Names of Persons*) and with a definitive standard in 1967 (*Names of Persons: National Usages for Entry in Catalogues*, revised in 1977 and undergoing a second revision in 1994). The standards were based on the results of a survey sent to all countries represented at the ICCP and to the national bibliographic agencies of a number of other countries. The support of the International Federation of Library Associations and Institutions (IFLA) and Unesco was vital to this effort to "enable cataloguers in all parts of the world to achieve a considerable degree of uniformity in the entry of names of persons" (Chaplin, 1967, p. iii).

The ICCP and the publication of a standard for name access points established IFLA as the organization that would take the lead in questions of international standardization for cataloging. Its Committee on Cataloguing and its International Office for Universal Bibliographic Control (UBC), later known as the Universal Bibliographic Control and International MARC Programme (UBCIM), became the organizing forces behind and the publishers of all new international standards. Without them, it is difficult to imagine that significant progress would have been made in these endeavors.

B. Standardization of Bibliographic Description

International standards for bibliographic description beyond the narrow bounds of personal name access points also were put in place beginning in the 1960s. A standard for the bibliographic description of physical items was essential to fulfill the dream of full international cooperation in cataloging. The principles enumerated by the International Conference on Cataloguing Principles regarding description also needed to be translated into practical form. The vehicle for this effort was the work of the Committee on Uniform Cataloguing Rules, which in 1966 began to seek "the establishment of an international standard for the descriptive content of catalogue entries" (IMCE in *Libri*, 1970, pp. 105–106). It enlisted the financial support of Unesco and the International Federation of Library Associations and Institutions in this effort, which eventually would result in the second legacy of the ICCP.

Attempts to establish a worldwide standard for bibliographic description were interrupted in 1967 by the success of an effort to establish such a standard for one linguistic corner of the world. The publication of *Anglo-American Cataloging Rules* (AACR, 1967) brought together American, British, and Canadian catalogers to subscribe to detailed rules for bibliographic description and access. The influence of those countries in the English-speaking world resulted in the wide adoption of AACR from Australia through Africa and beyond. In some respects this preempted and distracted interest from the concurrent attempt to establish a worldwide descriptive cataloging standard. The fact that separate and somewhat disparate British and North American texts were published pointed to limited success. LC's policy of superimposition (maintaining the use of incorrect access points for large files) meant that the new standard was not applied uniformly. At the same time, and despite the fact that only a fraction of the bibliographic world was adopting AACR, it did prove that as the result of the commonality of language, an international cataloging standard could be adopted in very distant corners of the world.

Most would date the beginning of serious attempts to establish a worldwide descriptive cataloging standard from 1969. In that year, the aforementioned International Meeting of Cataloguing Experts sought to establish a framework "designed to accommodate all the descriptive data commonly required not only in catalogues and bibliographies but also in other records used in libraries and elsewhere in the control and handling of books" (IMCE in *Libri*, 1970, pp. 111–112). A unique bibliographic entity with a unique and universally applicable bibliographic record finally was an expressed goal of a group that was empowered to make it a reality. A working group was assigned to "determine the framework of an international standard for bibliographic description" (Anderson, 1989, p. 20), and the international cataloging community awaited the results.

The conclusions of the working group were distributed as a set of recommendations in 1971. By 1973, those recommendations "had been adopted by a number of national bibliographies and . . . had been taken into account by a number of cataloguing committees in redrafting national rules for description" [ISBD(M), 1987, p. v]. The publication of *ISBD(M): International Standard Bibliographic Description for Monographic Publications* (1974), made official a standard that already had been put into practice. It was followed over the next 16 years by a general ISBD (1977) and by ISBDs for cartographic materials (1977; rev. ed. 1987), nonbook materials (1977; rev. ed. 1987), serials (1977; rev. ed. 1988), printed music (1980; 2nd rev. ed. 1991), antiquarian books (1980; 2nd rev. ed. 1991), and computer files (1990), as well as by updated editions of ISBD(M) (1st standard ed. rev. 1978; rev. ed. 1987). Each of the ISBDs specifies "the requirements for the description and identification . . . of publications, assigns an order to the elements and specifies a system of punctuation. . . . Its provisions relate first to the bibliographic records produced by national bibliographic agencies" [ISBD(M), 1987, p. 1].

The dream of full international cooperation in cataloging is put into words in the ISBDs. Although they relate only to description, the ISBDs aim "to aid the international exchange of bibliographic records between national bibliographic agencies and throughout the international library and information community" [ISBD(M), 1987, p. 1]. They have the explicit purposes of making records produced in one country readily acceptable in another, of breaking down language barriers in the interpretation of records, and of simplifying the conversion of bibliographic records to machine-readable form.

Unfortunately, the publication of the ISBDs has not led to a universal international standard for descriptive cataloging. Some nations use the ISBDs as their standards, but others adhere to influential national or international cataloging codes such as *Anglo-American Cataloguing Rules*, *Regeln für die alphabetische Katalogisierung*, and *Pravila sostavlenija bibliograficheskogo opisanija*. Each of these codes has been reissued since 1971 and while the influence of the ISBDs can be seen in them, the single standard that would allow each country to describe works published in that country according to a universal standard for the benefit of the world's catalogers still is not in place in 1995.

It is important to note that the ISBDs did not originate from a theoretical or philosophical framework. Although the ICCP provided a general framework of principles for personal name access, the committees that sprang from it found it more practical to agree upon practices than upon a detailed statement of principles to guide their work. Evidence of this approach is found in the fact that the ISBD for one form of publication, the printed monograph, was produced 3 years before a general ISBD. Seymour Lubetzky's philosophy of considering function before prescribing descriptive form was not followed. An internationally acceptable bibliographic description might not have arisen at all if a theoretical framework needed to be agreed upon first, but the likelihood of universal acceptance had to be hurt by the focus on practice over principle.

An attempt to return to a philosophical approach to bibliographic records, with special emphasis on description and access, has been made in the 1990s. A study group of the Standing Committee of the IFLA Section on Cataloguing has met to examine the primary uses and functional requirements of bibliographic records. It has looked at the functions of the catalog as defined by Charles Ammi Cutter and in the Paris Principles of 1961, and has attempted to define the functions of individual bibliographic records. It has examined the items and sets of items that exist in the bibliographic universe, the relationships that exist between those entities, and the functional attributes of bibliographic records. Its goal is to make international cataloging standards as cost effective as possible and to expand partnerships among libraries, publishers, and other agencies without sacrificing the vital functions of bibliographic records. It will be interesting to see if a more theoretical approach results in more widely accepted standards or, indeed, in any new standards at all.

C. Standardization of Subject Analysis

The cataloging world never has come as close to establishing an international standard for subject analysis as it has for personal name access points and bibliographic description. It was not until the 1990s that a working group of the Section on Classification and Indexing of the Division of Bibliographic Control of IFLA attempted to define the principles underlying subject heading languages. Such languages were defined in a draft document as consisting of "a controlled vocabulary of terms representing concepts and named entities and a semantic structure showing paradigmatic relationships among these; [they] may sometimes have syntax rules for combining terms into strings." The working group also defined the principles that should guide construction of subject heading languages.

International study of the theoretical underpinnings of subject analysis came many years after the construction of a variety of national systems for providing subject access to bibliographic works. The *Library of Congress Subject Headings* (LCSH), which contains headings created and assigned since 1898 by subject catalogers at the Library of Congress, is a primary example. LCSH was in its 17th edition in 1994 and contained more than 206,000 subject authority records (LCSH, 1994, pp. iii–vii). Although it is a large and well-recognized scheme, its usefulness as an international standard is limited by several factors. Among them are:

1. Subject authority records are created as needed to describe the collections of the Library of Congress instead of as a general framework for or construct of all subject disciplines. This gives them a decided bent toward the United States.

2. Subjects are in English using American spellings and reflecting terms used in American and other English-language publications.

3. LCSH is an enumerative precoordinate system, which makes it precise but expensive to apply and relatively inflexible.

Despite these drawbacks, LCSH was reported to be the basis for a number of national systems at the meeting "Subject Indexing: Principles and Practices in the 90's," sponsored by the IFLA Section on Classification and Indexing in 1993 (Holley, 1993b). Representatives from Brazil, Canada (both English and French speaking), France, Portugal, and England reported that some or all of each country's libraries use a system that is based on LCSH. In each case, local changes were incorporated, ranging from the addition of national terms to translation to a different language. Use of unrelated systems, such as *Regeln fur den Schlagwortkatalog* in Germany, MOTBIS in secondary school libraries in France, and local schemes in Iran and Spain, also were reported. Conference participants also considered current issues in subject indexing.

One promising new development reported in 1994 was an agreement between the Library of Congress and the National Library of Canada to allow the NLC to contribute records to LCSH. This is a limited area of cooperation, but it illustrates an intriguing new possibility. If the many national agencies that enhance LCSH for local use could begin to contribute those enhancements to the core scheme they all share, an international standard could eventually develop. The acceptability of strict LCSH structures and the ability of the Library of Congress to incorporate international contributions into its system remain to be determined, but this may offer the best hope yet for truly international cooperation in subject analysis.

In addition to discussions of principles and practices in subject analysis, and to limited international cooperation in practice, the 1990s have brought publication of *Guidelines for Subject Authority and Reference Entries* (1993). A working group of the Section on Classification and Indexing of IFLA's Division of Bibliographic Control designed the *Guidelines* to deal with the structure of entries instead of their form or punctuation. This is another case of principles being defined well after practice has been established. Where new subject analysis schemes are being established (as in Croatia), a draft of these guidelines has proven to be useful. Where national schemes already are developed, it is much too early to tell if publication of international guidelines will result in true international cooperation.

D. Standardization of Classification

Classification is the single major area in which the world's libraries are farthest from sharing a universal standard that would allow them to use bibliographic records from other countries without examination and enhancement. A number of major classification schemes are in widespread use. Each sprang from a particular set of circumstances, and so each has a different basis in principle. No serious attempt to reconcile them has been made. Furthermore, the appearance of a classification number on each of the physical items in a collection, as well as in the bibliographic records that represent them, makes it nearly impossible to move a large collection from one system to another in the interests of universality. At least three schemes are in widespread use.

The Dewey decimal classification (DDC), which first was published in 1876 and is in its 20th edition in 1995, was created simply because Melvil Dewey felt that no other appropriate classification scheme existed. It is built on a three-figure base, uses basic decimal division, and employs form (or standard) subdivisions. Its underlying principles include a hierarchical framework of all knowledge (as it stood in the 1870s, with some modifications beginning with the 15th edition in 1951), the possibility of great specificity, purity of notation, and practical utility and economy. A relative index "allow[ed] a great part of the work of classifying to be done in advance by experts in large central libraries with ample resources, thus securing, at a mere fraction of usual cost, better and more uniform results . . . and reducing labor to much narrower limits than ever before" (normalized spelling of Dewey, 1942, p. 14). DDC is the dominant classification system in the United Kingdom, Australia, India, Italy, France, Norway, and Latin America, as well as in public and school libraries in the United States. It is used by over 200,000 libraries in 135 countries.

The universal decimal classification (UDC) is a faceted system which took its main classes and divisions and the essential parts of its notation from DDC, but applied them to items in existing card indexes held at the Institut International de Bibliographie in Brussels (Tauber and Wise, 1961, pp. 189–194). Its development after 1895 and its publication in 1899 were based on the principles of bringing together related concepts, universality that allows linking simple main numbers with other numbers, and proceeding from the general to the more specific through decimal division. Ironically, its evolution away from the popular Dewey scheme published 23 years before guaranteed that neither it nor any other scheme would be universally applied. It is most commonly used in Eastern Europe and in the former Soviet Union.

The Library of Congress classification (LCC) began in 1897, and has been said to spring from no general principles other than the need to classify one of the largest collections of books in the world (Davison, 1966, p. 19). The Library of Congress had been classified according to the Jeffersonian scheme it inherited in 1815, which it had outgrown. Because the new system was to be applied to a large library already on the shelves, more consideration was given to the grouping of books than to the grouping of subjects. Alphabetical subarrangement took precedence over subject subarrangement. Publication commenced in 1902 and still is incomplete (at least in the area of law) in 1995. With the advent of printed catalog cards sold by LC and widely accepted by other libraries, LC's classification system became widely accepted as well. It is used by about 75% of academic libraries in the United States (usually the larger ones) and in scattered other libraries throughout the world.

In addition to DDC, UDC, and LCC, other systems are in more limited use worldwide. Those designed by Charles Ammi Cutter, Henry Evelyn Bliss, S. R. Ranganathan, and others contribute to the maze of classification systems that would need to be reconciled into an international standard. Each originated with an individual and a library that were not served by the schemes that already existed . In several cases, new (and, the authors thought, improved) principles of classification formed the bases of the systems. In these circumstances, it is difficult to imagine the quick emergence of a worldwide standard.

E. Standardization of Computer Formats

If all of the elements of a catalog record were subject to a single international standard, bibliographic records still would not be readily exchanged if they were not encoded into a standard machine-readable form that could be exchanged with other libraries in other countries. Entry of data elements using different conventions for tagging, coding, and recording the information for machine storage and transmission would not allow efficient (or any) on-line or batch exchange. The alternative is redundant data entry, which is inefficient and lends itself to error. These facts were recognized in the 1960s and were addressed with the creation of the MARC system.

MARC, an acronym derived from the term machine-readable cataloging, originated at the Library of Congress. According to Avram (1968, pp. 3–10), it grew out of a series of studies and conferences to investigate the possibility of recording cataloging data in machine-readable form. In 1965 and 1966, three conferences on machine-readable catalog copy were held at LC. These conferences focused on the fields to be represented in machine-readable form and possible magnetic tape formats to contain the data. Between 1966 and 1968, LC and 16 other North American libraries ran a pilot project to test the feasibility of producing and distributing machine-readable catalog records. The pilot was so successful that it evolved into a fully operational on-line system in a remarkably short time. The basic approach of the designers of MARC was accepted nationally and internationally.

Agreement with the concept and principles of MARC did not result in a universally accepted MARC, however. By 1971 it was stated that a universal MARC was "neither possible nor desirable. National systems have their own national characteristics and one must be careful not to . . . substitute a dull uniformity for the present anarchy. Indeed a reasonable diversity should be encouraged" (Coward, 1972, p. 19). That diversity has resulted in an amazing proliferation of MARCs. In a world that contains USMARC, UKMARC, CANMARC, IBERMARC, JAPAN/MARC, SAMARC, and many other MARCs there appears to be one standard with innumerable local variations. Those variations are overcome, to some degree, by acceptance of UNIMARC and by numerous individual agreements (which, ironically, have their own standards) relating to the transfer of MARC records between national bibliographic agencies.

The UNIMARC format first was published in 1977. It was an attempt to facilitate the international exchange of bibliographic data in machine-readable form by specifying the tags, indicators, and subfield codes for such data, as well as the logical and physical format in which the records and their content designators should be held on magnetic tape. The format was modified in 1980, a handbook to its use was published in 1983, and a manual was published in 1987. Although "several national libraries undertook projects to convert from an existing national format to UNIMARC or adopted UNIMARC for their national format needs" (Holt, McCallum, and Long, 1987, p. v), UNIMARC did not manage to supplant many of the various national MARC formats. It seems to remain as a viable international standard from which major deviations are not made, but to which very few national bibliographic agencies religiously adhere.

In an environment of minor deviations from a single international standard, the primary means of transferring MARC records between countries has become the direct one-way or two-way agreement. In addition to bridging the differences between formats, these agreements allow for negotiation of distribution rights within the country of receipt, possible cost recovery, the establishment of a selective record service or the transmission of all records produced in the originating country, and other differences. The agreements may be modeled on those presented by the International MARC Network Advisory Committee in *International Transfers of National MARC Records* (1987).

After more than two decades of following slightly divergent paths in their use of the MARC formats, and of negotiating individual agreements to allow records to be shared between countries, there is evidence that some national bibliographic agencies are becoming willing to set aside their "reasonable diversity" in the interests of true cooperation. Representatives of LC and the British Library (BL) met in June 1994 "to review principles for harmonization and simplification of USMARC and UKMARC" with the objectives of "increasing compatibility between the two formats with the ultimate goal of achieving a single MARC format" (Toward a Common MARC Format, 1994). Although their announcement of the meeting is cautious, including assurances that time will be needed to work out differences and that users of the formats will be consulted, LC and BL seem to be moving toward more efficient sharing of data. The fact that they are only two of the many national bibliographic agencies that might be working toward a common MARC format does not diminish their effort.

F. Standardization of Cooperative Cataloging Networks

In addition to the exchange of bibliographic data between national bibliographic agencies in the form of MARC records, international cooperative cataloging is facilitated by the use of bibliographic networks. These allow both national bibliographic agencies and individual libraries to use the catalog records of other libraries to minimize their own work. Where agreements between agencies fail to result in the full sharing of bibliographic data, cooperative cataloging networks can serve the purpose of facilitating the international exchange of bibliographic records.

OCLC, with well over 30 million bibliographic records, about 5000 members, and more than 18,000 participating libraries in 1994, is the largest cooperative cataloging network in the world. Although its origin and base are in the United States, OCLC has worked hard to expand its network, especially in Europe and Asia. Its usefulness beyond the English-speaking world is limited by network standards that require the use of AACR for description and access, by the fact that it reflects largely North American and Western European collections, and by the predominance of English language notes and subjects in its records. It is not the single global bibliographic database that can be consulted for cataloging copy, but it is as close as we come.

Other networks similar to OCLC but smaller in size, such as the Research Libraries Information Network (RLIN), exist in North America. Holley (1993a) has documented the cooperative cataloging networks outside of North America that serve the same functions as OCLC. He found very few to be multicontinental, or even to cross national boundaries. In such circumstances, and if a single dominant worldwide network is not to emerge, connectivity between networks might offer some of the benefits of a universally shared international database. In practice, they would fall far short of that ideal.

III. Why Full Cooperation Still Is in the Future

After more than thirty years of effort, there have been some remarkable gains in international cooperation in cataloging. The cataloger who had slumbered since 1963 might be surprised that we have managed to establish universal rules for the entry of personal names in catalogs. He or she never would have experienced the use of a cataloging code that is shared by a number of nations in all parts of the world, as AACR now is in common use in the English-speaking world. Since 1974, international standards for bibliographic description in a variety of formats have been established and largely are followed everywhere (although we talk less about ISBD than about the national cataloging codes that incorporate its precepts). The long-slumbering cataloger truly would be amazed that we are able to record and retrieve bibliographic information in computers, share it on-line with other libraries through bibliographic networks, and transmit it around the world through local variants of the MARC format. The growing influence of *Library of Congress Subject*

Headings and the lack of proliferation of new classification systems would seem to point to still greater success in international cooperation in cataloging.

On the other hand, the cataloger who had slumbered only since 1980 would be much less impressed with the level of progress in cooperation of the past fifteen years. There have been substantial gains in the power of computers, but there have not been corresponding significant gains in international cooperative cataloging. Much fine tuning has taken place, and there are undeniable advances in country-to-country cooperation, but the dream of the work cataloged only once in its country of publication and as a result cataloged for all the world is not much closer to reality than it was in 1980. These failures are failures of consensus, of will, of funding, and perhaps of imagination. They originate within and between countries. They must be overcome if serious progress in international cooperative cataloging is to resume.

A. Inherent Problems and Conflicts

There is no doubt that international cooperation in cataloging would have made greater strides in the past fifteen years (and well before) if there were only one language written in one script according to one orthography, if there were no national boundaries, if there were computers in every library in the world, and if libraries were the recipients of unlimited funding. The lack of each of these conditions can be seen as an inherent impediment to full international cooperation in cataloging.

There is no better evidence of the ability of common language to tie together cataloging agencies than the success of *Anglo-American Cataloguing Rules*. Since 1967, AACR has allowed much of the English-speaking world to share rules for bibliographic description and access. A common language allows for a high level of international understanding as rules are negotiated, written, and interpreted. Common language allows notes and subject headings recorded in one country to be used with little or no explanation in another country. It keeps cataloging leaders in one country in close communication with those in others, as exemplified by the workings of the Joint Steering Committee for Revision of AACR (JSC) and its continuous revision of AACR. Common language makes it easier to propose and implement cooperative efforts to align multiple MARC formats into a common MARC format, as representatives of the British Library, the Library of Congress, and the National Library of Canada met to do late in 1994. Given the historical relationships of these countries, a common language helps to cement a common bibliographic tradition.

It may be the ultimate irony, however, that AACR has had two titles in North America. The 1967 edition included the word cataloging while subsequent editions have used the spelling cataloguing. Even given a common language, a common cataloging code, and common bibliographic traditions, differences in orthography could prevent a catalog user from finding one of these editions in a single on-line search. Agreements between cataloging agencies to use a common spelling beginning in 1978, and to use such terms as "full stop" (which are common to some English-speaking ears and alien to others), have not caused authors or library users to use the same spellings or terms when they are searching catalogs.

Orthography is not the only thing that separates the countries which share AACR. A phenomenon that could be termed local interpretation (to be innocuous) or nationalism (to be unduly harsh) also has arisen. The creation of the *Library of Congress Rule Interpretations* (LCRI) serves as an excellent example of this problem. Designed to clarify AACR for Library of Congress catalogers, then distributed to other American libraries who contributed to LC's database and to national bibliographic utilities, LCRI proceeded to take on a life of its own that sometimes has brought United States cataloging practice into direct conflict with AACR. Although good-faith efforts were made to convince partners in JSC that a given rule needed to be clarified or changed, failure to do so occasionally led to local "interpretation" that negated a rule only within national boundaries. International cooperation in cataloging has suffered as a result.

If countries sharing a common language and descriptive cataloging code can have such problems in full cooperation, it is not surprising that the chasms caused by differences in language have been very difficult to bridge. Language differences make the process of negotiating international cataloging standards and writing them to the satisfaction of all parties very difficult. Subsequent interpretation of such standards can differ greatly if the standards are not equally clear in all languages. Notes and subject headings, which are of limited use if not written in the common language of local library users, require shared terminology and consistent translation if international cooperation is to be effective. Any proposed changes in standards require that many countries with many languages participate in the revision process. Each of these problems is compounded when not only languages, but the scripts in which those languages are written, vary.

Nationalism and differing bibliographic traditions also can be seen as an inherent impediment to the realization of full international cooperation in cataloging. If scripts, languages, bibliographic traditions, computer formats, requirements for national bibliographies, and bibliographic networks all change at a single border crossing, it is not surprising that cooperation in cataloging breaks down at the same historical and linguistic border. If political, ethnic, or religious differences make neighbors unfriendly to each other, they are unlikely to be fully cooperative in cataloging practice. Changes in national boundaries and governments in recent years have not ended age-old hostilities and have not resulted in a new era of international bibliographic cooperation. Libraries may seek better cooperation in these circumstances, but support and funds probably will not follow.

To the extent that libraries have limited influence over the moneys allotted to them, funding in gerneral is another inherent problem for international cooperation in cataloging. In many recently independent developing countries, money devoted to education and libraries cannot be shown to have resulted in economic gains. Illiterate populations are seen to be served better by investment in exportable commodities. Standard bibliographic records, although highly exportable, bring no hard currency in return. In many industrialized countries there has been a similar movement away from investment in education and libraries. The price of library services, including international cooperation, is seen as too high to justify. International standard cataloging will not thrive in libraries that cannot afford to buy new publications.

A final problem for international cooperation in cataloging that is beyond the control of libraries is the varying levels of computerization and telecommunication in the countries of the world. It is impossible to contribute useful records to the international cataloging community without the ability to store and transmit them electronically. If national bibliographic agencies are unable to afford computers, if national priorities direct computers to profit-making enterprises, ot if electrical supplies and telephone lines are not reliable, standard on-line bibliographic records may not be shared with the rest of the world.

B. Failures of Cooperation within Countries

There are many inherent impediments to progress in international bibliographic cooperation, ranging from language differences and national boundaries to funding shortages and inadequate computerization and telecommunication. As if these problems were not enough to impede the success of efforts to catalog each work only once in its country of origin and to share bibliographic records worldwide, failures of cooperation within countries also have slowed progress in shared cataloging. These failures are most evident when requirements for national bibliographies differ from international cataloging standards, when attempts to save money result in less than full catalog records, and when competing cataloging networks exist within the same country.

National bibliographic agencies, which often are associated with research libraries that are preeminent in their countries, are a natural source of catalog records created to the level of international standards. These agencies frequently acquire the full range of works published in their countries and are given the resources to provide good bibliographic access to them. They are more likely than other libraries to have established working relationships beyond their borders. The international usefulness of the records they create may be compromised, however, by the fact that national bibliographic agencies were established to produce national bibliographies. As previously noted, the IMCE recognized in 1969 that the requirements of the catalog and of the national bibliography often are different. The requirements for national bibliographies often have a long history and are less comprehensive than those for internationally shared cataloging copy. When conflicts arise and resources are short, relatively inexpensive service that will meet national needs often takes precedence over the concerns of international cooperation. A quarter century after the IMCE, there is little evidence that many national bibliographic agencies have worked diligently to bring conflicting requirements between international cataloging standards and national bibliographies into alignment.

One manifestation of the failure to match national bibliographic needs to those of the international cataloging community is seen in the persistence of various forms of minimal level cataloging. Because records that are less than complete by international standards may meet the needs of a national bibliography, some national bibliographic agencies have succumbed to the allure of less than full cataloging. Even for works published in the country of the agency, a record that omits selected data elements may be seen as a reasonable economy. There is no question that the short-term savings in recording less detail than required by international standards can be significant. The long-term costs that such savings may impose on users and other libraries also can be large. Reduced access, increased cost of upgrading minimal level records, and the failure of a system of international cooperation in cataloging loom large among those costs.

Failures to cooperate within countries are not the sole responsibility of national bibliographic agencies. If one agency is unable to afford to provide full standard cataloging for every work published in its country, there is nothing to prevent other cataloging agencies from contributing to a national cooperative effort that will meet both national and international needs. Bibliographic utilities have such opportunities built into them. Unfortunately, another failure to cooperate may be the result of multiple, competing utilities within the same country. If users of one utility never see the contributions of other libraries to a competing utility, duplicate effort certainly will be the result. If the essence of international cooperation in cataloging is the creation and sharing of a single bibliographic record to represent an item, that sharing does not get off to a good start if it fails within the national cataloging community. If a national bibliographic agency, which is almost always the entity through which international cooperation flows, must search several bibliographic utilities and its own local system to learn whether or not it is the first to catalog an item, its work cannot be very efficient.

C. Failures of Cooperation between Countries

Inherent impediments to full international cooperation in cataloging must be worked around because they will not be solved by the actions of libraries alone. Failures of cooperative cataloging within a particular country can be overcome if a single bibliographic agency is willing to fulfill the international obligation to provide standard cataloging for all works published in that country. The only arena in which libraries have the power to make prefect electronic records available throughout the world, but in which they must rely on other libraries for success, is the international arena. It is evident that large strides were made in this arena before 1980, but that many of the failures of cooperation at that time have not been overcome in the intervening years.

The litany of incomplete successes in cataloging cooperation is nearly as long as the number of areas in which cooperation is possible. To list them is not to ignore the many partial successes that have been achieved, but to point to the variety of areas where new initiatives and new successes could make a difference to the international cataloging community.

One of the areas in which a new initiative in cooperation is most needed is in the standardization of corporate name access points. In contrast to the relative success of standards for personal names, the formulation and assignment of corporate names remain subject to a wide variety of practices. Some of these are tied to linguistic differences, where use of the vernacular in headings causes conflicts between such terms as "Germany" and " Deutschland." Others are tied to historical bibliographic practice, in which some cataloging agencies barely recognize the concept of corporate authorship while possible partners in cataloging apply such headings liberally. The absence of an accepted standard leads to wide variation in practice, which is the antithesis of useful international cooperation. Establishment of an international authority file as advocated by Thomas and Younger (1993, pp. 246–247) would be a good step toward sharing forms of names, but would not overcome differences in heading application.

A second area in which new and effective cooperative initiatives would be welcome is in the standardization of subject analysis. To the extent that computers are able to be programmed to translate subject terms and that translation is facilitated by a fixed lexicon, subjects are more amenable to international acceptance than are corporate name access points. This assumes that there is a world standard thesaurus that could be applied in a world standard way. To the extent that LCSH is widely accepted outside the United States, it has taken on some of those characteristics. It is exceptionally far from being universal in coverage or acceptance, however. Discussion continues even within the United States on ways to make LCSH's enumerative and precoordinate system less expensive and more flexible.

Classification, like subject analysis, is important to the grouping function performed by catalogs and to the efficiency of efforts to share cataloging copy internationally. The multitude of classification systems in use, the absence of theoretical agreement on how classification should be applied, and the weight of billions of items already bearing relatively immutable call numbers argue against any short-term success in internationally shared classification. In the face of these problems, no attempt to bring classification under a common standard has emerged.

A last area in which a single internationally accepted standard would assist in achieving full cooperation in cataloging is in the area of shared bibliographic networks. Although a universal cooperative cataloging network is not essential to efforts to catalog each title only once, it could provide major assistance to libraries that were willing and able to cooperate (Mandel, 1992, pp. 45–47). Bibliographic networks frequently are under the control of government agencies or publicly held corporations and as a result are difficult to merge. Nationalistic or financial competitiveness may lead to duplication and competition among bibliographic networks that will continue to limit the cause of full cooperation in cataloging.

IV. Proposals for Improved Cooperation

If one assumes that international cooperation in cataloging was more success-ful in the period 1963–1980 than in the period 1980–1995, it is instructive to look at the major successes of the earlier period to see how they might be copied. The widely accepted standards for personal name access points, bibliographic description, and machine-readable bibliographic formats may provide clues for improved cooperation in the future.

In the case of personal name access points, acceptance came about through a combination of the initiative of a small group, the establishment of principles before publication of a standard, the willingness of libraries to allow local experts to set a standard for worldwide practice, and the relatively few varia-tions between past practice and newly standardized practice. The ICCP incor-porated "international" and "principles" into its name, and on the basis of its principles, conducted a survey to determine practices and preferences among a number of libraries from around the world. Using its own authority, it moved into a void and published a new standard. Both principle and practice assumed that the use of the author, especially in publications issued in his or her country, should be the primary factor in determining the form of the catalog entry. Success inspired revisions to the standard that have helped to keep it current and accepted for more than thirty years.

Internationally accepted standards for bibliographic description, especially as manifested in the ISBDs, followed a similar path to widespread use. The initiative of a small group, the IMCE, was vital to this success. As already noted, the IMCE was international in nature but was not obviously devoted to general principles. Like the ICCP, its conclusions resulted in relatively minor changes from past practice in most libraries of the world. This last factor may have played the most important role in its success. The need to record data found on the title page and other prominent sources within the work in much the same way as it is found on the work itself was a widely accepted practice in cataloging history. With the insertion of distinctive punctuation that sets off the various areas of the description (even for those who cannot read the language or the script), the ISBDs codified and formulated practices that already were in place. This made international acceptance and incorporation into local cataloging rules relatively simple. The creation of an ISBD for each format and the updates that have followed have led to widespread, if not universal, acceptance.

A third area of clear success in international cooperative cataloging was the establishment and acceptance of the MARC format. A small group of librarians at the Library of Congress and elsewhere took the initiative in this case. The inclusion of a single Canadian library made the effort modestly international. Principles seemed much more applicable to the data being encoded than to the method of encoding it, and so played an insignificant role in deciding the format. Where no standard and virtually no practice existed, it was easy to devise a system that did not challenge long-held local standards. The quick success and acceptance of MARC was a tribute to the ingenuity of its creators and to the urgent need for standards to encode and exchange machine-readable bibliographic information. Minor national variations have not been enough to overcome the overall accomplishment of establishing MARC standards.

Proposals for revived and improved international cooperation in cataloging, especially those that encompass subject analysis, classification, the assignment of corporate name entries, and greater cooperation between cataloging networks, have a difficult path to follow. Successes of the past imply that small groups with strong initiative, often working from the basis of shared principles and being truly international in nature, have the best chance to establish new international cataloging standards. Even more important than these elements, however, may be the similarity of proposed standards to an already established practice, a willingness to let local practice define international standards wherever that is possible, or the total absence of established standards to be overcome.

Small groups with strong initiative are less visible in the international cataloging arena since the emergence of IFLA and its UBCIM Programme as the international center of cooperative cataloging activities. Small groups continue to exist, but seem more bound by the structure and practices of a permanent organization than were the ICCP or ICME of the 1960s. To ascribe to IFLA any lack of success in establishing international standards would be an injustice, but it may be possible for dedicated small groups working outside its aegis to initiate more revolutionary changes.

Shared principles, like strong independent groups of experts, are difficult to find in the areas of subject analysis, classification, and corporate name access points. The disparate standards in each of these areas are based on historical practices, but perhaps not long-held principles. In most cases, principles have been defined at a later time to justify the practices. Although LCSH began as a practical system for analyzing the subject holdings of the Library of Congress, it now may be defended as an enumerative precoordinate system. In these circumstances it is difficult to get everyone to step back and agree to the abstract principles that could guide ideal international practices.

The groups that have considered shared cataloging standards over the past fifteen years truly have been international in nature. The successes of the period 1963–1980 have the best chance of being built upon in the future because of the broadening base of international participation. Groups such as IFLA's UBCIM Programme, while they may not generate revolutionary initiatives, have done an excellent job of bringing together North and South, developed and developing countries, and people with differing bibliographic traditions to discuss their common practices and their differences. It is possible that these efforts have planted the seeds for improved cooperation for decades to come.

Ultimately, the ability to establish widely shared bibliographic standards at the international level may depend on a willingness to accept minor variations based on existing national practice. In one of the areas of greatest success to date, personal name headings, experts took national practice and codified it for an accepting world. In another area, bibliographic description, experts took the largely shared practice of recording data as found on the item (including the order of the typical title page), added distinctive punctuation, and codified it for an accepting world. In a third area, the MARC format, experts saw a void, filled it well, and found the world rushing to accept the new standard. In the remaining areas where cooperation is much less complete, there is no apparent opportunity to take a predominant practice and convince the rest of the world that it is in the interests of all to accept it as a world standard. There is little opportunity to establish shared principles because conflicting principles already exist. There is no apparent opportunity to fill a void because none have emerged since the MARC format was created.

Given these circumstances, one must doubt that it is realistic to expect the international cooperative cataloging successes of 1963–1980 ever to be

repeated on the same scale. The best hope for continually improving cooperation may come from slow coalition building to alter existing principles and
practices. The efforts of individual national bibliographic agencies to forge
cooperative agreements with other agencies in areas such as subject access
points and fully shared MARC formats may prove to be the best strategy. In
the absence of an ability to get everyone in the world to agree upon a new
standard at the same time, it may be necessary to build one by one an alliance
of national bibliographic agencies with common practices. At some point in
the future such alliances should reach the critical mass necessary to convince
those outside their boundaries that a predominant international practice exists
and that all should join in its application.

The other crucial element in this mix is that libraries must be convinced
that international cooperation in cataloging practice is in their best interests.
If they already were convinced of this fact, there can be little doubt that
progress in cooperation would have been faster. In the absence of objections
to the theory of one-time cataloging of each item shared worldwide,
one must assume that recalcitrant libraries do not trust the application.
Doubts that international partners can be relied upon to hold up their
end of the cooperative exchange of bibliographic data must be eliminated
if further success is to be attained. In trust, as in agreement to new
practices, some critical mass seems necessary to make the theory become
a reality.

V. Conclusion

Progress made in the creation and acceptance of international cooperative
cataloging standards in the 1960s and 1970s may have raised unreasonable
expectations that such progress could be maintained indefinitely. Although
no standard seems to have gained acceptance in a totally unreserved way,
several that originated in the 1960s have come very close to achieving that
status. The remaining areas of difference, ranging from language and script
variations to subject analysis and classification practices and principles, are
beyond the control of libraries or do not exhibit qualities that make them easily
amenable to international standardization. In the absence of easy options, the
best hopes for improving long-term cooperation may rest in the coalition
building of national bibliographic agencies and in a growing willingness to
trust international partners. Neither of these approaches will result in a quick
payoff, but a diligent attempt to pursue both avenues may prove to be the
only way to make large gains toward the ideal world of each unique bibliographic entity being cataloged only once.

Glossary

AACR	Anglo-American Cataloguing Rules
BL	British Library
DDC	Dewey Decimal Classification
ICCP	International Conference on Cataloguing Principles
IFLA	International Federation of Library Associations and Institutions
IMCE	International Meeting of Cataloguing Experts
ISBD	International Standard Bibliographic Description
JSC	Joint Steering Committee for Revision of AACR
LC	Library of Congress
LCC	Library of Congress Classification
LCRI	Library of Congress Rule Interpretations
LCSH	Library of Congress Subject Headings
MARC	Machine-Readable Cataloging
NLC	National Library of Canada
OCLC	OCLC Online Computer Library Center, Inc.
RLIN	Research Libraries Information Network
UBCIM	Universal Bibliographic Control and International MARC
UDC	Universal Decimal Classification
UNIMARC	Universal MARC

References

Anderson, D. (1989). *Standard Practices in the Preparation of Bibliographic Records.* Rev. ed. IFLA Universal Bibliographic Control and International MARC Programme, London.

Anglo-American Cataloging Rules (AACR) (1967). North American text. American Library Association, Chicago. Later published under title *Anglo-American Cataloguing Rules* in 1978 (2nd ed.) and 1988 (2nd ed. rev.).

Avram, H. D. (1968). *The MARC Pilot Project: Final Report on a Project Sponsored by the Council on Library Resources.* Library of Congress, Washington, DC.

Chaplin, A. H., ed. (1967). *Names of Persons: National Usages for Entry in Catalogues.* IFLA, Sevenoaks, England.

Coward, R. E. (1972). MARC: National and international cooperation. In *The Exchange of Bibliographic Data and the MARC Format: Proceedings of the International Seminar on the MARC Format and the Exchange of Bibliographic Data in Machine Readable Form*, pp. 17–23. Verlag Dokumentation, Munich.

Davison, K. (1966). *Theory of Classification: An Examination Guidebook.* Clive Bingley, London.

Dewey, M. (1942). *Decimal Classification and Relativ Index.* 14th ed. rev. and enl. Forest Press, New York.

Holley, R. P. (1993a). Cooperative cataloging outside North America: Status Report 1993. *Cataloguing and Classification Quarterly* **17**(3/4), 201–236.

Holley, R. P. (1993b). Report on the IFLA satellite meeting "Subject Indexing: Principles and Practices in the 90's," August 17–18, 1993, Lisbon, Portugal. *Cataloging and Classification Quarterly* **18**(2), 87–100.

Holt, B. P., McCallum, S. H., and Long, A. B., eds. (1987). *UNIMARC Manual.* IFLA Universal
    Bibliographic Control and International MARC Programme, London.
International Meeting of Cataloguing Experts (IMCE) (1970). Report of the International
    Meeting of Cataloguing Experts, Copenhagen, 1969. *Libri* **20**(1–2), 105–132.
International Conference on Cataloguing Principles (ICCP) (1985). Report: International Con-
    ference on Cataloguing Principles, Paris, 9th-18th October 1961. In *Foundations of Cataloging:
    A Sourcebook* (M. Carpenter and E. Svenonius, eds.). Libraries Unlimited, Littleton, CO.
*International Transfers of National MARC Records: Guidelines for Agreements Relating to the Transfer
    of National MARC Records between National Bibliographic Agencies* (1987). IFLA Universal Biblio-
    graphic Control and International MARC Programme, London.
ISBD(M): International Standard Bibliographic Description for Monographic Publications (1987). Rev
    ed. IFLA Universal Bibliographic Control and International MARC Programme, London.
Library of Congress Subject Headings (LCSH) (1994). Library of Congress, Washington, DC.
Mandel, C. (1992). Cooperative cataloging: Models, issues, prospects. In *Advances in Librarianship*
    (I. Godden, ed.), Vol. 16, pp. 33–82. Academic Press, San Diego.
Tauber, M. F., and Wise, E. (1961). Classification Systems. In *The State of the Library Art.*
    (R. R. Shaw, ed.), Vol. 1(3), pp. 1–528. Graduate School of Library Service, Rutgers–The
    State University, New Brunswick, NJ.
Thomas, S. E., and Younger, J. A. (1993). Cooperative cataloging: A vision for the future.
    Cataloguing and Classification Quarterly **17**(3/4), 237–257.
Toward a Common MARC Format (1994). *LC Cataloging Newsline,* **2**(6).

Index

ISBN 0-12-024619-8